LATIN AMERICAN STATES
AND
POLITICAL REFUGEES

LATIN AMERICAN STATES
AND
POLITICAL REFUGEES

Keith W. Yundt

PRAEGER

New York
Westport, Connecticut
London

Library of Congress Cataloging-in-Publication Data

Yundt, Keith W.
   Latin American states and political refugees / by Keith W. Yundt.
    p. cm.
  Bibliography: p.
  Includes index.
  ISBN 0-275-92942-6 (alk. paper)
  1. Refugees, Political—Legal status, laws, etc.—Latin America.
I. Title.
KG564.Y86   1988
342.8′083—dc19
[348.0283]   88-15563

Library of Congress Catalog Card Number: 88-15563
ISBN: 0-275-92942-6

First published in 1988

Praeger Publishers, One Madison Avenue, New York, NY 10010
A division of Greenwood Press, Inc.

Printed in the United States of America

The paper used in this book complies with the Permanent
Paper Standard issued by the National Information Standards
Organization (Z39.48—1984).

10 9 8 7 6 5 4 3 2 1

Contents

Preface

I would like to thank Professor Jose Garcia for his support and encouragement in the undertaking of this book. Field research was made possible through the Geneva Program of the Center for International and Comparative Studies (CICP) at Kent State University, Ohio. My thanks to all in the CICP office who assisted me during my graduate student years. Also, I acknowledge the extreme helpfulness of the UN Library and UNHCR Documentation Center staffs in Geneva. A special thanks to Mr. Frank Field, whose contacts at UNHCR and enthusiasm for my project have made this a better study than my working alone. Finally, I express my deep appreciation for the sustained support of Professor Boleslaw Boczek. Many times his confidence in my abilities has been greater than my own.

The computer center staffs at New Mexico State University, Las Cruces, and Southwest Texas State University, San Marcos, cheerfully endured my lack of skill. My appreciation especially to Bill Bryson, who patiently answered questions and spent extra time to overcome what seemed to be unique difficulties in preparing this text. Finally, translations from the Spanish, unless otherwise cited, are my own; as are any and all mistranslations or misinterpretations.

Portions of this book previously have been presented at conferences or appeared as journal articles. The body of Chapter 6 was first presented at the Southwest Social Science Conference, Dallas, March 1987, and was subsequently published in the Inter-American Law Review, Volume 19, no. 1, Fall 1987. The substance of Chapters 5 and 9 was initially presented at the Western Political Science Association Conference, Anaheim, April 1987. A revised version of this presentation has been accepted for publication by the International Migration Review. I wish to express my appreciation to the editors of these journals, Judith Mellman and S. M. Tomasi, respectively, for persmission to use these two articles. Finally, I wish to thank Alison Bricken and Frank Welsch of Praeger, whose support and help made possible this publication.

List of Abbreviations

CCAS   Comision Coordinadora de Accion Social (Argentina)

CCPM   Comision Catolica Peruana de Migracion (Peru)

CEAR   Comision Especial para Atencion a Repatriados (Guatemala)

CEB   Conferencia Episcopal Boliviana (Bolivia)

CEDAS   Comite Ecumenico de Asistencia Social (Peru)

CEPARE   Comision de Elegibilidad para los Refugidos (Argentina)

CNR   Comision Nacional para el Refugiado (Dominican Republic)

CNR   Comision Nacional de Repatriacion (Uruguay)

COMAR   Comision Mexicana de Ayuda a Refugiados (Mexico)

CONAIN   National Council of Immigrtion (Bolivia)

CONAPARE   Comision Nacional para Refugiados (Costa Rica)

CONAR   National Committee for Assistance to Refugees (Chile)

DNM   Directoro Nacional de Migracion (Argentina)

ECOSOC   Economic and Social Council

EXCOM	Executive Committee of the High Commissioner's Program
FASIC	Fundacion de Ayuda Social de las Iglesias Cristianas (Chile)
IACHR	Inter-American Commission on Human Rights
IAJC	Inter-American Juridical Committee
ICEM	Inter-governmental Committee on European Migration
ICM	Inter-governmental Committee on Migration
IGCR	Inter-governmental Commission for Refugees
ICJ	International Commission of Jurists
ICRC	International Committee of the Red Cross
ILO	International Labor Organization
IRO	International Refugee Organization
LON	League of Nations
OAS	Organization of American States
ONPAR	Organizacion Nacional para la Atencion de los Refugiados (Panama)
SER	Servicio Ecumenico de Reintegracion (Uruguay)
UN	United Nations
UNDP	United Nations Development Programme

UNHCR   United Nations High Commissioner for Refugees

WCC   World Council of Churches

LATIN AMERICAN STATES
AND
POLITICAL REFUGEES

Introduction

The phenomenon of political refugees has a long history, but in the twentieth century the issue of political refugees has assumed a new magnitude as a consequence of the dramatic political upheaval in Europe and subsequently all over the world. Until the early 1950s, refugees were perceived and treated as a transient problem. Since then, however, political refugees as a permanent feature of international relations have been accepted as a sociological fact. This study investigates the practices of Latin American states toward political refugees within the context of international, regional, and national asylum and refugee law.

This area is virtually unexplored in the literature of political science and international law. There are two reasons for paucity of materials pertaining to political refugees in Latin America. First, until the relatively recent past, the overwhelming majority of political refugees in Latin America were Europeans fleeing the chaos of the two world wars. Compared with those in other refugee resettlement areas, these refugees were few in number and widely dispersed among the Latin American states. When this European "pool" of political refugees became exhausted in the mid-1950s, the Latin American states' involvement in refugee matters and international community attention to refugees in Latin America receded. Secondly, the political refugees from Chile, Argentina, and Uruguay in the 1970s were small in number compared with those from other "crisis" areas at the time, that is, Africa and Indochina. Moreover, the common European extraction of South America's refugees allowed for quick assimilation into neighboring states or resettlement to Europe. It is only since the Nicaraguan revolution (1978) and the subsequent violence engulfing the Central American states that mass migrations of persons seeking territorial asylum has refocused attention to questions of political refugees in Latin America. The concept of an international regime will be used to analyze the question of political refugees in Latin America. As conceptualized by Stephen Krasner, regimes encompass principles and norms and hence must embody some sense of general obligation. Consequently, by identification and analysis of the principles, norms, and general obligations due refugees, the identification of global and inter-American refugees regimes is possible.[1]

Among scholars who use regime analysis, a common

definition of regime has emerged: international regimes are
principles, norms, rules, and decision-making procedures around
which actor expectations converge in a given issue area.   On the
basis of this convergence, rules or social institutions are created,
or accepted, that regularize behavior and allow governments to
control transnational and interstate relations.   Such rules and
institutions are embedded in a broader social environment that
nurtures and   sustains   the   conditions   necessary   for   regime
functioning.[2] Within a causal model, a regime is an intervening
variable, represented by the diagram

CAUSE(S) ----> REGIME ----> BEHAVIOR/CONSEQUENCES

        Scholars of international relations have suggested a variety
of competing interpretations of international regimes.[3] Of these
interpretations, the one proposed by Oran Young is best suited
for investigation of a possible Latin American political refugees
regime.
        Young conceptualizes regimes as social institutions, that is,
as a fundamental part of patterned human behavior.   Social
institutions are recognized practices consisting of easily identifiable
roles, coupled with collections of rules or conventions governing
relations among the occupants of these roles.   Consequently,
norms are not the defining characteristics of a regime; rather,
rules, norms, or conventions acquire an aura of legitimacy which
is normative in character.[4] Such governed action, that is, patterned
behavior, inevitably generates convergent expectations on the part
of concerned actors.   In fact, Young states that the continuance
of all international regimes is dependent upon the maintenance of
these convergent expectations.   Furthermore, explicit formalization
of a regime, for example, a treaty, is not a necessary condition
for its successful operation.[5]
        The present study shows that a global regime governing
political refugees has been established.   The requisite rules,
norms, and procedures to regularize behavior and control its
effects are contained in international instruments (e.g., the 1951
Refugees Convention and its 1967 Protocol) and governing statutes
of international governmental and nongovernmental organizations
(e.g., the United Nations High Commissioner for Refugees and
the Intergovernmental Committee for Migration and International
Committee of the Red Cross).   Whether or not complementary,
compatible, or dissimilar rules, norms, procedures, and institutions
have been established or recognized by the Latin American states
is the central concern of this study.
        In strictly legal usage, a regime refers to a set of

international legal rules governing the behavior of states with regard to a specific issue.[6] To political scientists, however, the concept of regime is broader than it is to jurists, including not only legal norms but also declarations of principles. Despite the proliferation of political science literature on international regimes, only international jurists have investigated the global refugees regime, and virtually nothing has been written on refugees in Latin America.

Applying the model of an international regime to the case of political refugees in Latin America will fill a gap in the current political science literature. This study takes international regime as an intervening variable. Data used in this regime analysis are derived from primary and secondary sources. The primary sources used include documentation from international governmental organizations, the League of Nations, the United Nations, and the Organization of American States, and from international nongovernmental organizations such as Amnesty International, the International Committee of the Red Cross, and the International Commission of Jurists. Further sources include relevant national legislation available either through the UN Library, Geneva, or through contact with Latin American embassies in Washington, D.C., and personal interviews with officals of the United Nations and international nongovernmental organizations involved with refugees in Latin America. Finally, the secondary sources consulted are articles and books, mostly in Spanish, dealing with questions of asylum and refugees in Latin America.

Regime analyists suggest several causal variables, not necessarily mutually exclusive, for regimes, for example, egoistic self-interest, political power, norms and principles, usage and custom, and knowledge.[7] Following Young's emphasis on regimes as social institutions, usage and custom assume the greatest weight as causal varibles.

Young identifies three types of regime origin: spontaneous, negotiated, and imposed. These origins are not mutually exclusive; and over time it is possible for a regime to transform into another type.[8] Discussion of the global refugees regime will focus on its negotiated origin and subsequent, primarily spontaneous, transformation. For Latin America, emphasis is given to the spontaneous rules developed for political asylum, beginning in the late nineteenth century. Subsequent interwar efforts to negotiate an inter-American political asylum regime yielded only partial success. The central concerns of this study are

1. the spontaneous inter-American political asylum conventions compatible with, or complimentary to, the global refugees regime;

2. the negotiated inter-American instruments on political asylum compatible with, or complimentary to, the global refugees regime;

3. the conscious efforts the postwar inter-American system (OAS) has made to align these spontaneous and negotiated conventions with the global refugees regime, and to what effect; and

4. the transformation of inter-American social conventions that has occurred, or can occur, as a consequence of mass movement of refugees among the Central American states.

According to Young, regime transformation can be observed by alteration of regime components. No necessary conditions for regime transformation are identified: any of a variety of factors may be sufficient to precipitate major changes in prevailing social institutions. However, he does stress two points: first, prevailing social institutions are frequently victims of exogenous forces; and second, rapid social change tends to undermine spontaneous regimes without creating conditions for replacement.[9]

Three regime components are identified: substantive, procedural, and implementative. The substantive component concerns the norms, standards, or rules of any regime, four principal types of which are identified: authoritative international norms, international standards, with self-selected national exceptions, international guidelines and national standards.[10] The rules of a regime identify a relevant subject group, make behavioral prescriptions, and specify the circumstances under which a rule operates.

The second, procedural, component of a regime refers to the explicit organization of the regime, that is, the recognized social choice mechanisms, such as allocation or distribution decisions or a means of dispute resolution. The third component concerns compliance mechanisms and incentives for the actors' continued support of the regime, that is, decision-making activities for enforcing, implementing, and promoting regime rules.[11] Examples of six types of compliance mechanisms will be presented in this study: authoritative international decisionmaking, international monitoring, international policy coordination, international information exchange, international promotion or assistance, and national decisionmaking.[12] These three regime components will be presented first as they appear in the global refugees regime.

The most important substantive components are the United Nations High Commissioner for Refugees and especially the 1951

Refugees Convention and its 1967 Protocol. The definition of political refugee as contained in these two instruments is used to identify the relevant subject group. Examples of prescription rules of the global refugees regime are the guarantee of *non-refoulement,* that is, no forced return to a country of persecution of an asylum seeker, and minimum standards of treatment for recognized refugees. Finally, the global regime accepts an individual's well founded fear of persecution as specifying the circumstances that make other regime rules operative. The presence, or lack, of equivalent substantive components in Latin America is another concern of this study.

The procedural and compliance components of the global refugees regime are comprised of organs and agencies of the United Nations: the General Assembly, the Economic and Social Council, the Executive Committee of the High Commissioner for Refugees and the Office of the High Commissioner for Refugees. Similar, or equivalent, components of a Latin American regional refugees regime will be sought within the framework of the Organization of American States. Special attention is given to the Inter-American Commission on Human Rights and the Inter-American Court of Human Rights as procedural and compliance mechanisms central to a Latin American political refugees regime.

The final chapter of this study focuses on regime transformation. As stated earlier, the mass movement of persons seeking asylum in Central America is identified as the central force for regime change. This mass movement of asylum seekers has placed enormous political and economic strains on recipient states. Moreover, it has been suggested that the Latin American rules on political asylum are spontaneous in origin. If, as Young suggests, spontaneous regimes face exceptional difficulties in transformation, then one should expect this difficulty to be reflected by the inability of Latin American actors to establish, or agree to, regime components suitable for mass asylum situations.

Understanding regime transformation involves determining what methods and mechanisms are necessary to alter the regime, for example, group bargaining, unilateral action, or inaction by actors involved with the global or Latin American refugees regimes. In this study special emphasis is given to the role of human rights law as one element involved in regime transformation.[13] At the global level, the United Nations High Commissioner for Refugees, in part, relies on human rights law in exercise of its functions. What are the possibilities of enhancing its role vis-a-vis Central American refugees? At the regional level, the Inter-American Commission and Inter-American Court have broad statutory authority regarding human rights. How might these two agencies contribute to regime transformation? Finally, what have Latin American states done unilaterally or multilaterally to respond to the mass movement of asylum seekers in Central America?

NOTES

1. Stephen Krasner, "Structural Causes and Regime Consequences: Regimes as Intervening Variables," in Stephen Krasner. ed.. International Regimes (Ithaca, N.Y.: Cornell University Press, 1983), p. 2.

2. Ibid.. p. 9.

3. Especially useful for an overview of competing models for regime analysis is the special issue of International Organization 36, no. 2 (Spring 1982). which is devoted to the question of regime analysis. The contributions to this edition form the basis for Krasner's book International Regimes.

4. This model for regime analysis originally presented in Oran Young, "International Regimes: Problems of Concept Formation," World Politics 32, no. 3 (April 1980): 331-56. Refinement of the model appears in Young. "Regime Dynamics: The Rise and Fall of International Regimes," in Krasner, International Regimes. pp. 93-113. See also his review "International Regimes: Toward a New Theory of Institutions," World Politics 39, no. 1 (October 1986): 104-22.

5. Oran Young. "International Regimes: Problems of Concept Formation." pp. 331-33.

6. Boleslaw Boczek. "The Concept of Regime and the Protection and Preservation of the Marine Environment," Ocean Yearbook 6 (1986): 273-5.

7. Krasner. "Structural Causes." pp. 11-19; Young, "Regime Dynamics." pp. 108-11.

8. Young. "Regime Dynamics," pp. 98-105.

9. Ibid.. pp. 105, 110; Young,"International Regimes: Toward a New Theory of Institutions," pp. 114-15.

10. Jack Donnelly, "International Human Rights: A Regime Analysis," International Organization 40. no. 3 (Summer 1986): 603-4.

11. Young. "International Regimes: Toward a New Theory of Institutions." pp. 336-40. 344-46.

12. Donnelly, "International Human Rights," p. 604.

13. Over the last few years scholars have focused increasingly upon the possibility of internationally accepted human rights standards replacing international refugee law. To date. the Council of Europe and the European Communities have developed the most comprehensive instruments in this regard; hence the literature linking universally accepted human rights to political refugees has concerned primarily European practices and efforts. Also in the last few years. the Inter-American Commission on Human Rights and the Inter-American Court of Human Rights-- both modeled after the European human rights system--have received scholarly attention. but not to the depth or degree of that afforded the European institutions.

Chapter One

Latin American States and Refugees under the League of Nations

The various refugee organizations affiliated with the League of Nations were the first truly functional approaches to the refugee problem.[1] In 1919, the problem of displaced persons and refugees was not seen as a direct concern of the league. It was assumed that international voluntary and humanitarian organizations had sufficient experience and resources to adequately address the problem. With the creation of new nation-states from the former Austria-Hungary and Ottoman Empires, however, the magnitude of the refugee problem quickly overwhelmed the capacity of philanthropic organizations.

In 1920, Gustave Ador of the International Committee of the Red Cross (ICRC) repeatedly pressured the league for a coordinated international response to the refugee problem. He argued that only the league, as a intergovernmental organization, had the political authority capable of addressing the refugee problem, now beyond the ability of humanitarian organizations. Such action by the league could be taken pursuant to Article 25 of the league Covenant.[2]

As a result of pressure from the ICRC and the League of Red Cross Societies, the league appointed a High Commissioner for Refugees in 1921, and from 1921 to 1924, the High Commissioner's office provided legal and technical assistance.

From 1924 until 1929, the technical function was transferred to the International Labor Organization (ILO), where existing programs and expertise prevented a duplication of tasks. The technical functions were returned to the High Commissioner's Office for only one year, 1929-30. At the origin of the High Commissioner's office, no definition of "refugee" was agreed upon.[3]

Fridtjof Nansen of Norway was appointed as the first High Commissioner for Russian Refugees in 1921 and remained in this position until his death in 1930. While the office title indicated the original intent of dealing with refugees from the Bolshevik Revolution, the chaos in the Balkans and Near East soon compelled the High Commissioner to extend protection to other groups as well.[4]

The earliest reference found of Latin American attention to refugees is from 1923. After the formation of the Turkish Republic, the conditions of the mostly White Russian refugees in Constantinople required attention of the league in 1923. A force of 135,000, fleeing defeat in the Crimea, had entered the city. France had secured placement for 20,000 in Brazil; Peru had agreed to take 1,000. However, the general of these White Russians, Baron Pytor Wrangel, prevented any White Russians from leaving, as he considered his force as still representative of the Russian government.[5]

One of the major problems faced by Nansen was providing refugees with internationally recognized documents, essential for those requiring resettlement. Most refugees had lost their documentation in the chaos of civil war or revolution; or as with Soviet Russia, the juridical basis of recognized nationality had been denied. The Nansen passport was created as an internationally recognized document to replace lost or revoked documents of refugees. When recognized, the Nansen passport provided minimum juridical rights and guarantees in resettlement countries. Its recognition was obtained through negotiated arrangement with the High Commissioner and interested states.

Between 1922 and 1928 several international instruments regulating issuance of certificates of identity and the legal status of Russian and Armenian refugees were negotiated under the auspices of the High Commissioner. Recognition of these instruments by Latin American states was limited. Although several signed the instruments concerning identity certificates, none deposited ratifications; hence, these agreements never entered into force for any Latin American state. Subsequent efforts in 1928 to regulate the legal status of refugees brought no Latin American state's participation.[6] The only exception found in available League documents was a 1924 High Commissioner's Report, wherein Mexico was cited as the only Latin American state that recognized and had adopted the system of identity certificates for Russian refugees.[7]

The record of refugee resettlement to Latin American states during the 1920s is sparse. And what materials are available indicate that such resettlement efforts were generally disappointing, both for the league and the states. It was reported that "several thousand" refugee families were sent from Germany to Brazil in 1924. The nationalities and job classifications of these families were not specified.[8]

In 1925 an ILO mission visited several unspecified South American states to investigate opportunities for resettling refugees in agricultural colonies. Experimental colonies were established in Argentina, Brazil, and Paraguay in 1926. ILO offices were established in Buenos Aires and Rio de Janeiro to direct these settlements. In 1927 the first progess report was presented to the ILO. Argentina, Brazil, Cuba, Mexico, Paraguay, and Uruguay were listed among the countries receiving the majority of resettled refugees. No specific numbers or breakdown by ethnic group or nationality were provided. Difficulties of refugee assimilation, corruption, and infastructure underdevelopment were also reported. In 1929 these difficulties forced the ILO to cease all support for resettlement to Latin American agricultural colonies.[9]

In 1930 the High Commissioner's office was reorganized as the Nansen International Office for Refugees. The LON Council and Assembly had decided that the refugee problem was well on the way to solution: the reorganized Nansen Office was to liquidate its work within a ten-year period. This office functioned until 1938 and provided only technical aid to refugees. Legal protection was provided by the league secretariat.[10] No records or information on the Secretariat's role in extension of legal protection to refugees were found.

In August 1932, the Nansen Office presented the first report since its formation to the League Assembly. Few references to Latin American states were included. Argentina, the report indicated, had agreed to deliver to all foreigners without regular nationality, passports permitting the bearers to leave Argentina and return during a one-year period. Venezuela had informed the office that national problems prevented it from giving refugee concerns any priority. Nicaragua had maintained that the question of refugees was not of direct interest to countries of the American continent; however, for humanitarian reasons, it was prepared to adhere to league recommendations. In reply to Nansen Office inquiries, Colombia had claimed that the question of refugees required no attention on the part of the Colombian government.[11]

In May 1933, the Legal Committee of the League of Nations Assembly received a report from the Committee of Experts charged to investigate the current status of refugee law. The Committee concluded that the two 1928 arrangements no longer adequately dealt with refugee problems, and negotiation of a new international instrument was suggested. Further, the league should consider a gradual phase-out of the Nansen Office, as the refugee problem seemed essentially solved.[12] The suggestion for a new international instrument resulted in the Convention Relating to the International Status of Refugees of 28 October 1933. One provision of this convention required that states surrender the right to deny foreigners entry to their territory. The convention provided that a state party had to admit a refugee into its territory if the refugee was coming directly from the state at whose hands he feared persecution. No Latin American state was party to this convention.[13]

With the advent of the National Socialist regime in Germany in 1933, the league faced new refugee problems. As the Nazi regime began to implement anti-Jewish legislation, increasing numbers of Jews sought refuge outside Germany. To deal with these, an autonomous body, the Office of the High Commissioner for Refugees Coming from Germany, was created. This office had authority to raise funds and coordinate the resettlement and retraining of German Jews and was empowered to negotiate with governments on technical questions pertaining to refugees, as in the case of travel documents. From 1933 to 1935 it was staffed by an independent commissioner. The office remained effective until 1938. Uruguay was the only Latin American state among the twelve states composing the High Commissioner's Governing Board. Argentina and Brazil, among others, declined invitation to the Governing Board.[14]

In early 1935, the High Commissioner, James McDonald, and Doctor Samuel Guy Inman visited Argentina, Brazil, Chile, Colombia, Costa Rica, Ecuador, Honduras, Guatemala, Mexico, Panama, Paraguay, Peru, El Salvador, Santo Domingo, and Uruguay. They hoped to encourage the Latin American states to give special emphasis on accepting refugee intellectuals. While in Argentina and Brazil, they visited programs sponsored by the Jewish Colonization Agency. Upon their return to Europe, the High Commissioner reported that all the governments' ministries had expressed sympathy and support for his efforts.

Regarding the special appeal for accepting intellectuals, the Latin American states expressed interest only in displaced scholars and specialists, not rank-and-file professionals. The areas of law and medicine were already overcrowded. Only Ecuador and Chile agreed to specific placements. Arrangements were to be made through the German-based Notgemeinschaft Deutscher Wissenschafter im Ausland (Aid Society for Germans Studying Abroad). Approximately 3,000 German Jewish refugees were resettled to Latin America by 15 June 1935.[15]

Refugees from the Saar were also identified as a refugee group. Although no Latin American states became party to the Saar refugee instrument, refugees from the Saar were accepted in some Latin American states. In December 1935 the Nansen

Office received a settlement offer for Saar refugees from the colonization company Sul Brazil of Santa Catarina, Brazil. A representative from the Nansen Office in Rio was sent to investigate conditions. In his report, which included a copy of the draft contract with the company, he concluded that the area in Sao Paulo state was suitable for settlement for up to 50 Saar families.[16]

The Nansen Office 1935-36 annual report included a general description of Latin American refugee settlement arrangements. The countries generally provided free visas, exemption from entry fees, free accommodation for one week, and transport to settlement sites. Credit was usually available for agricultural goods. Additional settlement offers from Argentina and Brazil were presented to the Emigration Committee for study and possible approval. The report included replies to a questionnaire sent to resettlement countries by the Nansen Office. The questionnaire included a request for breakdown of refugees currently in country and inquired on certain points of refugee legal status. Among the Latin American states, only Peru, Nicaragua and Ecuador responded. As of 30 June 1936, the following breakdown of refugees was reported: Ecuador had 15 Russian, 12 Armenian, and 2 Saar; Peru had 39 Russian, 2 Armenian, and 27 Turkish; and Nicaragua had no recorded refugees. Peru provided the most comprehensive response to the questionnaire, but even here not all of the questions were answered. According to Peru, no refugees in Peru were unemployed (question 3), none were incapable of earning a living (question 4), and no public monies were required to support refugees (question 8). All three countries expressed unwillingness to provide credit to the Nansen Office for further resettlement.[17]

At the 1 July 1936 meeting of the Joint Management-Finance Committee of the Nansen Office, reports on refugee resettlement in Latin American states were presented. Paraguay had settled 200 Saar families. These families had been provided with free visas, 1,500 hectares, exemption from entry fees, free transport from point of disembarkation, and one week of accommodation.[18] However, the resettlement difficulties initially recorded in the ILO reports of the 1920s persisted. For instance, Brazil presented an Application on Behalf of a Group of Russian Refugees Transferred from India to Parana. In May 1935, there were 54 Russian refugees who settled in Parana. The Brazilian government reported one year later that these refugees had experienced difficulties of social adjustment and were unable to meet resettlement obligations.[19]

On 2 July 1936 the High Commissioner for Refugees Coming from Germany, Neill Malcolm, convened a conference designed to approve a draft agreement on the status of refugees coming from Germany. Ecuador and Uruguay were the only

Latin American states participating. On the questions of placement of refugees and consultations with the High Commissioner. Latin American governments informed the conference that they would give favorable consideration to individual refugees. No Latin American state became party to the resulting instrument.[20]

In 1938 all refugee functions were combined under a single office, by the creation of the office of High Commissioner for All Refugees under League of Nations Protection, which functioned until 1946, when it was replaced by the International Refugee Organization (IRO). It was limited to provision of legal protection to refugees.[21]

Also in 1938, the Evian (France) Conference addressed questions of refugees fleeing from the Eastern German territories. The conference created the Inter-Governmental Committee for Refugees (IGCR), functioning until 1947, when it was absorbed into the IRO. The IGCR was to promote orderly emigration and permanent resettlement. Although responsible for administering funds, it was not able to undertake operational expenditures. At its April 1943 Bermuda conference, the IGCR mandate was extended to all refugees in Europe. At the 4th Plenary of the IGCR in 1944, attention was given to Spanish Republican refugees. Prior to this attention, no official body had addressed the refugees from the Spanish Civil War.[22]

Several instruments pertaining to refugees were adopted following the Evian Conference. As with the majority of the refugee instruments concluded during the interwar period, no Latin American state participated in drafting, or became party to, these instruments.[23]

No additional information concerning Latin American states' involvement with refugees during the interwar years was found, and nothing in the available league documents that concerned refugees was dated beyond 1938.

NOTES

1. A comprehensive analysis of League of Nations (LON) documents pertaining to refugees has never been undertaken. The league's archives on refugee matters have not been catalogued or even filed in chronological order. Boxes of numbered documents are available, and the researcher must sift through with the hope of uncovering a reference to Latin American states' involvement with the league's refugee activities. Although English and French are the official languages, in neither language does complete documentation exist for league refugee matters from 1921-1938. The documents cited in this section were extracted from existing

league archival materials. In general, the lack of information corroborates the conclusion reached by the Inter-American Commission on Human Rights; in its 1967 Yearbook on Human Rights, the IACHR stated that "in all the League discussion, no instance was uncovered of any question arising regarding refugees in Latin America." See Organization of American States (hereafter OAS), Inter-American Yearbook on Human Rights 1960-1967 (Washington, D.C.: OAS, 1968) p. 479.

2. Louise Holborn, The International Refugee Organization. (Oxford: Oxford University Press, 1956), p. 8.

3. Atle Grahl-Madsen, "The League of Nations and the Refugees," paper presented at Symposium: 60th Anniversary of the Founding of the League of Nations, Geneva, November 1980, p. 2; Jacques Vernant, The Refugee in the Post-War World. (London: Allen and Unwin, 1953), p. 29; LON, ILO, Minutes of the 36th Session of the Governing Body of the International Labor Organization. May-June 1927, pp. 345-361; Dorothy Thompson, Refugees: Anarchy or Organization? (New York: Random House, 1938). pp. 30-31.

4. LON, The Refugees (Geneva: LON, 1938), pp. 11-13, 29-32. Armenian refugees were the concern of the league from 1921 to 1937. For general review of league efforts see John Hope Simpson, The Refugee Question. (New York: Farrar and Rinehart, 1939), pp. 7-13.

5. C. A. Macartney, Refugees-The Work of the League. (London: League of Nations Union, 1931), pp. 7-25, especially p. 13. For comments on resettlement of Armenians, Greeks, and Bulgarians see pp. 46-73, 74-112 and 113-22 respectively.

6. On 5 July 1922, the Arrangement with Regard to the Issue of Certificates of Identity to Russian Refugees was opened for signature. Argentina, Bolivia, Chile, Cuba, Guatemala, Mexico, and Paraguay were signatories. And on 31 May 1924 the Plan for the Issue of A Certificate of Identity to Armenian Refugees was concluded, with Brazil, Chile and Uruguay as signatories. For the 12 May 1926 Arrangement Relating to the Issue of Identity Certificates to Russian and Armenian Refugees, Cuba was the sole Latin American signatory state. Finally, two arrangements regulating the legal status of refugees were concluded in 1928: the Arrangement Relating to the Legal Status of Russian and Armenian Refugees and Arrangement concerning the Extension to Other Categories of Refugees of Certain Measures Taken in Favor of Russian and Armeinan Refugees. No Latin American state signed either arrangement. Full texts of all agreements are found in UN, UN High Commissioner for Refugees (hereafter UNHCR). Conventions, Agreements and Arrangements concerning Refugees Adopted before the Second World War (HCR/DC/42/1966; Geneva: UNHCR, 1966).

7. LON, Council of the League, Report to the 5th

Assembly of the League Work of the Council (A.8 1924), 10 June 1924, pp. 82-87.

8. Macartney, *Refugees-Work of the League*, p. 34. As noted by Thompson, the immigration countries assumed that the refugee problem would be short-lived and did not bother to keep exact statistics on the refugees' numbers and economic status. Thompson, *Refugees, Anarchy*, p. 4.

9. Macartney, *Refugees*, pp. 37-39; LON, ILO, Minutes of the 36th Session, pp. 350-52, 357.

10. Vernant, *Refugee*, pp. 24-30; LON, *Refugees*, pp. 32-33; Thompson, *Refugees, Anarchy*, pp. 37-38.

11. LON, Nansen International Office, *Report to the Governing Body* (A.24 1932), 16 August 1932, pp. 17-20.

12. LON, Inter-Governmental Advisory Committee for Refugees, *Report of the Inter-Governmental Advisory Committee for Refugees on the Work of its 5th Session* (C.266-M.136 1933), 18 May 1933, pp. 5-6.

13. Richard Lillich, *The Human Rights of Aliens in Contemporary International Law.* (Manchester, UK: Manchester University Press, 1984), p. 36; UN, UNHCR, *Conventions, Agreements and Arrangements*; LON, *Refugees*, pp. 33-35.

14. OAS, *Inter-American Yearbook*, p.484; LON, *Refugees*, pp. 36-41; Vernant, *Refugee*, pp. 24-30; Simpson, *Refugee Question*, pp. 14-15; Thompson, *Refugees*, p. 46.

15. LON, Office of the High Commissioner, *4th Meeting of the Governing Body of the High Commission for Refugees Coming from Germany*, London, 1935, pp. 6-10, 13-14, 24.

16. UN, UNHCR, *Conventions, Agreements and Arrangements.* On 30 July 1935 the *Plan for the Issue of a Certificate of Identity to Refugees from the Saar* was opened for signature.

17. LON, Nansen International Office, *Report of the Governing Body* (A.23 1936), 3 September 1936. This report covers the year ending 30 June 1936.

18. LON, Nansen International Office, *Management and Finance Committees: 20th Joint Session* (J.C. 214 1936), 1 July 1936. See Also LON, Nansen International Office, *International Assistance to Refugees* (A.73 1936), n. d., pp. 1-7 for reference to original offer.

19. LON, Nansen International Office, *22nd Joint Session* (J.C. 223 1936), 1 July 1936.

20. LON, Office of the High Commissioner, *Refugees Coming from Germany-Report to the 17th Session by High Commissioner Neill Malcolm* (A.19 1936), 1 September 1936, pp. 3-4; LON, *The Refugees*, pp. 41-43. The Provisional Arrangement concerning the Status of Refugees Coming from Germany was thus opened for signature on 4 July 1936, but no Latin American state became a party to this agreement. This

instrument used the 1933 Convention Relating to the International
Status of Refugees as a foundation.

    21. OAS, <u>Inter-American</u> <u>Yearbook</u>, p. 484; Vernant,
<u>Refugee</u>, p. 29.

    22. OAS, <u>Inter-American</u> <u>Yearbook</u>, p. 485; Holborn,
<u>International</u>, pp. 11-15; Vernant, <u>Refugee</u> pp. 58-59; Simpson,
<u>Refugee Question</u>, pp. 16-17.

    23. UN, UNHCR, <u>Conventions, Agreements and
Arrangements</u>; LON, <u>Refugees</u>, pp. 43-45. The Convention
concerning the Status of Refugees Coming from Germany was
concluded on 10 February 1938. Adopted on the same day was
the Additional Protocol to the Provisional Arrangement and the
Convention, Signed at Geneva on 4 July 1936 and 10 February
1938, Respectively, concerning the Status of Refugees Coming
from Germany. This 1938 instrument used the 1936 Provisional
Arrangement as its basis.

Chapter Two

Prewar Asylum Policies of
the Latin American States

The Latin American states' involvement at the international level, either through the League of Nations or by participation in relevant international conventions, reveals no agreement among Latin American states on the global rules for asylum or on recognition of refugee status. The general unwillingness of Latin American states to become involved with the league on refugee matters, however understandable given their political and economic conditions, reinforces this disparity between Latin American pronouncements and actual state behavior. Moreover, the unwillingness of Latin American states to become involved with the league's efforts to standardize and regularize the treatment of refugees reflected the general disinterest in the problem on the part of Latin American states. This chapter will focus on the Latin American states' domestic policies, which had a bearing on asylum and refugee status prior to creation of the global refugees regime.

For the interwar period the available record of domestic policies of the Latin American states can be grouped into four clusters of states. The largest cluster (Argentina, Bolivia, Brazil, Chile, the Dominican Republic, Paraguay, and Venezuela) dealt with refugees under colonization and immigration laws. Of these states, Argentina, Paraguay and Venezuela did not specifically target league refugees. The Dominican Republic, however, designed a colonization scheme (discussed later in this chapter) specifically designed to accomodate German Jewish refugees.   A second cluster of states (Uruguay, Peru, and later Argentina) had strict racial requirements as part of their immigration criteria. A third cluster (Colombia and Nicaragua) expressed the opinion that refugees were not a concern for the Latin American states.   The final cluster (Ecuador, Guatemala, and Mexico) recognized asylum in domestic laws but were not involved with league refugees. Mexico, however, did make special exception for selected Republican refugees from the Spanish Civil War.

The historical record of domestic policies before creation of the global refugees regime is sparse, and the available documentation is often incomplete. Hence what follows has certain gaps.   Unless specifically stated, it is assumed that all of the laws and documents cited remained in force throughout the time period covered.   The specifics for each cluster of states are presented below.

COLONIZATION AND IMMIGRATION LEGISLATION

Argentina

Throughout the interwar period, the treatment of aliens in Argentina, including asylees (*asilados*,) and refugees, was addressed by the Argentine Immigration Code. In 1876 the Central Immigration Department was established.   From its establishment, free immigration into Argentina was permitted until entry restrictions were imposed in 1923. It was renewed in 1938, remaining in force until 1947.   Ostensibly, entry restrictions were imposed to protect domestic labor; however, entry requirements included approval based on ethnic background, so these restrictions clearly had a racialist basis.   In 1941 a three-member board was established to review the status of entry applications and was made responsible for drafting directives for the Central Immigration Department.[1]

Argentina used immigration as a source of population growth.   Entry restrictions, which applied to league refugees, allowed the government to ensure that immigrants would have needed skills and benefit Argentine growth and development. Overall, however, the experience of immigrants was not favorable; many, especially league refugees resettled to Argentina, remained reluctant to acquire Argentine nationality.   Their reluctance stemmed from incomplete assimilation rather than from legal barriers to naturalization.[2]

There was no direct Argentine involvement with league efforts for refugees; nor was Argentina party to any league-sponsored instrument concerning refugees. All actions involving league refugees were undertaken on a strictly unilateral basis by the Argentine government. For example, a decree of 1931 agreed to deliver to all foreigners without regular nationality, passes permitting the bearers to leave Argentina and return during a one-year period of validity. The only record found of specific Argentine recognition of European stateless persons and refugees was in a note sent to the league's Inter-governmental Advisory Committee for Refugees in 1933. This note merely restated the Argentine willingness to introduce a special "passport" for foreigners unable to obtain a passport because of statelessness. The granting of this special passport did not remove the holder from immigration restrictions.[3]

Bolivia

In Bolivia, the earliest codified provisions incorporating the concepts of asylum and refuge appeared in the Bolivian Penal Code of 1834. Prior to enactment of this code, the constitution had articulated the legality of refuge and asylum as innate rights without discrimination as to class, creed, race, or nationality.[4]

Bolivia took extensive action to promote agricultural settlements in the early twentieth century. The first law pertaining to agricultural ventures was a decree in 1905 allowing foreign nationals to become part of agricultural colonies. Amendment of this Decree in December 1926 instituted a series of benefits for those individuals, groups, or organizations stimulating entry of immigrants whose objective was colonization but added no express recognition of refugee or *asilado* status.[5]

The Bolivian government expressly recognized the right of asylum in 1937. *Asilados* were required to be politically neutral. Extradition for political offenses was prohibited, but expulsion could occur for reasons of public security. Additional regulations on aliens, including *asilados* and refugees, were contained in the Bolivian constitution, which provided for equality of status in labor, commerce and industry, education, private property, wages, and social security. Naturalization of non-Hispanics was possible after two years of residence and obtaining of a naturalization card.[6]

Brazil

The Brazilian Constitution of 1891, as amended in 1926, permitted recognition of *asilados* and refugees on a case-by-case basis. It also prohibited extradition for political crimes.[7]

Brazil encouraged agricultural colonies, with the greatest surge of settlers occurring before 1930. Most settlers were attracted to the southern states of Rio Grande do Sul, Santa Catarina, and Parana. No records were uncovered to indicate how many of the agricultural settlers had LON refugee status.

During the depression years of the 1930's, entry restrictions for Asians, especially Japanese, and Germans were imposed. A decree of 1938 provided for expulsion of foreigners for endangering public order or security. Extradition was prohibited for political crimes, except anarchist activities and attempts on the life of a chief of state.[8] No exceptions were contained in this legislation for *asilados* or refugees.

Chile

In Chile, refugees were treated under the provisions of that nation's land settlement laws. The Land Settlement Bureau was established in 1928, and absorbed by the Department of Agricultural Colonization in 1935. All immigrant movements were planned by the Chilean government. A total of 3,000 Spanish Republican and 15,000 German Jewish refugees had been accepted by 1939.[9]

The Dominican Republic

The Dominican National Constitution of 1844 provided equal rights for foreigners so long as they did not take arms against the Republic. The first laws dealing specifically with refugees were adopted in the 1930s. Only a small number of Spanish Republican and Jewish refugees took advantage of Dominican refugee status.[10]

At the 1938 Evian Conference on Refugees Coming from Germany, the Dominican Republic made a generous offer to resettle up to 100,00 refugees. Agreement on conditions was reached in 1940 between the Dominican government and the Jewish-sponsored Dominican Republic Settlement Association. Refugees under this program would be exempted from normal entry taxes and were guaranteed full freedom of economic activity. The first 400 refugees arrived in 1940 and settled at Sosua; however, due to an unfavorable report by the Brookings Institution, discussed below, few additional refugees had arrived by the end of 1942.[11]

In the fall of 1940 the Brookings Institution received a grant to study the feasibility of the Dominican offer. Its study indicated that the situation of the Spanish Republican refugees in the Dominican Republic was exceedingly difficult, a reflection of the usual failure of colonization attempts for Europeans in a tropical or subtropical climate. Moreover, the majority of Europeans awaiting resettlement were of urban origin, and thus ill-suited for both agricultural work and rural life. Historical circumstances had created sentiments hostile to foreigners in the Dominican Republic. French occupation in 1802 and Haitian domination until 1844 had left lasting hostility to non-Hispanic Europeans and to blacks in general. These sentiments were reflected in a law of 1938 that imposed a tax of $500 on all immigrants, including stateless persons. Furthermore, a 1938 labor law required all work places to hire at least 70 percent of their work force from Dominican labor. Special exceptions could be granted, but only for one-year contracts. The law made no exclusions or special provisions for refugees.[12]

Paraguay

In Paraguay, numerous agricultural colonies in the interwar period were established by religious, primarily German-speaking, minorities, especially Mennonites and Hutterites. Available records indicate that the prime motivation for these groups was the desire to practice religious beliefs without persecution. Germans have traditionally been welcomed as immigrants to Paraguay.[13]

In 1926, feeling that their religious life was threatened, 1,743 Mennonites left Canada and established the Meno colony in the Chaco. Also in the late 1920s, Mennonites living along the lower Volga felt threatened by Stalinist policies. Granted permission to leave, 1,481 established the Frenheim colony, also in the Chaco. During the interwar years, numerous groups of European political refugees resettled to Paraguay. In 1927, 200 Russians from Volhynia entered Paraguay. The colony of Sudetia was founded by Sudeten German refugees in 1934, and an additional 48 Sudeten families (190 persons) arrived in 1938. In 1935 a Nansen Office was opened in Paraguay. Through this office 158 Saar refugees were resettled in 1938.[14] In total, 3,000 Jews, mostly refugees, arrived during the interwar years. Also, up to 10,000 Nansen-status refugees, mostly Ukrainians and Balts, found refuge in Paraguay. Of the latter groups, most chose to obtain Soviet passports in 1945, responding to the Soviet victory over Nazi Germany.[15]

Venezuela

     The earliest information available on Venezuelan refugee
policy is the 1918 Law on Immigration and Colonization. There
are no references to *asilados* or refugees nor any possible
provisions linked to asylum status in this law. The aliens law of
1919 contained several references to *asilados*. Regarding general
rights, it guaranteed aliens the same civil rights as nationals.
Aliens were prohibited from engaging in political activity. Entry
to those who might disturb the public order or the foreign policy
of the republic was denied. *Asilados* were designated a town of
residence, were prohibited from travel to specific areas, and could
be expelled for violation of any of these conditions, but if
expelled, they would not be compelled to travel to any territory
under the jurisdiction of the persecuting government.[16]
     In the 1930s Venezuelan scholars gave serious attention to
controlled immigration and settlement policies as a means to
foster development. Consequently, during the late 1930s, a strong
immigration policy was put into place. Refugees were not a
priority under this immigration policy.[17] The Immigration and
Colonization Act of 1936 established the Technical Institute of
Immigration and Colonization. The modified laws and regulations
contained no mention of *asilados* or refugees, nor any provisions
for special dispensations to encourage immigration of refugee
groups.[18]
     The Aliens Act of 1936, revised in 1942, and the
accompanying regulations of 1943, defined the rights of all
foreigners in Venezuela. Oversight and regulation of aliens was
entrusted to the Identification Bureau of the Ministry of the
Interior.[19] Aliens were guaranteed the same civil right as
nationals. No mention of recognition of Nansen passports was
contained in this law and regulations. A deposit of 500 Bolivars
was required upon entry, and there were no exemptions for
asilados or refugees.
     The duties of aliens included a strict neutrality in politics.
Moreover, in general, public employment was prohibited to aliens,
with the executive branch empowered to review the merits of
exceptional cases. Aliens could be expelled for threats to public
order or for endangering the foreign policy of the republic. A
recognized *asilado* would be designated a place of residence and
subjected to travel restrictions. Failure to obey these restrictions
would result in expulsion.[20] During the interwar years, between
10,000 and 12,000 refugees came to Venezuela. Of this number,
about 6,000 were Spanish Republican refugees; the remainder was
divided between Jews, Russians, and Poles.[21]

RACIAL RESTRICTIONS

Bolivia

In response to the massive migration to Bolivia of Jews from Germany and Central Europe, many of whom sought refuge in Latin American states, the government issued decrees banning the entry of Jews: 15 March 1939, 3 May 1939, 6 April 1940, May 1940, 14 January 1941, and 17 April 1942. Prior to the first Decree, 10,000 Jews had entered Bolivia.[22]

Peru

By decree in 1936, Peru created the National Immigration Board. Subsequent decrees in 1937 and 1945 detailed the functioning of the board, which was responsible for establishing an entry quota system and enforcing the prohibition of entry for specific racial groups. An estimated 2,500 Jewish refugees arrived during the interwar period. No additional information was obtained for Peru.[23]

Uruguay

The basic immigration law of Uruguay was enacted in 1890. Under this law, Asians were excluded from entry. Modifications were enacted in 1932 and 1936. By 1939 approximately 7,000 German Jews resettled to Uruguay.[24] No additional information for Uruguay was uncovered.

EXPRESSED NO CONCERN

Colombia

In 1929 Sebastian Moreno Arango compiled the Colombian laws and executive decrees governing foreigners. In this compilation, no specific treatment of *asilados* or refugees was found. However, he did note numerous bi- and multi-lateral extradition treaties, all of which contained a political offense exception to extradition.[25]

The Law of Immigration of 1920 contained no reference to *asilados* or refugees. A law in 1922 laid the groundwork for agricultural colonies in Colombia, but no special clauses pertaining to *asilados* or refugees were included. Nor was evidence uncovered of special efforts by Colombia to recruit refugees for colonial settlement. Approximately 6,000 Jewish refugees had been admitted by 1939, and a select group of Spanish Republicans were admitted in 1938-39. The size of this latter group, and the total numbers of refugees admitted, is not known.[26]

When contacted by the Nansen Office, Colombia responded that no problem relating to refugees required the attention of the Colombian government and that the legal and administrative dispositions in force in matters of passports did not admit holders of Nansen passports.[27]

Nicaragua

In 1931 Nicaragua informed the Nansen Office that the question of refugees was not of direct interest to the countries of the American continent. Nicaragua pledged to adhere to league recommendations for humanitarian reasons, so long as such recommendations were consistent with national laws and vital interests.[28]

LEGAL TRADITION

Ecuador

Although the first domestic legislation specifically concerned with refugees was not enacted until 1941, Ecuador has a history of recognizing *asilados* through political exception clauses in extradition treaties.[29] Materials referring to Ecuadoran legislation pertaining to extradition and naturalization before 1940 were not found. The first comprehensive treatment of naturalization found was in a law of 1940; as revised in 1941, it expressly recognized the right of asylum by stating that

those condemned or persecuted for political or religious crimes or for acts connected with these crimes or those that seek asylum in order to save their lives from immediate danger, will be able to enter the territory of the Republic and their temporary or permanent residence will be regulated by the Director of Immigration.

Moreover, they were exempt from extradition, except for the *attentat* clause; that is, assassination of a chief of state or members of his family. Also, a refugee would not be returned who was likely to be tried, *inter alia*, for a crime other than that contained in the extradition request or subject to special tribunal or proceedings. A returned asylee was prohibited from being turned over to a third country without the express consent of Ecuador.[30]

A decree in 1941 regulated passports. Nansen certificates of identity or other similar certificates granted by the League of Nations to Russian and Jewish refugees were accepted with the same requirements and considerations as ordinary passports. Interwar refugees in Ecuador totaled 2,500 Jews, of whom 500 resettled to other countries.[31]

In 1943 Ecuadoran jurist Rodrigo Jacome Moscoso proposed a plan to coordinate the Latin American laws on nationality within the existing framework of the continental system. His plan would also have extended constitutional and civil rights to immigrants and provided for regularization of work permits and licenses.[32] He argued that such regularization on a continental basis was necessary, as

> especially in the epochs of exodus, provided by racial, religious or political persecutions, all the fugitives abandon their place of origin or habitual residence, totally or partially deprived of the necessary documentation . . . The neighboring countries should receive without discrimination (such) a mass of refugees . . . Also, the authorities of the receiving state must regularize the permanancy of the refugee in its territory and issue each person an identity document.[33]

No reference to the work or suggestions of Jacome Moscoso was found in later works on the subject. It is unknown whether the author's ideas or framework were ever presented, or acted upon, in either the Pan-American Union or a Latin American Congress concerned with private international law.

Guatemala

Information on Guatemala during the interwar period is sparse. The first consolidation of national laws dealing with foreigners was done in 1894. In this work, Guatemala was recognized as an asylum to all foreigners, but *asilados* could be expelled for "the health of the nation."[34] No information is found indicating the number or places of origin of refugees that came to Guatemala during this time.

Mexico

General protection of all inhabitants of the United States of Mexico is found in its 1917 Constitution, which provides for the right to enter and leave Mexico, although foreigners are prohibited from engaging in the politics of the country.[35] A 1928 extradition treaty between Mexico and Panama prohibited extradition for press, military order, or political crimes. The exception to this for attempts against the life of a chief of state was included.[36] The Federal Labor Act of 1931 contained provisions discriminating between aliens and residents. According to the Restriction on Professional Practices Act of 1944, refugees could receive temporary permission to practice their profession. Children of refugees that met Mexican qualifications could also exercise a profession.[37]

In 1939 Mexico announced an open door for Spanish Republican refugees. A special delegation was sent from the Paris embassy to refugee camps in the Pyrenees. For those wishing to settle in Mexico, normal regulations for immigration were suspended. An estimated 16,000 men, 4,000 women, and 8,000 children who were Republican refugees entered Mexico in 1939. Government support for the Republicans and the open door for refugees scandalized the Mexican middle class and church hierarchy, and these groups engaged in a vitriolic campaign against the "Godless numbers" taking jobs from Mexicans.[38]

INTERPRETATIONS

No information on refugees or *asilados* is available for El Salvador, Honduras, Panama or Cuba. Few provisions of the institutions of diplomatic and territorial asylum, as contained in numerous Latin American extradition and asylum treaties, had been incorporated into domestic legislation at the close of the interwar period. Thus, while formal recognition was extended to the institution of political asylum, the actual protections afforded to *asilados* by individual states were uncoordinated and not uniform.

With the chaos resulting from the First World War, the international community began to identify and define the concept of refugee. While this term obviously overlaps in certain respects with the Latin American concept of *asilado*, the Latin American states were not actively involved in interwar refugee affairs. Efforts by Latin American states during the Spanish Civil War were an understandable exception. Spain remained the mother country of culture, religion, and language. But the generosity shown to the Spanish Republican refugees was not extended to the groups that the LON recognized as refugees.

This lack of uniform response had several causes. Religious and ethnic prejudices led to restrictions or prohibition of Jewish and non-European, nonwhite refugees. Political suspicions prevented acceptance of Russian and other refugees from the Bolshevik Revolution.

Except for the Dominican Republic's offer in 1938, no Latin American state made provisions in its immigration and colonization legislation for the settlement of groups of refugees. During the interwar years many Latin American states designed extensive national development plans most of which included an agricultural component, yet no Latin American state made a serious effort to recruit acceptable personnel from the interwar refugee populations.

This failure to actively recruit refugees as settlers can partially be explained by several factors. By the mid-1930's, the political climate in Latin America was not hospitable for Jewish refugees. Also, refugees from Europe were primarily of urban origin and did not possess the requisite skills sought by Latin American states. The few that were accepted by Latin American states as agricultural colonists soon proved unadaptable to their conditions, thus making the Latin American states less inclined to continue or expand such programs.

In sum, while inter-American instruments regulating asylum were concluded, Latin American states' practices were haphazard and not uniform, and the standards contained in these instruments were not translated into the member states' domestic legislation. Also, the Latin American states had little interest, need, or involvement with helping to form the rules or principles of international refugee law during the interwar period. Considered next are Latin American responses to the European refugee crisis that followed World War II; any change of perception of this issue at that time will be indicated in terms of their involvement with the IRO.

NOTES

1. Jacques Vernant, The Refugee in the Post-War World. (London: Allen and Unwin, 1953), p. 598.
2. Jorge Hechen, "The Argentine Republic," in The Positive Contribution of Immigrants (Paris: UNESCO, 1955), p. 148, 158.

3. LON, Resolution Submitted by the Committee of Experts to the Intergovernmental Advisory Commission for Refugees, (Legal [V] 1-8 C.266.M136 1933), 18 May 1933, p. 3; LON, Nansen International Office. Report to the Governing Body (A.24 1932), 16 August 1932, p. 17.

4. UN, ILO, Anexo al diagnostico migraciones laborales e integracion del refugiado en Argentina (RLA 83/VAROV), Buenos Aires, 1984. p. 49; Marcelo Hurtado Villa, Jaime Prudencio Cossio and Reynaldo Peters Arzabe. "Pautas para una legislacion Boliviana sobre el refugiado," in Asilo politico y situacion de refugiado (La Paz, Bolivia: Ministerio de relaciones exteriores, 1983), p. 93.

5. Vernant, Refugee, pp. 609, 612. Numerous abuses were recorded under this law: false declarations by refugees seeking resettlement, schemes selling unuseable land, and in 1938-39, the selling of illegal visas to German Jews in Hamburg. See also UN, ILO, Migraciones laborales e integracion del refugiado en Bolivia (RLA 83/VAROV), Buenos Aires, May 1984, p. 46.

6. Mario Roncal Antezana, "Tratamiento legal del refugiado dentro orden interno," in Asilo politico, pp. 49-51, 55-62.

7. Ernest Hambloch, "Brazilian Constitution of 1934," in Bound Volumes of Miscellaneous Pamphlets on Constitutional Law 3, no. 35., pp. 5-74.

8. Vernant, Refugee, pp. 617, 620-21.

9. Ibid., pp. 630-31.

10. UN, ILO, Migraciones laborales e integracion del refugiado en Republica Dominicana, Buenos Aires, July 1984, pp. 1-3.

11. Ibid., pp. 84-85; Vernant, Refugee, pp. 645-46; Louise Holborn, The International Refugee Organization (Oxford: Oxford University Press, 1956), pp. 405-06. The first 400 refugees had demonstrated great difficulties due to their lack of agricultural skills. Eventually this lack of skill was traced to false statements made by the refugees while still in Germany; fear and urgency for leaving had precluded consideration of the difficulties in adaptation to the agricultural lifestyle.

12. Brookings Institution, Refugee Settlement in the Dominican Republic (Washington, D.C., the Institution, 1942), pp. x, 7, 23, 63-69, 87, 143-44, 146.

13. Joseph Fretz, Immigrant Group Settlement in Paraguay (New York: ICEM, 1962), pp. 18-38.

14. Ibid., pp. 15, 51-53, 71-72, 81-91; LON, The Refugees (Geneva: LON, 1938), pp. 27-28.

15. Vernant, Refugee, pp. 668-69.

16. Venezuela, Ley de inmigracion y colonacion, Caracas, 1918, pp. 5-19, 42-58.

17. Holborn, International, p. 688; LON, Nansen Office, Report, 1932, p. 19.

18. Venezuela, Decreto que crea el Instituto Tecnico de Inmigracion y Colonizacion, Caracas, 1938, pp.   23-30, and Decreto Reglamentario del Instituto Tecnico de Inmigracion y Colonizacion, Caracas, 1938, pp. 33-89.

19.   Saskiam   Sassen-Koob,   "Economic   Growth   and Immigration in Venezuela," in International Migration Review 13, no. 47 (1979): 468.

20. Venezuela, Ley de extranjeros y su reglamento, Caracas, from Editorial La Torre, 29 June 1942.

21. Vernant, Refugee, pp. 686-87; Holborn, International, p. 409.

22. Vernant, Refugee, pp. 609, 612.

23. Ibid., pp. 671, 674.

24. Ibid., pp. 677, 679, 682.

25. The bilateral treaties listed were France-New Granada (23 July 1892, Article 5), Great Britain-Colombia (27 October 1888, Article 6), Spain-Colombia (23 July 1892, Article 5), Belgium-Colombia (21 August 1912, Article 4), Colombia-Chile (16 November 1914, Article 3, with the proviso that the crime is not considered political if the principle motive constituted a common crime), and Colombia-Panama (24 December 1927, Article 4 with the asylum state to determine the nature of the crime).   Sebastian Moreno Arango, Codificacion de las leyes y disposiciones ejecutivas sobre extranjeros (Bogota: Imprenta Nacional, 1929), pp. 49-87.

26. Vernant, Refugee, pp.   33-37, 642; LON, Nansen Office, Report, 1932, pp. 17, 20.

27. Luis Esguerra Camargo, Introduccion al estudio del problema inmigracion en Colombia (Bogota: Imprenta Nacional 1940), pp. 19-33.

28. LON, Nansen Office, Report, 1932, p. 18.

29. Ecuador-Brazil (1853, Articles 2 and 3), Ecuador-United States (1873, Article 3), Ecuador-Peru (1874, Article 9), Ecuador-Great Britain (1875, Article 8), Chile-Ecuador (1897, Article 6), and the Bolivarian Agreement of 1911. Luis Alfredo Robayo, Extranjeria, inmigracion, extradicion y naturalizacion (Quito: Imprenta Nacional, 1949), pp. 181-95, 216-28.

30. Ministerio de Gobierno, Recopilacion de la ley y regamentos de extranjeria y naturalizacion.   (Quito: Imprenta Nacional, 1941), pp. 25-78; Vernant, Refugee, p. 648.

31. Ministerio de Gobierno, Recopilacion, pp.   79-122; Vernant, Refugee, pp. 648, 657.

32. Rodrigo Jacome Moscoso, Nacionalidad y extranjeria (Quito: Imprenta Nacional, 1943), pp.   89-92, 170-71.   For comparisons of nationality categories restricted to Hispanic states and those states that provided categories in their constitutions or laws see pp. 93-118.

33. Ibid., p. 155.

34. Secretaria de Gobernacion y Justicia, Leyes de inmigracion y extranjera, Guatemala City, 1931, pp. 95, 100.

35. Filipe Tena Ramirez, ed., Leyes fundamentales de Mexico 1808-1978. Mexico City, 1978, pp. 821, 836.

36. Secretaria de Relaciones Exteriores, Memoria 1928-29, Tomo I. Mexico City , 1929, pp. 294-99.

37. Vernant, Refugee, p. 659.

38. Ibid., pp.   661-63; Judith Adler Hellman, Mexico in Crisis. (New York: Holmes and Meier, 1978), p. 39.

Chapter Three

The International Refugee
Organization and the
Latin American States

The Inter-Governmental Committee for Refugees (IGCR) sent four resettlement missions to Latin America in 1946. The impetus for these missions came from the announcement by Brazil that it was interested in admitting refugees to fill manpower needs. One mission went to Brazil; a second to Argentina, Paraguay, and Uruguay; a third to Bolivia, Peru, and Ecuador; and the fourth to Chile, Colombia, and Venezuela. Consequently, IGCR reception missions were established in Venezuela and Brazil.[1]

The experience of the IGCR well served the International Refugee Organization (IRO), which was established after World War II.[2] Something had been learned by the international community from its experience with refugees during the interwar years. For unlike in the period immediately following the First World War, refugee issues were among the first issues addressed by the newly created United Nations.

Postwar refugee issues were debated in the 3rd Committee of the UN General Assembly during 1946. A committee resolution of 12 February 1946 laid the groundwork for the treatment of refugees. Brazil, Colombia, the Dominican Republic, and Peru were included as countries of resettlement, which allowed them to participate on the Economic and Social Council (ECOSOC) Special Committee on Refugees and Displaced Persons. This

committee held sessions from April through June 1946, discussing
definitions of the word "refugee," the scope of the international
agency to deal with refugee problems, and the relationship of this
agency to the United Nations.[3] On 15 December 1946 the
constitution of the IRO was approved by the General Assembly,
with a vote of 30-5-18.[4] To smooth the transition from the IGCR
to the IRO, a preparatory committee of the IRO was created in
1947. The first IRO General Council was held on 13 September
1948. The Dominican Republic, Guatemala, and Venezuela were
members of this council; Brazil participated as an observer.[5] As
under the League of Nations, it was assumed that the postwar
refugee problem was temporary and would be solved in a
relatively short time. With this assumption, however, a conflict
was built into the operations of the IRO. Short-term institutional
provisions prohibited long-term planning, and the planned life
expectancy of the IRO was only until 30 June 1950. The main
receiving countries quickly fell behind in managing the influx of
European refugees. This backlog of refugees awaiting resettlement
created the need to extend the life of the IRO for the so-called
supplementary period, until 30 September 1951. Actual
operations continued until 1 March 1952, when the IRO was
succeeded by the UN High Commissioner for Refugees
(UNHCR).[6]

The IRO Constitution demonstrated the complexity of
defining a refugee, and of distinguishing a refugee from a
displaced person. In an expansion of the interwar refugee
criteria, which had focused on group membership or nationality,
under the IRO Constitution the term refugee applied to a person
who had left, or was outside of, his or her country of origin or
of former habitual residence and who, whether or not nationality
was retained, belonged to one of the following categories:
victims of Nazi or Fascist regimes; Spanish Republicans; persons
considered refugees prior to the Second World War; persons of
Jewish origin; foreigners or stateless persons who were victims of
Nazi persecution; and unaccompanied children, 16 years of age or
under. Excluded as refugees were war criminals, quislings
(collaborators with Nazi Germany) and traitors, ordinary criminals
extraditable by treaty, and any person who could be shown to
have assisted the forces of the enemies of the Allies. Articles 2,
4, and 13 of the constitution provided for legal and political
protection of refugees and granted the IRO legal capacity in the
territory of member states. Taken together, these articles enabled
the IRO to exercise a quasi-consular function. IRO responsibility
ceased when a refugee was repatriated, had acquired a new
nationality, or became well established in the country of
resettlement.[7]

All individuals eligible for refugee status under the IRO
Constitution were automatically granted legal and political

protection.   Thus eligibility determination was declaratory, not constitutive.   The IRO was charged to ensure that governments remained willing to grant asylum and the rights of nationality and immigration.[8]

Article 20 of the IRO Constitution transferred the functions of the IGCR to the IRO.   Travel arrangements and documentation were governed by the London Travel Agreement of 15 September 1946.   Concerning travel documents, stress was placed on inclusion of a return clause, which would enable a refugee to reenter a country on the same terms as individuals holding valid passports.   Repatriation also received detailed coverage, especially the principle of *non-refoulement*.[9]

Negotiations for resettlement agreements were complex and difficult.   Success and favorable terms often depended upon the good will between the IRO and resettlement governments.   Also, voluntary societies in resettlement states were necessary to ensure resettlement.   Resettlement agreements detailed the the basis for selection of refugees, number to be selected, age, family size or status, medical condition and standards, employment rights and duties, state guarantees, transportation, and administration services.[10]

Strict criteria of qualifications and country need had to be met for selection of resettlement to Latin America.   In general, resettlement to Latin America had severe limitations, as the countries concerned lacked the financial resources to undertake the burdens of sponsoring large numbers of refugees.   Most of the countries lacked adequate reception facilities.   Also, their economies lacked the dynamism to ensure that the refugees would rapidly attain self-sufficiency.   The chosen resettlement sites would place the refugees in pioneer conditions. Although Latin American countries preferred agricultural workers, most of the European refugees came from urban backgrounds and had no skills for such a life.[11]

Once refugees were resettled in Latin America, their successful integration remained difficult.   The most difficult point was providing the legal means for integrating them into the economic structure of the concerned country.   Unless special exemptions were made in domestic legislation, entry into the work force changed the person's status from refugee to that of an ordinary immigrant.   While the vast unsettled areas made a strong case for immigration, there remained the history of groups having difficulty with assimilation during the League of Nations period of refugee activities.

Of the European refugees resettled in Latin American states by the IRO, most indicated Latin America as their second choice of destination.   Follow-up studies showed that strong nostalgia for a return to Europe persisted in these refugee groups.   Even among those who were economically successful, psychological problems of adjustment to Latin society persisted.   A notoriously slow bureaucracy exacerbated these general problems.[12]

There is noted change between the Latin American states' interwar policy clusters and those under the IRO.   Colonization and immigration schemes were developed by several states (Argentina, Brazil, Venezuela), specifically targeting refugees. Brazil and Venezuela sustained close cooperation with the IRO throughout its lifetime.   For the remaining Latin American states, involvement with the IRO varied.   However, unlike in the interwar period, no state expressed indifference to the refugee issue.   Rather, the responses are clustered either as limited or select involvement with the IRO (Bolivia, Chile, Colombia, the Dominican Republic, Ecuador, Guatemala, Paraguay, Peru, Uruguay) or recognition of the refugee issue without involvement (Costa Rica, El Salvador, Nicaragua, Honduras, Mexico).   Mexico is an exception, having used bilateral agreements outside the IRO to resettle Spanish civil war refugees.

The three identified policy clusters are discussed in greater detail below. A summary of country participation with the IRO is presented first, followed by the domestic legislation.

COLONIZATION AND IMMIGRATION SCHEMES

Argentina

From 1946 until 1948, when an IRO office in Buenos Aires was opened, the Argentine government had no selection missions in the European refugee camps.   The IRO was given lists of acceptable refugees by national voluntary societies; visas and landing permits were granted to individuals on these lists.   The most active agencies were the Slovak League of America, the Holy Synod of the Orthodox Church, and the Slovene Welfare Society; all were headquartered in Buenos Aires.   During this initial period there was nominal government sponsorship for refugees, and many hardship cases were accepted.   There was also a separate arrangement to resettle Poles exiled in Great Britain during the war. The Polish Resettlement Office, working through the British Consulate General, functioned in the years 1948-50.[13]

Representatives of Argentine voluntary agencies were sent to IRO assembly centers in Germany, Austria, and Italy in 1947. Initially, a liberal visa-granting policy was followed. By August 1947, numerous Croats and Slovenes from Italian camps had been selected.   Following the signing *ad referendum* to the London Travel Agreement in 1947, permission for the entry of Russian

Orthodox refugees was granted.   Moreover, all these actions were taken prior to the reaching of a selection agreement with the IRO in 1948.[14] This agreement soon proved inadequate.   In late 1948 Argentina imposed restrictive entry laws, suspended the issuance of visas, and no longer accepted refugees sponsored by voluntary societies.   Instead, only individual sponsors with status as a first-degree relative were recognized.   Also, despite the signing of the London Travel Agreement, Argentina refused to accept any substitute document for a national passport.   No explanation for these actions was given to the IRO.   The healthy state of the Argentine economy provided no justification for such restrictions, which had a political motive, since the majority of the refugees accepted by Argentina had come from Central and Eastern Europe.[15]

By December 1948 all issuance of visas in the German zones had ceased. In January 1949 visa issuance was halted in Austria; and by the end of the month no Argentine consulate was issuing visas to European refugees.   A new selection agreement was negotiated only in August 1949.   Under this agreement, refugee resettlement was permitted only after conditions of strict skill criteria were met, and then approval was granted on a case-by-case basis.   During the same time, Argentina negotiated a series of bilateral migration agreements for individuals mostly of German, Italian, or Spanish origin. While not excluded from these bilateral arrangements, refugees were required to have private sponsors or critical skills before being accepted for resettlement.[16]

Two decrees in 1949 modified the 1941 immigration law. The Central Immigration Department was reorganized as the National Directorate General and was responsible for implementing the strict selection policy, ostensibly to safeguard the moral and economic health of the country. Admission required a visa from an Argentine consulate and certificates of good health. good behavior, and nonmendacity from competent authorities in the country of origin.   Refugees and *asilados* entering Argentina on an individual basis generally were not subject to special treatment. Argentina recognized as *asilados* only individuals coming from states parties to the 1889 Montevideo Convention on International Penal Law.   They were required to report to the authorities and declare their status within 72 hours of entry. An identity card would be issued, along with a list of restrictions on movement, residence, employment, and so on, and they had to report to the police every thirty days.   A decree in January 1945 provided for the expulsion of any refugee or *asilado* for reasons of public security.   Sentencing for a crime subject to more than three years imprisonment would lead to automatic expulsion and, if applicable, loss of citizenship.   After Argentina signed the London Travel Agreement *ad referendum*, immigration authorities were empowered to recognize IRO travel documents. Aliens passports would be issued to stateless persons or those unable to secure proper papers. Personal status was governed by the laws of the country of domicile.[17]

In the economic sphere, refugees were accorded equality before the law and, theoretically, allowed to carry out occupations for which they were qualified.   Restrictions were imposed on certain occupations, such as, law and medicine, and certain provinces required a minimum length of residence before allowing practice of an occupation.   There were no distinctions between nationals and aliens in such matters of social legislation as social security or hours of work. A decree of May 1946, as modified in June 1946, guaranteed insurance and pension rights and permitted a pension at the age of sixty if the person was a naturalized citizen or had been a resident alien for more than five years.[18]

The Argentine Constitution of 1949 included provisions on nationality and naturalization. To obtain naturalization a minimum two years of residency was required; naturalization was automatic after five years of residency unless an individual expressly requested otherwise.[19]

A 1949 amnesty decree, which regularized the status of illegal entrants, affected approximately 30,000 interwar, mostly Jewish, refugees.   Most of these were settled in Buenos Aires, which was the country's largest city and greatest job market and was also more attractive for settlement than provincial towns because the towns required more extensive documentation for residence, such as a provincial identity card in addition to the national identity card.[20]

Brazil

In 1946 Brazil announced its intention to admit refugees to meet labor shortages.   Consequently, a series of resettlement agreements were reached with both the IGCR and the IRO.   The IGCR agreement of 1947 provided for the admission of 1,000 families (15,000 individuals).   First arrivals landed in May 1947. Brazil expressed a preference for skilled labor and agricultural settlers for pioneer areas.   The Brazilian law that denied the right to practice a liberal profession to those trained in foreign countries was not relaxed to encourage refugee selection.[21]   In November 1947 Brazil signed *ad referendum* to the London Travel Agreement.[22]

An administrative agreement was reached with the Preparatory Committee for the International Refugee Organization on 30 April 1948.   It established a joint IRO/Brazilian committee to study questions of colonization, refugee assimilation and social welfare needs, employment, and legal status.   For budgetary reasons Brazil never ratified the IRO Constitution; hence there was no legal foundation for the joint committee. Nevertheless, a permanent secretariat had already been established, which can be credited with the successful coordination between government ministries.[23] The available documents indicate that Brazil was actively involved in IRO activities, participating in numerous sessions of the General Committee, and willing to support the flexible and expansive efforts of the organization.

An elaborate reception system for refugees was established. They would disembark at the Federal Reception Center on the Ilha das Flores near Rio de Janeiro. After the best placement for their skills had been determined, the refugees would be sent to state reception areas for placement. Most were settled in the states of Rio Grande de Sul, Parana, Santa Catarina, Rio de Janeiro, Guias, and Bahia.[24]

A resettlement agreement with the IRO was reached on 24 June 1948. This agreement guaranteed treatment of refugees "generally not less favorable than that enjoyed by Brazilian citizens under similar conditions and aptitudes." The rights of protection of refugees established in Brazil would be overseen by the IRO as long as the refugees remained stateless or for other reasons had lost protection.[25] The agreement was originally in force for only six months, but although never formally renewed, it continued until June 1949, when the Brazilian colonization schemes were declared bankrupt, necessitating the recall of all its selection missions. The joint committee was terminated on 15 December 1949. A change in federal administration brought renewal of the joint agreement, and new selection missions arrived in Europe in February 1951.[26]

An *asilado* or refugee seeking individual admission and residence in Brazil required a valid passport and health certificate. All persons over the age of 18 were required to register with the authorities within eight days of entry. Upon registration, an identity card would be issued, good also as a work permit. All changes of address or occupation had to be reported for a period of four years, and annual registration was required during this period. The London Travel Document was recognized. Stateless persons were issued an aliens passport or an IRO document of indeterminate nationality. Reentry was permitted only if the refugee had a permanent residence permit. Naturalization for non-Portuguese persons was governed by a 1949 law that which required five years of continued residency, or three years for critical occupations. Additional requirements for naturalization included knowledge of the Portuguese language, a minimum age of 18, a record of good behavior, good health, and a means of subsistence.[27]

Initially the National Immigration Department of the Ministry of Labor delt with the selection, reception, and placement of refugee groups. By 1949, group arrivals at the Rio center had been surpassed by individual refugee arrivals. Consequently, the placement of individuals became haphazard. Moreover, those settled as independent farmers or in agricultural colonies found life exceedingly difficult, since lack of basic infrastructure was a constant and severe problem.

In 1949 legislation was proposed to reorganize the several Brazilian government agencies handling immigration and refugee resettlement. A National Institute of Immigration and Colonization, attached to the president's office, absorbed the Council of Immigration and Colonization, the National Immigration Department, and the Colonization Bureau of the Ministry of Agriculture.[28] No further information on this reorganization was uncovered.

Venezuela

Venezuela reached a settlement agreement with the IGCR in 1947, but no specific number of refugees to be accepted was listed. Rather, the government would submit periodically a list of needed skills, and appropriate refugees would be screened. By an exchange of letters in April 1948, the agreement was continued under the IRO.[29]

In November 1947 Venezuela signed an unconditional travel document agreement with the IRO, and in January 1948 a selection mission was sent to the U.S. Zone in Germany. From January 1948 until the suspension of refugee airlift operations in November 1948, Venezuela accepted an average of 200 refugee families each month. The airlift was halted pending reorganization of the Venezuelan immigration department, which was undertaken in cooperation with the IRO.[30] The selection missions returned to Europe in July 1949, and 650 refugee families each month were selected until termination of the program on 30 November 1951.[31]

Prior to reorganization of the Venezuelan immigration policy in 1948, refugee resettlement was handled by the Technical Institute of Immigration and Colonization. Subsequently, the National Agrarian Institute assumed the functions and duties of the Technical Institute. Admission required a valid passport and visa and payment of an entry deposit. Venezuela did not recognize the Nansen Passport or statelessness. Individuals in either of these categories were classified according to country of birth. Refugees selected in Europe were issued an entry permit by the Agrarian Institute; residency permits were issued by the Ministry of the Interior.[32]

An *asilado* could be expelled for reasons of peace and

security of the Republic.   Violation of the residency restrictions imposed on *asilados* also resulted in expulsion.   The principle of *non-refoulement* was recognized.   No distinction between aliens and nationals was made in social legislation; however, liberal professions could be practiced only on the basis of reciprocity. Refugees and their families had access to free schooling and university education.   Naturalization required only two years residency and literacy in Spanish.   Since the paperwork for naturalization was costly, however, few refugees applied.[33]

Refugees encountered serious difficulties in the labor market in Venezuela.   While the selection missions in Europe screened the refugees for needed skills, the selection was not recognized by the Venezuelan Ministry of Labor.   Hence, many refugees anticipating employment upon arrival were confronted with an intransigent Minister of Labor.   Existing labor legislation granted Venezuelan nationals priority in filling critical or specialist occupations, and the Ministry of Labor refused to relax these conditions for selected refugees.[34]

SELECT AND LIMITED INVOLVEMENT

Bolivia

Bolivia had little involvement with the IRO.   In September 1947 the IRO received notice from the Bolivian Development Corporation that it was seeking agricultural settlers of Italian descent, and lists of other needed specialists were sporadically forwarded.   Due to unfavorable experience with some refugee groups, Spanish extraction for specialists was required beginning in 1949.[35] Admission required a permanent passport; a certificate of good behavior, lawful occupation, and medical status; and payment of an entry tax, plus deposit of a minimum sum.   All individuals arriving as refugees or *asilados* were required to register with the police within 48 hours of entry.   The Ministry of Immigration would issue an identity card.   Since Bolivia was not a party to the London Travel Agreement, a special decree regulated travel documents.   While no distinction was made between aliens and nationals in questions of social legislation, refugees had difficulty in practicing liberal professions even after recertification.   Naturalization required only a three years' residence.[36]

Chile

Chile signed a resettlement agreement with the IGCR in 1947. Refugees would be selected to fill skilled and semiskilled positions in the work force. The number of refugees selected would be determined by labor shortages, but a preference was given to Balts and Ukrainians. The General Directorate of Social Services issued identity cards and temporary residence permits. In general processing was slow, and selection teams sent to Europe were small and infrequent. The first Chilean selection missions arrived in Austrian camps in October 1947, but selection was halted in late 1948, pending development of a new selection process. The Chilean selection missions resumed operations in Austria and Germany in 1950. The IRO was disappointed at the small total number of refugees eventually resettled to Chile.[37]

The Standing Immigration Board was created in 1948, superseding the Coordinating Commission, which had been formed in 1946. For admission, individuals were required to possess a valid passport, visa, statement of abstention from domestic politics, and immigration card for employment and had to pay a set immigration fee to guarantee subsistence during the first six months in Chile. Residency permits were issued by the police, and immigrants were required to report within three days of entry. Social legislation, codified in 1945, made no distinction between aliens and nationals.[38]

As a party to the London Travel Agreement from 1947, Chile accepted unconditionally the travel documents issued by the IRO. If a refugee's documents expired, new identity and travel documents would be issued, but a return clause would not be included with the travel document. Naturalization required five years' continued residency in Chile.[39]

Colombia

Colombia signed a resettlement agreement with the IGCR in 1947. The 1,500-peso immigrant tax was waived for refugees, but only a small number eventually resettled. Also, political instability slowed economic development, thus making Colombia a less attractive destination. In 1948 Colombia informed the IRO that while it could offer no opportunities for mass resettlement, it was willing to consider refugees on an individual basis.[40]

In 1948 the Directorate for Immigration and Colonization was created. It was charged, *inter alia*, with determining areas best suited for colonization and was to act as a labor exchange. Admission required refugees to have a valid passport and certificates of good behavior, health, and personal status. While not a party to the London Travel Agreement, Colombia did grant visas to the holders of such documents. Entrants were required to report to the authorities within five days of entry to receive identity and residence cards. *Asilados* were assigned a residence and could be expelled for violation of the restrictions. Naturalization required five years of continuous residency (three years for those in a colonization scheme). No distinction between aliens and nationals was made in Colombian social and labor legislation.[41]

Dominican Republic

No reference to the Dominican Republic is found in the IRO documents. However, in March 1949 the Dominican government agreed to provide temporary admission for up to 800 European refugees stranded in Shanghai, and 200 White Russians arrived in October. Their Russian background created suspicions as to their political affiliations and loyalties; consequently, assimilation was difficult and never complete.[42]

Ecuador

Ecuador signed a resettlement agreement with the IGCR in 1947. While interested primarily in specialists to fill skilled job shortages, Ecuador was willing to consider settlement of small families as well. The 1947 Law on the Status of Aliens established an Immigration Board, responsible for fixing annual quotas for immigrant groups. However, this act contained no specific mention of refugees or *asilados*. Ecuador signed *ad referendum* to the London Travel Agreement, recognized as valid only if containing a reentry visa.[43]

In his 1949 study of Ecuadoran aliens policy, the jurist Luis Alfredo Robayo criticized the lack of special provisions for *asilados*. He recognized that their special situation involves ideological conflict and sudden social convulsion in their home country and that under these circumstances, host countries are required to extend special treatment. In his draft Aliens Law, Robayo suggested that they receive all the personal guarantees and protections extended to Ecuadoran nationals and special treatment to promote their assimilation.[44] No further mention of this study, or concrete government actions in response to these suggestions, was found.

Regulations for the Application of Provisions concerning

Naturalization, Extradition, and Deportation were adopted by Ecuador in 1950. No mention was made of refugees. Under these regulations, Ecuador was not obliged to extradite for political crimes or common crimes connected therewith. If deportation of an alien was impossible, then the Ministry of the Interior would order confinement in an agricultural or penal colony.[45]

To be admitted as an *asilado* required a valid passport, visa and health certificate. Upon entry, a set sum would be deposited as a guarantee of solvency. Residence permits were obtained through the appropriate provincial authorities. Naturalization required only two years' continued residence.[46]

Guatemala

An IRO mission was established in Guatemala City by an exchange of letters in 1948. The majority of refugees accepted by Guatemala were Spanish Republicans from southern France. Few of them adapted successfully, and in 1949 the Guatemalan delegate to the IRO General Committee announced that immigration plans were impossible to implement due to lack of funds.[47]

Guatemalan domestic law contained no provisions on refugees; they were covered by the aliens legislation. *Asilados* were exempt from having a valid passport for entry into the territory. They were required to report to the police within 48 hours of entry. Those without travel documents would receive an identity card from the police. All could be subject to residence restrictions; failure to abide by which would lead to expulsion, but not to a persecuting country.[48]

Paraguay

There is no mention of Paraguay in the available IRO materials, but a Paraguayan decree of 1946 granted identical advantages to all categories of immigrants. Refugees were exempted from the aliens entry deposit. While in principle there was no discrimination for entrants, in practice the authorities discouraged the entry of certain racial groups. Admission required the possession of a valid passport and medical, occupational, and good behavior certificates. Upon entry, refugees were required to register with the Department of Agriculture and Land Settlement, where they would be issued a six-month visa. Personal status was governed by the Argentine

Civil Code, which made no distinction between aliens and nationals in matters of social legislation. Expulsion for reasons of state security was permitted. While Paraguay was not a party to the London Travel Agreement, it did recognize that document for select groups of refugees.[49]

Peru

An agreement with the IGCR was reached in 1947, and an IRO field office was opened in Lima in 1948. However, visa issuance and transport of refugees to Peru were halted in early 1949. Most of the refugees who resettled in Peru were concentrated in the cities, and not on agricultural settlements as expected. Peruvian authorities discovered that many of the refugees had made false occupational statements to IRO personnel.[50]

Admission required a certificate of good behavior and a deposit sufficient to cover a return trip to the country of origin. Those of communist, anarchist, or totalitarian persuasion were denied entry. Upon registration at the Aliens Office, an identity card was issued that also served as a residence permit. Aliens were required to renew this card annually for two years and pay an annual residence tax. Naturalization required only two years of residency and literacy in Spanish. Aliens, including refugees, could be expelled for reasons of state security or public peace.[51]

Uruguay

Available IRO materials contain no mention of Uruguay. Under a decree issued in 1947, the Ministry of Interior was made responsible for refugees. In 1948 the National Colonization Institute assumed this responsibility. Admission to Uruguay could be on a temporary or permanent basis. IRO refugees were provided with free residence permits, of which only 100 were issued, all to the Central Mennonite Committee. Naturalization required three years of residence, five years if single. After an additional three years of residency, naturalized citizens acquired the full rights granted Uruguayans by birth. Uruguay was not a party to the London Travel Agreement.[52]

LEGAL RECOGNITION, NO INVOLVEMENT

Costa Rica

No mention of Costa Rica is found in the available IRO documents, but the Costa Rican constitution of 1949 recognizes the territory of Costa Rica as an asylum for all persecuted for political reasons. Extradition for political crimes was prohibited, and the language used in the articles relating to personal, economic, and social guarantees was clearly based on the wording of the corresponding articles of the 1948 Universal Declaration of Human Rights.[53]

El Salvador

No mention of El Salvador is found in available IRO documents. The only references applicable to refugees were contained in the 1950 Constitution of El Salvador. It embodied a number of the economic, social, and cultural rights proclaimed by the Universal Declaration.[54]

Honduras

A Honduran Decree of 1946 provided for the expulsion of aliens for totalitarian, communist, or subversive activities. In 1949 Honduras reached agreement with the IRO to recognize the IRO travel documents for holders in transit through the Honduran territory.[55]

Mexico

Mexico had little involvement with the IRO. Refugees were selected by Mexico according to bilateral agreements with other countries. Thus, pursuant to an agreement signed with the Polish exile government in London in 1942, Mexico established the Colonia Santa Rosa for Polish refugees from Iran and India. By the end of the Second World War, 1,490 Poles had resettled to Mexico; 769 found work in Mexico. The camp was closed on 1 January 1947. In 1948, Mexico sent a mission to Portugal for selection of a limited number of refugees, and in the years 1945-52, approximately 28,000 Spanish Republican refugees were accepted.[56]

In 1947 the General Population Law was enacted. Under Mexican law *asilados* were classed as nonimmigrants and were the responsibility of the Ministry of the Interior. They could remain in Mexico depending on the circumstances in their country of origin, reviewed annually. Also, they were subject to a lesser entry fee than aliens generally. Their visas could be revoked for reasons of public order, and the federal executive reserved the right of expulsion without due process. Otherwise, *asilados* were guaranteed the same rights as nationals. Naturalization required five years' residency, but a naturalized citizen had a lesser status than a Mexican by birth. Mexico was not party to the London Travel Agreement and did not recognize its travel document.[57]

Nicaragua

The available IRO documents contained no mention of Nicaragua. The only information applicable to refugees is found in the 1950 constitution, which accepted the American Declaration of the Rights and Duties of Man and recognized the right of asylum. Aliens had the same rights and guarantees as nationals. Extradition for political crimes was prohibited, and the territory of Nicaragua was recognized as an asylum for those persecuted for political reasons. The principle of *non-refoulement* was recognized.[58]

INTERPRETATIONS

Compared with the interwar period, some improvement in policies pertaining to refugees and *asilados* can be noted. However, this improvement was confined to the larger, more developed states of South America, that is, Argentina, Brazil, and Venezuela, and among these, domestic political turmoil soon forced Argentina out of active involvement with the IRO.

Despite occasional difficulties, the undertakings of Brazil and Venezuela were relatively successful. The vast pool of skilled unemployed refugees resulting from the Second World War presented an opportunity for accelerated economic development. Hence, active involvement with refugee concerns by Brazil and Venezuela was determined primarily by economic policy goals and not philanthropic sentiment. This does not deny the acceptance of added burdens of hard-core refugees along with the greater numbers of economically active individuals.

The remaining states of South America had little involvement with refugee resettlement. Their interest was limited for a variety of reasons: lack of economic growth and a tight labor market (Chile, Colombia, Ecuador), lack of space (Ecuador, Uruguay), and unfavorable experiences with refugees in the past (Peru). The Central American and Caribbean states lacked the resources to become involved with refugees. Guatemalan plans for large-scale resettlement soon collapsed for financial reasons, and after its unsuccessful colonization scheme of 1938, the Dominican Republic had little incentive to become involved with refugees again.

Mexico's behavior toward refugee concerns was consistent with its overall international profile: high salience on humanitarian questions, but caution in practical undertakings. Perhaps the hostility generated by the Mexican open-door policy for Spanish Republicans during the interwar years had made the authorities more cautious of renewed involvement with refugees. Yet additional Spanish Republicans were accepted between 1945 and 1950, and apparently this group was far better received. A second reason for Mexico's attitude was reluctance to get involved with international institutions in the early postwar years. Perhaps active involvement with the IRO could be perceived as compromising Mexican sovereignty, hence the preference for refugee selection on a bilateral basis.

In all the Latin American states, domestic legislation lacked specific provisions for refugees. The experience with refugees under the League of Nations and Nansen Office had been insufficient to have an impact on domestic legislation. This does not imply that the Latin American states were lagging behind the international community in this regard. The guiding assumption of the IRO was that the refugee problem was temporary and solvable.

Where the issue of asylum was dealt with in domestic legislation, its conditions were regulated within the framework of the inter-American treaties on asylum. However, the protection accorded *asilados* is not directly comparable to the protection provisions of the IRO Constitution. While certain legal categories did overlap, essentially the IRO and the inter-American asylum treaties dealt with different situations. The Latin American states' concern with refugees would not be sparked for another two decades, and then only in response to events within the Western hemisphere itself.

Although successful in easing the burden of postwar European refugees, the IRO had a limited mandate and was dissolved. However, since refugees remained a concern of the international community, the IRO was replaced with components that subsequently evolved into a global refugees regime. This global regime is the subject of the next chapter.

NOTES

1. International Refugee Organization (hereafter IRO), Migration from Europe. (Geneva: IRO, 1951), pp. 20, 26; Louise Holborn, The International Refugee Organization (Oxford: Oxford University Press, 1956), p. 368; Holborn, Refugees: A Problem in Our Time, Vol. 1, (Metuchen, N.J.: Scarecrow Press, 1975), p. 171.
2. Holborn, International, pp. 19, 25-27, 56-61.
3. Ibid., pp. 29-39.
4. Ibid., pp. 45, 54. For general review of amendments, debates, and passage of the IRO Constitution, see pp. 43-46. Cuba, the Dominican Republic, Ecuador, Guatemala, Honduras, Mexico, Nicaragua, Panama, Paraguay, Peru, Uruguay, and Venezuela voted in favor; Argentina, Bolivia, Brazil, Chile, Colombia and Costa Rica abstained. El Salvador was not present for the vote. Guatemala, Honduras and the Dominican Republic adhered to the constitution that same month.
5. Ibid., pp. 54, 627; IRO, Migration, op. cit. p. 1.
6. Holborn, International, pp. 54-67; Organization of American States (hereafter OAS), Inter-American Yearbook on Human Rights 1960-1967 (Washington, D.C.: OAS, 1968), p. 485.
7. Holborn, International, pp. 47-53, 203, 311-12, Appendix I: Constitution of the IRO.
8. Ibid., pp. 313-19, 321-22.
9. IRO, Report on the Policy of the IRO Regarding Repatriation and Resettlement (GC/4), 13 September 1948.
10. Holborn, International, pp. 127-28, 144-52, 157.
11. IRO, The Facts About Refugees. (Geneva: IRO, 1948), pp. 14- 15.
12. Jacques Vernant, The Refugee in the Post-War World. (London: Allen and Unwin, 1953), pp. 579-93.
13. Vernant, Refugee. p. 603; Holborn, International, pp. 401-2.
14. IRO, General Committee. Preparatory Committee Information Bulletin 23 (PC/PI/IB:23), 12 July 1948, p. 65; IRO, General Committee, Report of the Director General on the Activities of the Organization since 1 July 1948, Information Bulletin 60 (IRO/GC/60), 22 March 1949, p. 46. Signature ad referendum is a provisional acceptance of an international agreement, pending government approval.
15. Vernant, Refugee, pp. 603-05.
16. IRO, Information Bulletin 7 (IRO/PI/IB/7), 15 December 1948, p. 2; IRO, Information Bulletin 9 (IRO/PI/IB/9), 1 February 1949, p. 3; IRO, Information Bulletin 21 (IRO/PI/IB/21), 1 August 1949, p. 8; UN, General

Assembly, 9th sess., Report of the United Nations High
Commissioner for Refugees (1954) (A/2648/Add. 1/Add. 2), UN:
New York, 1954, p. 17.
    17. Vernant, Refugee, pp. 598-601.
    18. Ibid., pp. 601-2.
    19. Ibid.
    20. Ibid., p. 605.
    21. IRO, Migration, pp. 26-27; Holborn, International, p.
402.
    22. IRO, Preparatory Committee Information Bulletin 12
(PC/PI/IB/12), 15 November 1947, p.   3; IRO, Preparatory
Committee Information Bulletin 13 (PC/PI/IB/13), 24 November
1947, p. 8.
    23. IRO, General Committee, Summary Record of the First
Session (IRO/GC/SR 1), 13 October 1948, p.   10; IRO,
Semi-Annual Report 1 July 1951 to 31 December 1951
(IRO/GC/256), January 1952.
    24. IRO, Migration, p.   73; Holborn, International, pp.
402-4; IRO, Preparatory Committee Information Bulletin 22
(PC/PI/IB/22), 26 May 1948, pp. 22-23; Vernant, Refugee, p.
622.
    25. UN, Department of Social Affairs, A Study of
Statelessness, (Lake Success, New York: UN, 1949), p. 50.
    26. IRO, Information Bulletin 11 (IRO/PI/IB/11), 1 March
1949, p. 8.
    27. Vernant, Refugee, pp. 616-17, 619, 626-27.
    28. Ibid., pp. 620-21, 624-25.
    29. Holborn, International, pp. 407-09.
    30. IRO, General Committee, Summary Record of the
Second Meeting (IRO/GC/SR 2), 13 October 1948, p.   1; IRO,
General Committee, Summary Record of the Third Meeting
(IRO/GC/SR 3), 12 November 1948, p. 8-9.
    31. IRO, Preparatory Committee 12, p.   45; IRO,
Preparatory Committee Information Bulletin 16 (PC/PI/IB/16), 24
January 1948, p. 64; IRO, Preparatory Committee 23, p. 64;
IRO, Information Bulletin 19 (IRO/PI/IB/19), 1 July 1949, p.   5;
IRO, Semi-Annual Report 1951, p. 8.
    32. Vernant, Refugee, p. 698; Holborn, International, pp.
407-9.
    33. Vernant, Refugee, pp. 688-92; Holborn, International,
p. 408.
    34. Vernant, Refugee, p.   693; Holborn, International, p.
409.
    35. IRO, Information Bulletin 15 (IRO/PI/IB/15), 30 April
1949, p.   4; IRO, Information Bulletin 20 (IRO/PI/IB/20), 15
July 1949, p. 8.
    36. Decree of 20 May 1947; see Vernant, Refugee, pp.
609-11, 613.

37. Vernant, Refugee, pp. 635-38; Holborn, International, p. 16, 401-5; Holborn, Refugees, p. 637; IRO, Preparatory Commitee Information Bulletin 9 (PC/PI/IB/9), 9 October 1947, p. 3; IRO, Information Bulletin 16 (IRO/PI/IB/16), 15 May 1949, p. 5; IRO, Report of the Director General 1949, pp. 46-47; IRO, General Committee, Report of the Director General to the General Committee of the IRO, 1948-1949 (IRO/GC/100), March 1950, p. 43.

38. Vernant, Refugee, pp. 631-5; Holborn, Refugees, p. 637.

39. IRO, Preparatory Committee 12, p. 45.

40. Agreement of 15 March 1947; see IRO, Report of the Director General 1949, p. 47.

41. Vernant, Refugee, pp. 639-42; UN, Yearbook on Human Rights for 1951 (New York: UN, 1953), pp. 49-50; Decree 2662 of 5 August 1950, amended by Decree 3743 of 20 December 1950. Article 2 provided that the Labor Code applied throughout the territory to every inhabitant, irrespective of nationality. Article 8 guaranteed the freedom of choice of work. Article 10 provided for equality of protection and guarantees to all employees. And Article 22 stated that where doubt or conflict in application of the code arose, the provisions most favorable to the employee were to be applied.

42. Holborn, International, pp. 405-06.

43. Agreement of 21 April 1947, Aliens Law of 20 February 1947; see UN, Yearbook on Human Rights for 1947 (New York: UN, 1949), pp. 92-94; Holborn, International, p. 406; IRO, Preparatory Committee 12, p. 45.

44. Luis Alfredo Robayo, Extranjeria, inmigracion, extradicion y naturalizacion (Quito: Imprenta Nacional, 1949), pp. 20-21, 149.

45. UN, Yearbook on Human Rights for 1950, (New York: UN, 1952), p. 73.

46. Vernant, Refugee, pp. 648-51.

47. IRO, General Committee, Summary Record of the Twenty-fifth Meeting (IRO/GC/SR 25), 21 April 1949, pp. 15-16; IRO, General Committee, Summary Record of the Forty-first Meeting (IRO/GC/SR 41), 4 July 1949, p. 5; IRO, General Committee, Summary Record of the Fifty-eighth Meeting (IRO/GC/SR 58), 22 October 1949, p. 9.

48. Vernant, Refugee, pp. 652-53.

49. Decree 13.979 of 6 June 1946, see Vernant, Refugee, pp. 665-68; Holborn, International, pp. 406-07.

50. IRO, Preparatory Committee Information Bulletin 1 (PC/PI/IB/1), 8 September 1947, p. 5; IRO, Preparatory Committee Information Bulletin 24 (PC/PI/IB/24), 27 August 1948, p. 3; IRO, Report of the Director General, 1949, p. 47.

51. Decree 110409 of 1949; see Vernant, Refugee, pp.

671-73; ICJ, States of Emergency (Geneva: ICJ, 1983), pp. 251-52.

52. Vernant, Refugee, pp. 677-82; Holborn, International, p. 407.

53. UN, Department of Social Affairs, The Impact of the Universal Declaration of Human Rights (New York: UN, 1953), p. 31; Pan American Union (hereafter PAU), Constitution of the Republic of Costa Rica, 1949 (Law and Treaty Series no. 35), (Washington, D.C.: PAU, 1951), p. 6.

54. UN, Department of Social Affairs, Impact, pp. 31-32.

55. Honduras, Decree 95 of 7 March 1946; IRO, Information Bulletin 18 (IRO/PI/IB/18), 15 June 1949, p. 9.

56. IRO, Preparatory Committee 23, pp. 48-49; Holborn, International, p. 176;

57. Vernant, Refugee, pp. 657-58, 660-61.

58. PAU, Constitution of the Republic of Nicaragua, 1950, (Law and Treaty Series no. 36), (Washington, D.C.: PAU, 1954).

Chapter Four

The Global Refugees Regime

Contemporary refugee law has its foundations in the League of Nations system. The various refugee organizations affiliated with the league from 1920 to 1946 were the first truly functional approaches to the refugee problem. However, the negotiated instruments and practices of these organizations remained insufficient to qualify as an international regime.

In 1946 all refugee functions of the league were turned over to a newly created agency of the United Nations, the International Refugee Organization (IRO). The IRO was given a time-limited mandate to solve the problem of postwar European refugees. At the expiration of this mandate, some member states of the United Nations realized that more permanent action for refugees was required. Toward this end, in the early 1950s the international community agreed to minimum standards applicable to refugees. These standards are stated in a convention and are protected by an office of the United Nations system, that of the High Commissioner for Refugees (UNHCR).

Legal questions pertaining to refugees fall into three usually overlapping categories. The first is refugee law, as such, as reflected in international instruments, including the 1951 Refugees Convention, 1954 Stateless Persons Convention, 1967 Protocol to the Refugees Convention, Statute of the United Nations High Commissioner for Refugees and those resolutions of the General Assembly that refer to and interpret any of the foregoing. The second is international declarations that recognize universal human

rights, such as the 1948 Universal Declaration. The third
category is the humanitarian law of armed conflict, best reflected
in the 1949 Geneva Conventions and the two Protocols Additional
of 1977.[1] (For Latin American states-parties to the global refugees
regime, see Table 2 of the appendix to this book.)

COMPONENTS OF THE GLOBAL REFUGEES REGIME

The substantive component of the global refugees regime has
expression in two dimensions. First, the negotiated dimension is
reflected by the 1951 Refugees Convention and its 1967 protocol
and the 1954 Stateless Persons Convention. These global
instruments establish definitions, minimum standards of treatment,
and requirements for implementation of treaty provisions for all
those individuals governed by the instruments. As shown below,
this negotiated dimension includes authoritative international norms
(e.g., the principle of *non-refoulement*) and international standards
with self-selecting national exceptions (e.g., the geographic
limitation of the 1951 convention). Since provisions of the 1954
Convention on Stateless Persons dovetail very closely with
provisions of the 1951 Refugee Convention, the two will be
discussed together.

The prevailing assumption during the conference drafting the
1951 Refugees Convention was that refugees were a short-lived
disturbance in the international system. Postwar European
refugees were the major concern. Consequently, the parties to
the convention are given a choice of geographic scope of its
provisions. If a state applies the global convention only to events
in Europe, this means that it has adopted the "geographic
restriction" or "geographic limitation" of the convention.[2]

The preambles to both the 1951 and 1954 instruments
invoke the international guidelines of the UN Charter and the
Universal Declaration of Human Rights, so to ensure the widest
possible exercise of fundamental rights and freedoms. Neither
instrument grants refugees or stateless persons an affirmative right
to enter the territories of states parties; however, in the case of
refugees there is a restriction on returning persons to states where
they may face persecution. This restriction on *refoulement*
operates indirectly to grant a right of entry if it happens that the
only choice facing a state party is admission or *refoulement*.
Under the Refugees Convention only this situation requires that a
state party admit the person. Although the Stateless Persons
Convention contains no reference to *non-refoulement*, the delegates
at the conference agreed that explicit restatement of
non-refoulement was unnecessary, since it was recognized as a
general principle of international law.[3]

Both conventions list particular rights and freedoms to which refugees and stateless persons are entitled. Basic rights are laid down in absolute terms; equated rights are rights equal to those possessed by other groups of persons. Thus, equated rights vary from host state to host state, while basic rights are common to all refugees and stateless persons in all states parties to the conventions.[4]

As far as basic rights of refugees and stateless persons are concerned, nondiscrimination on the basis of race, religion, or country of origin is required; these persons have the right of access to courts of the host country; after three years' residence they are to be free from labor legislation designed to protect host country nationals; host states may not apply restrictive measures to refugees who have either a spouse or a child who is a national of the host state. Refugees have the right to be issued with valid identity papers and travel documents by the host state. Upon resettlement to another state, they are entitled to take with them any assests brought from the host country. Expulsion is prohibited except on the grounds of national security or *ordre public*; the latter term is vague, corresponding in general to the term public policy.[5]

Under the Refugees Convention illegal entry has no bearing on an individual's status as a refugee and thus is classed as a basic right. However, the mode of entry does have a bearing on treatment by the host state, that is, national standards of treatment may become operative. Thus the convention states that if an unlawful entrant presents himself or herself without delay to host state authorities and shows good cause for illegal entry or presence, then the host state shall not impose penalities. It is not clear whether this phrase prohibits prosecution and conviction for unlawful entry. It may mean that after convicting a refugee the state may not impose penalties. Private employers, however, would be free to discriminate against a refugee on the grounds of possession of a criminal record. Nor is the host state required to recognize the person in question as being lawfully in the territory after he has presented himself to the proper authorities. The host state thus remains free to withhold certain benefits expressly guaranteed only to refugees lawfully in the territory: rights of association, most favorable treatment regarding wage-earning employment, self-employment, exercise of liberal professions, housing, public relief, application of labor and social security legislation, freedom of movement, issuance of travel documents, and protection from ordinary expulsion.[6]

Equated rights form four categories: rights afforded nationals of the refugee's or stateless person's home state, national treatment; most-favored-alien status, and rights granted aliens generally. Under both conventions personal status is governed by the law of the country of domicile. National treatment is afforded the following rights: freedom of religion and religious education, ownership of artistic and industrial property, legal assistance, participation in rationing systems, elementary education, and labor and social security legislation.[7] Refugees only are entitled to most-favored-alien treatment with regard to formation of nonpolitical and nonprofit associations and trade unions and wage-earning employment.[8] Both refugees and stateless persons are granted rights generally available to aliens with respect to property, self-employment and practice of liberal professions, housing, public education above the elementary level, and freedom of movement within the host state.[9]

Both conventions also have substantive deficiencies; that is, where the international instrument is silent, national standards operate. Refugees are recognized as such on the basis of their well-founded fear of persecution, but the Refugees Convention does not define persecution. Determination is left to states parties, and no coherent practice exists on this question.[10] Nor does either convention contain provisions requiring implementation of regime norms, that is, legislative incorporation or establishing procedures for determination of status. States have discretion as to means of implementation: legislative incorporation, administrative procedures, informal and ad-hoc procedures, or a combination.[11]

Procedural and implementation mechanisms for enforcement, implementation, and promotion of the substantive standards expressed by these conventions are found in the institutional dimension of the global regime. Both conventions require states parties to inform the secretary-general of the United Nations of laws and regulations adopted to ensure application of convention provisions. Only the Refugees Convention, however, requires cooperation of national authorities with UN agencies for application of the provisions.[12] The key UN agencies and bodies forming the procedural and implementation mechanisms of the global refugees regime are the General Assembly, the Economic and Social Council (ECOSOC), the Executive Committee of the High Commissioner for Refugees (EXCOM), and the Office of the High Commissioner for Refugees (UNHCR).

The UNHCR initially was established as the institutional mechanism to enforce the 1951 Refugees Convention. ECOSOC is charged with monitoring and oversight of UNHCR activities, and reports annually to the General Assembly, which has ultimate responsibility for UNHCR. With regard to the global refugees regime, both the General Assembly and ECOSOC primarily have been concerned with promotion of regime standards. Promotion activities include, frequent commendation of UNHCR activities, ex post facto expansion of UNHCR prerogatives (essentially necessary responses to emergency situations) by General Assembly Resolutions, and annual reports from UNHCR to ECOSOC and the General Assembly. These reports are a form of information exchange, but they seem to have little consequence for regime enforcement or implementation. Insufficient time and attention is given to UNHCR specifically, or refugees generally, by ECOSOC or the General Assembly. In the early years of refugee affairs (1959-64), ECOSOC had sufficient time and interest for some detailed involvement with UNHCR annual reports, but with the rapid proliferation of refugee crises in Africa (1960s) and Indochina (since 1975), ECOSOC involvement has declined. Since 1970, the UNHCR annual reports have been routinely accepted by ECOSOC and passed to the General Assembly without debate. Normally the General Assembly accepts the ECOSOC recommendation of acceptance of the UNHCR annual report without substantive debate as well. Review of ECOSOC records for 1952-1984 found no question or references to questions about legal protection in Latin America or concern for political refugees in Latin America.[13]

The more effective components of procedure and implementation are found within UNHCR: the EXCOM and the Office of the UNHCR. The EXCOM is composed of 41 states parties to the global refugees regime, elected by the General Assembly. Decisions are taken by consensus, and this body is responsible for direction of UNHCR activities, both internally and internationally. As such, then, the EXCOM is involved with promotion, implementation, and enforcement of the global refugees regime. Under certain circumstances (see below), EXCOM promotion and implementation activities have substantive consequences, which are incorporation of new or additional international guidelines and standards into the global regime.

Several decision-making procedures are used by the EXCOM and UNHCR in performance of their promotion and implementation activities.

1. International promotion and assistance of the regime is done through annual meetings of the EXCOM, its sponsoring of special committee reports on newly emergent issues, and its general support of UNHCR's expansive legal protection activities.

2. Information exchange is encouraged by calling upon states parties to comply with reporting and cooperation requirements.

3. International policy is coordinated by supporting UNHCR efforts to draft model legislation for regime implementation, sponsoring regional colloquia to identify shared standards and harmonization of national policies.

4. There is international monitoring of state practice, as reported by UNHCR field personnel or by interested member states.

Actual enforcement activities must be inferred; this assumes that continued political and moral pressure from the EXCOM and UNHCR eventually can lead to a change in state behavior toward compliance with requirements of the global regime. A degree of self-regulation is also assumed: states will comply with regime requirements on the basis of reciprocity.

In 1952 the ECOSOC established the High Commissioner's Advisory Committee on Refugees. Brazil and Venezuela were the only original Latin American member states. In 1955 this committee was restructured and renamed the Executive Committee (EXCOM). Since 1955 Brazil, Colombia, and Venezuela have always been members. Argentina and Nicaragua became members with the latest expansion of EXCOM members in 1983.[14]

A review of EXCOM records for 1955-79 indicated no recorded comments relating to international protection made by any Latin American state, either as member or observer. Even the events in Chile following the 1973 coup elicited no recorded comments from the Latin American states.   It is only in connection with the turmoil in Central America since 1979 that Latin American states have more frequently appeared before the EXCOM; for example, in 1979 both Honduras and Nicaragua sent observers to explain their countries' asylum policies. The refugee problem in Central America received detailed scrutiny from the EXCOM in 1985.[15]

OFFICE OF THE HIGH COMMISSIONER

As mentioned previously, UNHCR is the agency intended to enforce the 1951 Refugees Convention.   Until 1986 its structure was comprised of the executive office of the High Commissioner; the four divisions of protection, assistance, external affairs, and administration and management; eight regional sections, which provide the geographical coverage of UNHCR activities; and UNHCR field offices.

The executive office is headed by the High Commissioner, who is elected by the General Assembly and reports to it through the ECOSOC.   He is responsible for the overall policy and direction of UNHCR in accordance with the provisions of the statute and the relevant General Assembly resolutions.   In 1986 the Division of International Protection was reorganized and renamed the Division of Refugee Law and Doctrine.   Under this reorganization, first, the five regional bureaus were given direct day-to-day responsibility for all aspects of UNHCR office activities, including protection matters; second, the title change emphasizes a new orientation. The division is linked with and gives support and advice to the regional bureaus in their protection activities. It also carrys out research, promoting refugee law and developing doctrine.

The Division of International Protection had three functional sections:

1. the General Legal Section, responsible for matters concerning refugee instruments (global and regional), instruments relating to stateless persons and such matters as asylum, determination of refugee status, *refoulement*, expulsion, extradition, voluntary repatriation, nationality, and naturalization;

2. the Conferences and Treaty Section, responsible for the promotion of international humanitarian law and international instruments on human rights as they affect refugees; and

3. the Research and General Legal Advisory Unit is responsible for research and study of longer-term protection policy objectives and general legal problems.

The 1986 reorganization provided the Division of Refugee Law and Doctrine with additional capacity, both in terms of staff and material support, to provide additional professional advice on matters relating to refugee law and international protection. Computer facilities were introduced, to support these activities and to monitor states' practices and legal developments in the field of protection. Furthermore, a group of regional advisers provide the link between the regional bureaus and the division and ensure uniform application and respect for protection principles internationally. The unit in charge of promotion and dissemination of refugee law develops training program for UNHCR staff members, government officials, and other personnnel outside UNHCR. Finally, the Center for Documentation on Refugees has been brought under the Division of Refugee Law and Doctrine and is currently establishing an international network for the exchange of information with other documentation centers.[16] Regional sections are the operational backbone of the office and are most directly involved with regime implementation. The chiefs of the regional sections are responsible, under the overall direction of the protection and assistance divisions, for coordination of the UNHCR field establishment. Within their regions, they are responsible for ensuring that the policies of UNHCR are fully implemented, compiling and analyzing information on refugee situations and on legal, social, and economic developments relevant to refugee affairs and formulating, managing, monitoring, and evaluating assistance projects and protection measures. Each section distributes responsibilities to country desks and has at least one protection officer attached.[17] UNHCR field representatives are responsible, under the guidance of the regional sections, for all actions required to attain the overall objectives of UNHCR in the countries they cover. They promote liberal asylum policies and an adequate legal status for refugees, review or examine local procedures relating to the recognition of refugees, and extend to them international protection. They maintain close contact with governments, intergovernmental and nongovernmental organizations, diplomatic missions, and information media and follow administrative and legislative practices concerning social, economic, and educational matters of potential benefit to refugees. In countries where UNHCR is not represented, these responsibilities are discharged to the extent possible and necessary by the appropriate regional section.[18]

The legal bases for UNHCR protection activities are the 1950 Statute of the Office of the UNHCR, designating the High Commissioner responsible for providing international protection to individuals falling within the scope of the statute and for seeking durable solutions; the 1951 Refugees Convention; and its 1967 Protocol. "Mandate refugees" receive international protection pursuant to the Statute of the UNHCR and subsequent General Assembly resolutions. The principal difference between mandate refugees and convention refugees is that mandate refugees do not have the benefit of the legal system established by the 1951 Refugees Convention.[19] Since the High Commissioner's protection responsibilities have been bestowed by the General Assembly, the international protection activities of the UNHCR are not dependent upon government request. The right of initiation of activities reflects international recognition of UNHCR responsibilities as entirely nonpolitical and humanitarian in nature.[20]

The need for international protection arises from the fact that refugees do not have the protection of their former home country. Persons who meet the criteria of refugee found in the statute are refugees irrespective of whether they have been formally recognized as refugees by a national authority or UNHCR.[21]

Persons seeking admittance to a country as refugees are referred to as asylum seekers. Until the mid-1970s UNHCR concerns generally focused on individual cases and the global refugees regime mechanisms were appropriate for the task.

However, since the mid-1970s UNHCR has faced increasing numbers of asylum seekers in the form of mass movements (massive influx). Members of massive influx situations seeking asylum seldom meet the prima facie conditions for recognition as refugees. Consequently, states, whether regime members or not, grew increasingly reluctant to grant asylum and refugee status. In response to these new circumstances, transformation of the global refugees regime was required, and this transformation would have to occur within the institutional dimension of the regime, as support for negotiating new, or revised, standards to address massive influx situations was not apparent in the international community.

From 1977 to 1985 UNHCR has undertaken spontaneous transformation of the global refugees regime to address the phenomenon of massive influx of asylum seekers. Transformation of implementation mechanisms has relied on monitoring, policy coordination, and information exchange. Legitimacy for these spontaneous transformations has been sought through approval by the EXCOM and the General Assembly, as well as by states' acceptance of changed UNHCR practices. Obtaining legitimacy has the consequence of incorporating new norms into the global refugees regime, because the strength of conclusions of the EXCOM is not limited to the states members, since its members are elected by and act on behalf of the international community as a whole.

In a massive influx situation, determination of status is a central issue. When determination on a group basis is required, UNHCR intervenes to ensure that asylum seekers are granted at least temporary asylum and are not subject to *refoulement*[22] until a determination of status has been made. The EXCOM agreed to universal minimum standards for determination of status only in 1977, stating that determination of status was an inherent part of UNHCR's protection function.[23]

As the number of mass-asylum incidents increased, states more frequently resorted to granting temporary asylum. No specific provision of the UNHCR statute, subsequent General Assembly resolutions, or provisions of the 1951 Refugees Convention addressed the question of temporary asylum. Consequently, the EXCOM established a group of experts to investigate minimum standards for temporary asylum.

Reporting in 1981, the group of experts recognized that granting temporary asylum was a lawful act of state, but that for a state to refuse a mass entry of asylum seekers would undermine the principle of *non-refoulement*. UNHCR, then, should stress admission of refugees rather than the granting of asylum, since asylum could be interpreted as a durable solution.

Minimum standards suggested by the group of experts were adopted by the EXCOM as UNHCR norms in 1981. Further, the

EXCOM stated that these norms were applicable regardless of states' adherence to the 1951 Refugees Convention. These standards include

1. nondiscrimination,

2. access to a recognized legal system in the country of refuge,

3. unrestricted UNHCR access to asylum seekers to enable exercise of its legal protection function,

4. promotion of voluntary repatriation, and

5. location of refugee camps at a "reasonable" distance from the frontier of the country of origin.[24]

The first two standards grant basic civil capacity to asylum seekers; the fourth and fifth standards received further refinement from EXCOM special committees. Point 5 is designed specifically to address the phenomenon of armed attacks against refugee camps and was the subject of a special study in 1982-83. This study reiterated that refugees were protected as civilians in armed conflict situations by provisions of the 1949 Geneva Conventions and Protocol No. 1 of 1977. To lessen the possibility of armed attacks on refugee camps, UNHCR should

1. promote conditions that ensure that camps and settlements were not exposed to the dangers of attack, that is, it should have full and regular UNHCR presence and access to camps;

2. maintain contact with all parties involved in armed attacks and with political organs of the UN;

3. consider placing the political aspects of certian attacks before the Security Council; and

4. increase UNHCR influence by stressing the humanitarian and nonpolitical dimension of UNHCR activities.

And at the 38th session of the EXCOM (1987), a consensus conclusion on military attacks was adopted.[25]

The UNHCR also has a recognized role in legal protection during refugee repatriation. International action to promote voluntary repatriation requires consideration of the situation within the country of origin as well as within the receiving country. UNHCR has a legitimate concern for the consequences of return, and the EXCOM has stated that to "monitor fullfillment of amnesties, guarantees or assurances on the basis of which the refugees have returned . . . should be considered as inherent in his (UNHCR) Mandate."[26]

A global refugees regime is in existence, but the Latin American states have their own earlier institutionalized principles of asylum. Therefore the question arises of the compatibility of the concept of asylum, as defined by the Latin American states, with the principles of the global regime. This problem is investigated in the next two chapters, one dealing with asylum and refugees under the Organization of American States and the other with a comparison between the principles of the global refugees regime and the Latin American concept of asylum.

NOTES

1. UNHCR, Handbook for Emergencies, Part One: Field Operations. (Geneva: UNHCR, 1982), pp. 11-12 section 2.4; Article 73, Protocol 1 Additional to the 1949 Geneva Conventions. Article 48 of the 1977 Protocol Additional to the 1949 Geneva Conventions made an explicit distinction between combatants and population groups; Article 51 entitled civilians to enjoy general protection against the dangers of military operations; and Article 57 required precautionary measures to be taken by the military. Article 13 of Protocol 2 reiterated the general protection of civilians. Under Article 85 of Protocol 1, an attack on civilians was recognized as a grave breach of Protocol 1. In addition, the UN Charter places certain general obligations on member states. And certain provisions of the International Covenant on Civil and Political Rights are applicable to refugees. See "Refugee Rights Human Rights," Refugees, No. 38 (February 1987): 5.
2. By Resolution 429 (V) of 14 December 1950, the General Assembly decided to convene in Geneva a Conference of Plenipotentiaries to complete the drafting of and to sign a convention relating to the status of refugees. This conference met in Geneva from 2 to 25 July 1951. It is instructive to note that Brazil, Colombia, and Venezuela were the only Latin American states participating in the conference, and Cuba was the only such state with observer status. The geographic scope of the global convention is determined by the words "as a result of events occurring before 1 January 1951." For purposes of the 1951 convention, these words can mean either events in Europe before 1 January 1951 or events occurring in Europe and elsewhere

before 1 January 1951. Each state party to the global convention
was to submit at the time of signature, ratification, or accession a
declaration specifying which meaning applied.

3. Atle Grahl-Madsen, Territorial Asylum (New York:
Oceana, 1980), p. 41. Reference to *non-refoulement* in the final
act of the 1954 conference does not grant a legally binding
character to the principle as it applies to stateless persons; it is
an expression of moral authority.

4. On additional human rights and international instruments
applicable to refugees, see also Atle Grahl-Madsen, "Refugees and
Refugee Law in a World in Transition," in Michigan Yearbook of
International Legal Studies: Transnational Legal Problems of
Refugees (New York: Clark Boardman, 1982), pp. 65-88.

5. Richard Lillich, The Human Rights of Aliens in
Contemporary International Law (Manchester, U.K.: Manchester
University Press, 1984), pp. 66-69; see also Atle Grahl-Madsen,
The Status of Refugees in International Law, Vol. 2 (Leiden,
The Netherlands: A. W. Sitjhoff, 1972), chapter 6; Louise
Holborn, Refugees: A Problem in Our Time, Vol. 1 (Metuchen,
N. J.: Scarecrow Press, 1975), pp. 164-71; S. Prakash Shina,
Asylum and International Law (The Hague: Martinus Nijhoff,
1971), pp. 99-115. Scholars' review of the preparatory text and
travaux preparatoires of the 1933 Convention relating to the
International Status of Refugees, from which *ordre public* was
taken, shed no light on the intended scope or meaning of the
term. For basic rights, see Refugees Convention Articles 3,
16-17, 27-32; Stateless Persons Convention Articles 3, 16-17,
27-31.

6. Atle Grahl-Madsen, "The Expulsion of Refugees," in
Bound Pamphlets on Refugees, UN Library Code, n.d., pp.
99-100. See Convention Articles 15, 17-19, 21-24, 26, 28, 32.

7. Stateless persons have no equated rights of the most-
favored-alien category. See both conventions, Articles 4, 14, 16,
20, 22 and 24.

8. Refugees Convention Articles 15, 17; Stateless persons
are granted treatment no less favorable than that accorded aliens
generally.

9. UN, Office of Public Information, United Nations Action
in the Field of Human Rights (New York: UN, 1974), pp. 75-76.
See also Shina, Asylum, pp. 99-128.

10. Guy Goodwin-Gill, The Refugee in International Law
(Oxford: Clarendon Press, 1983), pp. 38, 43; Organization of
American States (hereafter OAS), Subsecretariat for Legal Affairs,
A Study Comparing United Nations International Instruments and
Inter-American Instruments on Asylum, Refugees and Displaced
Persons (SER/ser.D/5.2), 20 September 1984, pp 11-12.

11. Goodwin-Gill, Refugee, pp. 22, 140-48; World Peace
Through Law Center. Towards the Second Quarter Century of
Refugee Law (Washington, D.C.: WPTLC, 1976), pp. 7, 11.

12. Gilbert Jaeger, Status and International Protection of Refugees (Geneva: UNHCR, 1980), internal memo, pp. 21-22.

13. UN, General Assembly, 14th sess., Report of the Economic and Social Council (A/4143), 1959, pp. 93-94. See bibliography, UN section, for full listing of ECOSOC reports consulted.

14. UN, General Assembly, 7th sess., Report of the Economic and Social Council (A/2172), 1952, pp. 70-71; UN, General Assembly, 7th sess., Report of the United Nations High Commissioner for Refugees and Addendum (A/2126), 1952, p. 11; UNHCR, Press release (Ref 258), 22 November 1955; UN, General Assembly, 10th sess., Report of the Economic and Social Council (A/2943), 1955, pp. 68-70; UN, General Assembly, 10th sess., Report of the United Nations High Commissioner for Refugees (A/2902/Add. 1), 1955, p. 21 and annex, p. 28; Holborn, Refugees, pp. 382-83. For 1986-87 EXCOM membership list see "Dossier: The 37th Session of the EXCOM," Refugees, no. 35 (November 1986): 19.

15. UNHCR, Report on the 24th Session of the Executive Committee of the High Commissioner's Programme (A/AC.96/497), 18 October 1973, p. 8; UNHCR, 24th sess., Executive Committee (hereafter EXCOM), Summary Records of the 239th-249th Meetings (A/AC.96/SR 239-249), 14 December 1973; UNHCR, Report on the 25th Session of the Executive Committee of the High Commissioners Programme (A/AC.96/511), 31 October 1974, pp. 5, 14, 21; UNHCR, Report on the 30th Session of the Executive Committee of the High Commissioners Programme (A/AC.96/572), 19 October 1979, p. 22. Summary Records for EXCOM activities after 1983 were not available at time of on-site research.

16. "Interview: Ghassan Arnaout," Refugees, no. 34 (October 1986): 16-17.

17. M. Landall, The Organization of UNHCR (Geneva: UNHCR, June 1980) pp. 1-9; Interview, Americas Section assistance personnel, July 1985. As of late 1986 there were three regional offices in Latin America, under the Americas Secion: San Jose, Costa Rica deals with countries of Central America and the Caribbean; Lima, Peru is concerned with Colombia, Ecuador, Venezuela, Peru, Suriname and Guayana; and Buenos Aires deals with Bolivia, Brazil, Paraguay, Chile, Uruguay and Argentina. As of July 1985, branch offices were located in Mexico City and Tegucigalpa, Honduras.

18. Landall, Organization, p. 9, see also UN, UNHCR, 35th sess., Report on UNHCR Assistance Activities for 1982-1983 (A/AC.96/620), 1 August 1983, pp. xlii-xliv.

19. OAS, UN and Inter-American Instruments, pp. 21-22, 124-30. Criteria for recognition as a "convention refugee" are a well-founded fear of persecution for reasons of race, religion,

nationality, membership of a particular social group or political opinion; being outside the country of nationality; inability or, owing to such fear, unwillingness to avail oneself of the protection of that country; or, for stateless persons, being outside the country of former habitual residence and inability or, owing to such fear, unwillingness to return to it.   Nor may the individual(s) fall under criteria of the cessation clauses (Article 1, Section C) or the Exclusion clauses (Sections D-F) of the Refugees Convention. It is understood, however, that states must accord to Mandate refugees the fundamental human rights. UNHCR is not competent to intervene on behalf of active combatants and persons bearing arms.   Protection of these persons may fall within the competence of the International Committee of the Red Cross (ICRC).   Also, protection cannot be extended to individuals subject to the exclusion clauses of Chapter II Article 7(d) of the Statute. For further discussion see UNHCR, Handbook, p. 10 section 2.3.

20. OAS, UN and Inter-American Instruments, pp. 127-28; UNHCR, Handbook, p. 8 section 2.1; Atle Grahl-Madsen, "Identifying the World's Refugees," in Gilburt Loescher and John Scanlan, eds., The Global Refugee Problem: US and World Response (Beverly Hills: Sage, 1983), p. 14.   Governments are responsible for the security and safety of, assistance to and law and order among refugees in their territory.

21. Atle Grahl-Madsen, "International Refugee Law Today and Tomorrow," in Archiv des Volkerrechts 20, no. 4 (1982): 425; Paul Weis, "The Development of Refugee Law," in Michigan Yearbook, pp. 34-37; "Protection: Twenty Years After the Protocol," Refugees, no. 46 (October 1987): 17-34. Refugee status is declaratory and not constitutive, which means that an asylum seeker cannot lose the status of refugee on procedural grounds, such as failure to register in the asylum state.

22. Guy Goodwin-Gill, International Law and the Movement of Persons between States (Oxford: Clarendon Press, 1978), pp. 140, 218-19 and "Entry and Exclusion of Refugees: The Obligations of States and the Protection Function of the Office of the United Nations High Commissioner for Refugees," in Michigan Yearbook, pp.   302-6; International Commission of Jurists (hereafter ICJ), An Application in Latin America of International Declarations and Conventions relating to Asylum (Geneva: ICJ, 1975), p.   13.   The General Assembly expressed recognition of non-refoulement as a part of general international law by Resolution 34/60 of 1979, which applies, however, only to countries of first refuge. Goodwin-Gill concludes that after this General Assembly action there is substantial, if not conclusive, authority that the principle is binding independent of specific assent.   And the International Commission of Jurists (Geneva), citing Paul Weis, has stated that non-refoulement has become a

rule of international law recognized by civilized nations. Alternatively, the Legal Subsecretariat of the OAS has concluded that the principle of *non-refoulement* of Article 33 of the 1951 Refugees Convention establishes asylum as a human right by making it an international obligation to grant asylum to those meeting the criteria of Article 1. For discussion on this point see Grahl-Madsen, "International Refugee Law," pp. 411-2 and "Refugees and International Law," pp. 71-3; Goodwin-Gill, Refugee, pp. 97-100; ICJ, Application, p. 14; OAS, UN and Inter-American Instruments, p. 36; UN, General Assembly, 33rd sess., Report of the United Nations High Commissioner for Refugees (A/33/12), 1978, pp. 4-6. Temporary asylum had been used by Argentina and Peru during the Chilean crisis.

23. UN, UNHCR, 28th Session, Report on Meeting of the Sub-Committee of the Whole on International Protection Held Monday 30 October 1977 (EC/SCP/6), 7 November 1977, pp. 6-9. The recommended procedures are:

1. competent officials present at the border or in the territory have clear instructions and are required to act in accordance with the principle of *non-refoulement*;

2. all applicants for refugee status are to receive necessary guidance as to procedures;

3. states should have a clearly identified authority with responsibility for examining such requests;

4. all applicants are to be given the necessary facilities, including an interpreter, and opportunity to contact UNHCR;

5. if recognized as a refugee, each individual will be so informed and issued documentation;

6. if not recognized, individuals are to be allowed reasonable time for appeal and

7. applicants are to be permitted to remain in the country pending decision on the appeal.

See UN, UNHCR, 32nd sess., Follow-up on Earlier Conclusions of the Sub-Committee: The Determination of Refugee Status (EC/SCP/22/rev. 1), 3 September 1982, p. 3.

24. UN, UNHCR, 30th sess., Report on the 30th Session of the Executive Committee of the High Commissioner's Programme (A/AC.96/572), 19 October 1979, p. 18; UN,

UNHCR, 31st sess., Report on the Meeting of the Expert Group on Temporary Refuge in Situations of Large-Scale Influx (EC/SCP/10/Add. 1), 17 July 1981, pp. 5-6, 12, 14; "Current Problems in International Protection," Refugees, no. 22 (October 1985): 5; "Refugee Rights," p. 5.

25.   UN, UNHCR, 32nd sess., Note on International Protection of Refugees in Armed Conflict Situations (EC/SCP/25), 4 October 1982, pp. 1-5; UN, UNHCR, 32nd sess., EXCOM, Summary Record of the 347th Meeting (A/AC.96/SR 347), 14 October 1982, p. 11; UN, UNHCR, Report by Ambassador Felix Schnyder (EC/SCP/26), 15 March 1983, pp. 3-5.   Despite the background of Guatemalan, Salvadoran and Honduran attacks on refugee camps during the period of this study, Ambassador Schnyder gave no attention to, or suggestion of, regional organization involvement.   Debate on the question of armed attacks on refugee camps ended in frustration at the 36th Executive Committee Session.   Since presentation of the Schnyder Report, informal governmental working groups, the Subcommittee of the Whole on International Protection, and the Executive Committee have attempted to identify a set of principles that could be adopted by states for dealing effectively with the problem.   Only after six years of continuous negotiation was consensus language finally achieved. See "Agreement on Military Attacks," Refugees. no. 47 (November 1987): 13 and "Armed Attacks on Refugee Camps: No International Consensus," Refugees, no. 24 (December 1985): 5.

26.   "UNHCR's Executive Committee- The 36th Session," Refugees, no. 24 (December 1985): 17-18; UN, UNHCR, 30th sess., Note on Voluntary Repatriation (EC/SCP/13), 27 August 1979, pp. 3-6.   The Subcommittee of the Whole on Protection cited Article 5 of the OAU Refugees Convention as providing general guidance.   This article makes specific reference to return and arrangements for information on the country of origin.   Such information would be supplied by a delegation visit prior to any return, thus facilitating the choice of return.   Also, UNHCR devised norms for mass voluntary repatriation of Nicaraguan nationals in 1979.   In this case UNHCR provided for adequate reception arrangements.

Chapter Five

Asylees and Refugees under the Inter-American System

Following the First World War, efforts by private and public international organizations provided the experience and helped shape the character of contemporary refugee law. Prior to the First World War there were no international legal norms protecting political refugees as this concept is understood today. Rather, states dealt with those seeking refuge or asylum under constitutional provisions and domestic laws regulating immigration and naturalization, through political offense exception clauses in extradition treaties, or in Latin America, through institutions of diplomatic and territorial asylum. It is thus appropriate first to review the political offense exception and the institutions of asylum as developed by the Latin American states.

One should look for sufficient continuity in the behavior of the Latin American states to identify elements of an international regional territorial asylum regime. The possible presence or absence of a political asylum regime operating among the Latin American states will provide the starting point for (1) providing evidence for the continuity and change in Latin American states' behavior under the global refugees regime and (2) investigating the practicability of establishing a regional refugees regime as articulated by the Latin American states.

INTERNATIONAL LAW IN LATIN AMERICA

The doctrine of natural law provides the basis and framework for "Spanish international law." Based on the tenets of scholastic philosophy, Spanish international law provided protection for the individual. Indeed, the individual as a subject of international law reaffirmed the postulates of Catholic philosophy.[1] Francisco Suarez, a 16th century jurist of the Spanish school, is cited as its most characteristic exponent.

Another jurist of the 16th century Spanish school was Francisco de Victoria. His writings reflect the central themes identified with Suarez, but more importantly, he addressed himself to concerns that have direct bearing on questions raised today: refugees, statelessness and humanization of war. Writing in The Indians, de Victoria, citing *jus gentium*, stated that "it is rekoned among all nations inhumane to treat visitors and foreigners badly without special causes." Regarding forced exile, he stated that "banishment is one of the capital forms of punishment. Therefore it is unlawful to banish strangers who have committed no fault."[2] This prohibition of banishment of strangers may be juridically equivalent to the principle of *non-refoulement* in contemporary international refugee law.

Regarding the lack of citizenship, that is, statelessness, de Victoria observed that failure to have a nationality was a violation of both natural law and the law of nations. Finally, in On The Law of War, he noted that "with regard to harmless agricultural folk, and also with regard to the rest of the peaceable civilian population, during war these are presumed innocent until the contrary is shown."[3] This latter statement touches several points of humanitarian law that have a bearing on this study. In broadest terms, the innocence of civilian populations has been recognized in the 1977 Protocol Additional No. 1 to the 1949 Geneva Conventions. Also, failure of a state to recognize the innocence of rural populations can be cited as a root cause of mass refugee movements in Central America. In the last few years, state-directed counterinsurgency and development strategies have presumed the hostility of rural popopulations. Subsequent state-directed actions to subordinate these supposedly hostile populations have resulted in mass refugee flows.

EXTRADITION AND ASYLUM IN THE PREWAR
INTER-AMERICAN SYSTEM

Cited as first examples of principles of a continent-wide international law were the principles contained in a series of

Treaties of Union, Alliance and Confederation. These instruments spelled out specific rignts of continental citizenship, employment, and justice and, with their prohibition of slavery, demonstrated that the Latin American states had taken the lead in acknowledging the role of the individual in international law.[4]

Treaties resulting from the Montevideo Congress of 1888-89 were the first to sanction acceptance of political asylees (*asilados*).[5] (see Table 1 of the appendix) This congress was followed by the First Inter-American Conference, held in Washington, D.C., 1889, where, for one thing, national treatment of foreigners with regard to civil rights was recognized.[6] The Second Inter-American Conference, in Mexico City in 1901-2, turned to the codifiction of international law. The first concrete result of this codification was the 1911 Bolivarian Treaty of Extradition.[7] Under this agreement, extradition would not be granted if the act on which it was based was considered by the asylum state as a political offense or related act. The decision of the asylum state was final. Asylum was recognized as a juridical institution under international law, but several crucial unresolved questions remained, such as, defining political persecution and the obligations of safe conduct for the asylee.[8]

A congress that took place in 1867 on the initiative of Peru was the first attempt at specifically regulating and defining the concept of asylum. It was not until the Montevideo Congress of 1889, however, that for the first time a treaty on international penal law included legal standards on diplomatic asylum.[9] This congress stipulated that the laws of extradition governed the return of those charged with a political offense. Also, *asilados* were to be afforded an inviolable asylum, but it was the duty of the host state to ensure that they did not commit from its territory acts that could endanger the public peace of the nation against which the offense had been committed.[10] Political offenses, offenses subversive of the internal and external safety of the state, or common offenses connected with these, would not warrent extradition. Determination of the character of the offense was incumbent upon the asylum state and was to be made under and according to provisions of the law that proved most favorable to the accused.[11]

The aforementioned principles on extradition and asylum were reiterated and incorporated into treaties at the 6th (1928) Inter-American Conference. Moreover, delegates at this conference stated that the institution of asylum was not an interference in the internal affairs of another state.[12]

With the onset of economic depression in the 1930s, the domestic political conditions of Latin American states deteriorated rapidly. Economic problems and political tensions often resulted in acts of violence. In such tumultuous conditions, many individuals previously holding political power were forced to seek asylum, and the provisions of the 1928 treaty were proved inadequate.

Revision of the 1928 treaty was done at the 7th Inter-American Conference (1933).[13] The 1928 treaty had failed to qualify exactly what constituted a political crime. Also, the instrument did not establish with precision the fundamental bases for asylum as a humanitarian institution. In light of the then present circumstances, it was necessary to explicitly state those conditions demanding protection due to political opinions or revolutionary upheaval.[14]

The 1933 revision failed to resolve these concerns. While asylum was expressly recognized as an institution of humanitarian character, it could be denied to those accused or prosecuted by ordinary courts. The ability to deny asylum on the grounds of mere accusation of criminal activities inhibited successful appeal for asylum by those pursued for political reasons.[15]

Meeting in Montevideo in 1939, the Second Latin American Congress on Private International Law addressed this deficiency. New instruments on extradition and asylum were adopted.[16] Uruguay, the host state, argued that asylum should be recognized as a human right; other delegates at the conference did not share this position.[17] Under the 1939 treaty, asylum could be denied to individuals indicted or condemned for common crimes.

Furthermore, this instrument addressed for the first time the difficulties confronting an asylee in the country of refuge. An asylee was placed in a difficult position vis-a-vis the domestic laws of the Latin American states in terms of the exercise of rights and access to facilities and guarantees of the society where the *asilado* must function as an individual, seeking employment, education, transfer of assets, and so on. So that states would not be assuming an indefinate burden by granting of asylum, the treaty states that it is entirely up to the granting state to decide how long an asilado may remain.[18]

Following this congress, the politics of the Latin American states became increasingly polarized, a reflection of the ideological conflict engulfing the European continent. Attention to the widening world war superseded attention to questions of extradition and asylum at Inter-American Conferences. These concerns were renewed, however, following the Second World War, under the framework of the Organization of American States.

ASYLEES AND REFUGEES UNDER THE OAS

Following World War II, the inter-American system was reorganized as the Organization of American States (OAS). Questions of extradition, asylum, and human rights are now dealt with by OAS-sponsored treaties. Political refugees have been a phenomenon within the inter-American system since the early 1960s. However, the OAS did not give its attention to refugees until the violence in Central America since 1979 resulted in mass exodus of individuals seeking asylum in neighboring states. This section reviews the OAS instruments and guarantees applicable to refugees and relates specific actions taken by the OAS to deal with the mass exodus of asylum seekers.

The general concern for human rights expressed by the OAS member states provides the broadest framework of rights and guarantees that can be applied to refugees.   A 1945 Draft Declaration on Human Rights, directed against conditions of the Peron regime in Argentina, faltered against the concern for nonintervention in internal affairs.   Reintroduced as the American Declaration of the Rights and Duties of Man (American Declaration) in 1948, heated argument ensued as to whether it should be incorporated as part of the OAS Charter or simply adopted as a resolution of the conference. Finally adopted as a resolution of the conference, the American Declaration was not initially a legally binding instrument but the recognized statement of international guidelines for the inter-American community. Subsequent to the 1967 OAS Charter amendments, however, some jurists strongly argue that the American Declaration had been incorporated as part of the charter and thus was binding upon member states. Argument on this point remains inconclusive.[19] Pertaining to refugees and stateless persons, the American Declaration gives explicit recognition to the right to a nationality and a right to asylum.[20]

Efforts to establish mechanisms to promote, implement, or enforce the standards of the American Declaration were delayed a decade; only in 1959, with the creation of the Inter-American Commission on Human Rights (IACHR) and the initiation of preparing a Draft American Convention on Human Rights, did the inter-American community establish compliance mechanisms for its nascent human rights regime.[21] A negotiated human rights regime was finally created by the 1969 American Convention on Human Rights (American Convention).   However, until adoption of the American Convention, IACHR human rights promotion and protection activities relied on the not binding American Declaration. Consequently, from its first session the commission established a tradition of broadly interpreting its powers pursuant to its original statute.[22]

This broad interpretation was possible as Statute Article 1 designated the IACHR as an autonomous body. Designation neither as an organ nor a specialized agency of the OAS, the commission's status remained ambiguous.   Moreover, the statute granted no enforcement powers. Yet the ambiguous phraseology left room for broad interpretation, reflected by the commission's opinion that its function was to protect human rights, while OAS member states accepted the less effective function of promotion of human rights.[23]

The statute of the IACHR was strengthened in 1965 at the Second Special Inter-American Conference, whereby the commission's powers of investigation and initiative were broadened.[24] And in 1966 Mexico proposed an additional amendment to the statute, calling for explicit recognition of the commission's competency to examine petitions presented by individuals. This latter amendment was effected by the Protocol Amendment to the OAS Charter, adopted by the 1967 Third Special Inter-American Conference.[25] This amendment converted the IACHR into a consultative organ of the OAS and raised its status to that of a principle organ. Thus, despite continued objections of member states to commission protection activities, it is doubtful that the IACHR can be abolished or its powers curtailed without formal amendment of the OAS Charter.[26]

Despite the increased stature and powers of the IACHR, its enforcement activities are stymied by Chapter 6 of the revised charter. Its Article 16 provides that the state "shall" respect the rights of individuals. The use of "shall" establishes a legal obligation that member states respect the rights of any individual, not only its citizens. However, this obligation conflicts with Article 18, dealing with nonintervention in internal affairs, which gives preference to the rights of states; that is, to their sovereign prerogatives. This conflict in the charter text clearly displays the unresolved dilemma of whether collective action can be undertaken without violating the key concept of nonintervention.[27]

The adoption of the American Convention in 1969 was an important step in the history of human rights in Latin America.[28] This instrument created a court of human rights and, by providing for means of enforcement, albeit with state consent, has greater chance of eventually being implemented. However, the American Convention has a recognized hierarchy of rights, civil and political rights receiving greater attention. (For Latin American states-parties to the convention, see Table 3 of the appendix)

The Inter-American Court of Human Rights became operational with the entry into force of the American Convention on 18 July 1978. The court is an autonomous judicial institution the purpose of which is application and interpretation of the American Convention. The convention confers two distinct functions on the court: adjudication of disputes relating to charges that a state party has violated the convention (contentious jurisdiction) and interpretation of the convention and certain other human rights treaties in which it is not called upon to adjudicate a specific dispute (advisory jurisdiction).

Regarding contentious jurisdiction, a state party to the convention does not subject itself to this jurisdiction upon ratification of the convention. Rather, the court acquires jurisdiction with regard to a state only when it has filed a special declaration or has concluded a special agreement with the court. Private parties do not have standing to initiate proceedings.[29]

Regarding judgments, the court must decide whether there has been a breach of the convention, what rights the injured party should be accorded, what steps should be taken to remedy the breach, and the amount of damages to which the injured is entitled.   In addition to regular judgments, the court has the power to grant temporary injunctions as an extraordinary remedy. Judgments are final and not subject to appeal.   Enforcement is with action by the General Assembly of the OAS.[30] An advisory opinion may deal with the American Convention or any other treaty "concerning the protection of human rights in the American states."[31]

As far as rights of refugees in the inter-American system are concerned, the American Declaration states that an individual is not required to leave the national territory except by his own will; every person has the right to be recognized everywhere as a person having rights and obligations and to enjoy the basic civil rights; the right to a nationality and asylum in accordance with domestic laws and international treaties are guaranteed.[32] The right to a nationality cannot be suspended even by constitutional exceptions, such as a state of seige. However, deprivation of nationality frequently recurs in the practice of Latin American states. Often done to silence political opponents, such deprivation has the effect of creating stateless persons, forcing them to seek refuge in another country.

Under the American Convention, states are obliged to treat all persons subject to their jurisdiction without discrimination for reasons of national or social origin.   The rights of the convention are to be given domestic legal effect by legislative or other measures as necessary.   The right to nationality shall not be arbitrarily taken away, nor can a national of a state be expelled from the territory of that state or be deprived of the right to reentry.   And the right to seek and be granted asylum pursuant to   domestic   legislation   and   international   agreements   is guaranteed.[33]

Where asylum is concerned, the American Convention is not as broad as the American Declaration.   While the declaration recognizes asylum for numerous causes of persecution, the convention has provisions only for persecution for political offenses   or   related   common   crimes.   The   principle   of *non-refoulement* is specifically endorsed in the convention and applies to any alien within the territory of a state and not just *asilados.*   Collective expulsion of aliens is prohibited, a provision without precident in other inter-American instruments and the global refugees regime.   Suspension of guarantees under certain extraordinary circumstances, such as a state of seige, is permitted;

however, not all of the guarantees of the convention may be suspended. For example, while the right to nationality may be suspended, the right to asylum cannot.[34]

Of more specific concern for refugees and asylum seekers is OAS revision to the tradition of political and territorial asylum, as developed by the prewar inter-American community. The OAS has sponsored modification and harmonization of inter-American asylum and extradition instruments, so that their provisions reflect changes in states' practices.

Efforts to revise inter-American extradition principles began in 1954. Between 1956 and 1977 the Inter-American Juridical Committee (IAJC) circulated five draft extradition texts before the OAS General Assembly convened a conference that adopted the 1981 Caracas Extraditon Convention.[35] This convention reiterates that the state of refuge has unilateral determination of what constitutes a nonextraditable offense. Moreover, a strengthening from earlier inter-American agreements is inclusion of the principle of *non-refoulement.* Finally, no provision of the convention may be interpreted as a limitation on the right of asylum when its exercise is appropriate.[36]

Regarding territorial asylum, the 1954 Caracas Territorial Asylum Convention reaffirms the unlimited right of states to control entry into their territory. This jurisdictional right was equally applied, without restrictions, to persons who entered from a state "where they were persecuted for their beliefs, opinions or political affiliations, or for acts which may be considered as political offenses." No state is obliged to surrender, expel, or extradite recognized *asilados.* And the principle of *non-refoulement* is stated as a right of, rather than a duty or prohibition imposed upon, the state of refuge.[37] However, in a change from previous inter-American asylum instruments, surreptitious or illegal entry no longer provides grounds for denial of asylum or protection. Freedom of speech and assembly for asylees is guaranteed, unless their purpose is to incite violence against the home state. *Asilados* identified as "notorious leaders of a subversive movement" must be held at a reasonable distance from the frontier, as determined by the asylum state.[38]

Although the OAS has modernized inter-American extradition and asylum instruments, they are generally applicable only to individuals seeking asylum for political offenses. These conventions contain no definition or concepts applicable to political persecution, as defined by the global refugees regime. Moreover, OAS records disclose that since 1954 the issue of territorial asylum has never been delt with by the OAS Council or its General Assembly. Prior to 1970, when the IACHR began to present annual reports to the General Assembly, questions concerning human rights in general, and political refugees especially, were of insufficient merit to warrant attention. Nor has the commission been presented with an overabundance of cases or complaints alleging denial of the right to asylum contained in either the American Declaration or, American Convention.[39]

Nevertheless, since the early 1960s the inter-American system has had to cope with increasing numbers of political refugees as recognized by the global refugees regime. As a consequence of the 1959 Cuban Revolution, large numbers of Cubans fled to Europe, the United States, and other Latin American states. In 1963 a message to the Secretary-General of the OAS from the Madrid-based Commission on Cuban Refugees expressed concern about the continued flow of refugees from Cuba and the lack of response by the American states. In turn, the Secretary-General requested the IACHR to investigate the issue of political refugees in the Americas.[40] The commission agreed to study how generation of political refugees was directly related to the violation of human rights, how territorial and diplomatic asylum created different problems for the asylee, the economic dimension of refugees, and the domestic legislation in the Americas pertaining to refugees. Member states were requested to forward information concerning political refugees to the commission and to issue travel documents consistent with the 1951 global convention. Attempts to obtain cooperation from Cuba were unsuccessful.[41]

Draft conclusions on the report on refugees were presented by the commission at the Second Special Inter-American Conference in 1965. The commission found that

1. there was a lack of domestic legislation pertaining to refugees in the American states;

2. an inter-American Convention on Political Refugees was desirable;

3. the OAS lacked a protection agency for refugees;

4. travel documents pursuant to the 1951 Refugees Convention were not issued by member states; and

5. refugees were not accorded the right to work in host states.

Moreover, the report stressed the fundamental change in the nature of the refugee problem in the Americas. Historically, *asilados* had been the few and wealthy; now the refugees were poor and and moved in masses; a direct consequence of political instability. To meet these changed conditions, the commission suggested that states adopt uniform legislation to regularize refugees' civil status;

review the inter-American Asylum Conventions, since the 1954 Caracas Territorial Asylum Convention was inadequate; reognize that economic and, more generally, development problems could not be divorced from the issue of political refugees; and until the inter-American community undertook independent action, validate expired passports when individuals were unable to obtain new ones and issue travel documents consistent with the global refugees regime.[42]

In response to the IACHR report, the conference first expressed recognition of the changed nature and circumstances of political refugees in the Americas, especially those fleeing Cuba,[43] and second, it initiated the process of preparing an inter-American refugees convention. Such a convention was deemed necessary because the 1954 Caracas Territorial Asylum and the global 1951 Refugees Conventions had not been ratified or acceded to by a sufficient number of American states. Moreover, these instruments did not adequately deal with new aspects of the refugee problem such as mass exoduses. The draft convention was to focus on legal concerns of refugees, such as a definition of refugee; a refugee's rights, duties, and personal status; issuance of travel documents; and coordination of assistance and protection.[44]

The OAS International Council of Jurists, charged with drafting a refugees convention, stated that "the inter-American system shows sufficient maturity for the regional community as a whole to be able to participate fairly effectively in assistance to refugees." The Draft Refugees Convention defined a refugee as "any person who, upon entering the territory of one of the Contracting Parties because of pursuit not resulting from ordinary crimes, is recognized as such by the territorial state." The refugee would have a duty to conform to the laws and regulations of the host state; personal status would be governed by the laws of the host state. All contracting parties were to grant refugees at a minimum the rights that their laws granted aliens. The convention would supplement the 1954 Caracas Territorial Asylum Convention, but its application would be independent. A designated authority within the OAS would be responsible for assistance and protection to refugees; having direct contact with refugees so to carry out its functions, coordinate legal protection with UNHCR, negotiate with host states for issuance of work permits, establish an international employment information service, coordinate the activities of voluntary agencies, and study relocation and repatriation of refugees. If any state were unable to issue travel documentation consistent with the 1951 Refugees Convention, then the OAS would issue the documentation. Recognition of these travel documents would be obligatory. The convention would enter into force for each state when its instrument of ratification was deposited. The IACHR was identified as the most appropriate organ to fullfill convention functions.[45]

Initially a special conference on a convention relating to refugees had been anticipated. In 1967 the OAS-ICJ circulated its draft; the UN General Assembly had just approved the 1967 Protocol to the 1951 Refugees Convention.   Consequently, the project of an OAS refugees convention was shelved and a special conference never convened.[46] It has been argued that the global 1967 Protocol, appearing at the same time as the OAS draft convention, quashed any immediate hopes of a Latin American regional refugees instrument, first because separate instruments appeared redundant and second, because the UN protocol had the virtue of being a global instrument.   If adhered to, the protocol would remove any possible inconsistencies between the regional instrument and the 1951 Refugees Convention.   Unfortunately, few Latin American states chose to adhere to the protocol.   This failure of adherence was cited as demonstrating the difficulties of a regional refugees convention being adopted and implemented effectively.

Although the inter-American community discontinued efforts for a regional Refugees Convention in 1967, the IACHR continued to monitor the refugee situation in the American states. By relying on relevant global and regional instruments, the commission has attempted to promote adherence to international standards for refugees and encourage states parties to the global refugees regime to more fully comply with regime obligations. Also, the commission has continued to promote means to bring the practices of the Latin American states into accord with the guidelines of the global refugees regime.   For instance, in the first Inter-American Yearbook on Human Rights (1968), the commission reported that Inter-American Conventions on economic and social rights and personal status did not contain rights similar to those under the global refugees regime. Moreover, despite repeated IACHR and UNHCR suggestions, relatively few provisions concerning political refugees existed in the domestic laws of American states; most states continued to rely on the liberal treatment accorded to foreigners by their constitutions and in the relevant inter-American conventions. Generally, domestic legislation made no distinction between immigrants and refugees. Treatment of refugees was subsumed by immigration departments and settlement or development schemes.[47]

Between the Chilean coup of September 1973 and the last stages of the anti-Somosa Nicaraguan civil war in 1978, IACHR attention to refugee questions entered a new phase: it was now necessary to deal with expulsion of individuals for political reasons, denial of reentry, and revocation of nationality, which had the effect of creating stateless persons.   These state actions were addressed by provisions of the American Declaration and the American Convention.   Thus the commission, relying on its legal authority, engaged in activities designed to achieve fuller implementation of these inter-American guarantees.[48]

Faced with the ongoing violence in Central America, the commission has returned its attention to the broader questions concerning political refugees in Latin America, especially the phenomenon of massive influx of asylum seekers in Central America. A comprehensive review of refugees in Central America was presented to the OAS in 1982. Essentially this report reiterated the findings and suggestions of the 1965 commission report on refugees: the change in socioeconomic status of refugee groups from the few and wealthy to poor and in masses, the lack of an adequate inter-American instrument or agency to deal with these changes, and the lack of appropriate domestic legislation or customary practices that recognized this new type of political refugee.[49] In sum, twenty years after receiving a warning that the problem of political refugees had undergone a fundamental change, the inter-American community proved unable to devise any effective response.

To strengthen the inter-American response to the Central American refugees, the commission suggested

1. that the OAS and its member states reaffirm the obligation of *non-refoulement* and its derivative, nonrejection at the frontier;

2. that the nonpolitical nature of asylum be reaffirmed;

3. that the member states ratify the global refugees instruments and expand domestic legislation concerning refugees;

4. that the definition of refugee be expanded to include those fleeing from a breakdown of social order;

5. that the member states guarantee at least temporary asylum in massive influx situations; and

6. that an inter-American authority for refugees be created by the OAS, not by convention but by a resolution of an OAS political body.

Creation of the IACHR by a resolution of the meeting of the Minister of Foreign Affairs served as precedent for this last suggestion.[50]

The commission repeated these criticisms and suggestions in each of its 1981-1985 annual reports. And while the OAS General Asembly each year has noted, and accepted, the commission suggestions, no substantive actions have been taken.[51] Consequently, the enforceable principles of legal protection for massive-influx situations remain those enunciated by the global refugees regime and inter-American asylum instruments. When combined, how effective are these principles in the Central American case? What are the areas of agreement between the two sets of standards? And what means of reconciling any areas of incompatibility are available? These questions will be addressed in Chapter 6.

NOTES

1. Diego Uribe Vargas, Los Derechos humanos y el sistema inter-americano. (Madrid: Ediciones Cultura Hispanica, 1972), p. x.

2. Ernst Nys, ed., De Indis et de Jure Belli Relectiones (New York: Oceana, 1964), p. 151.

3. Ibid., pp. 154, 179.

4. Uribe Vargas, Derechos humanos, pp. 121-23. These treaties, which united Colombia-Peru (1822), Mexico (1823), Chile (1823), and the Central American Republic (1825), were reaffirmed at the Congress of Panama of 1826.

5. Ibid., pp. 124-25.

6. Jose Joaquin Caicedo Castilla, El Derecho internacional de el sistema interamericano. (Madrid: Ediciones Cultura Hispanica, 1970), pp. 33-37.

7. Jesus Maria Yepes, Del Congreso de Panama a la Conferencia de Caracas (Caracas: Imprenta Nacional, 1976), pp. 260-61, 265-67.

8. German Cavelier, La Politica internacional de Colombia, Vol. 4, El Asilo Diplomatico (Bogota: Imptenta Nacional, 1960), p. 21, 28-9; International Commission of Jurists (hereafter ICJ), An Application in Latin America of International Declarations and Conventions Relating to Asylum (Geneva: ICJ, 1975), p. 55; Jose Augustin Martinez Viademonte, El Derecho de asilo y el regimen internacional de refugiados (Mexico City: Ediciones Botas, 1961), p. 26.

9. ICJ, Application, p. 49; Organization of American States (hereafter OAS), Subsecretariat for Legal Affairs, A Study Comparing United Nations International Instruments and Inter-American Instruments on Asylum, Refugees and Displaced Persons (SER/ser.D/5.2), 20 September 1984, pp. 52-54.

10. Martinez Viademonte, Derecho de asilo, pp. 24-25; OAS, Inter-American Treaties and Conventions on Asylum and Extradition (ser. XII-Series no. 34), Washington, DC, 1967, pp. 3-4.

11. ICJ, Application, p. 55; OAS, Inter-American Treaties and Conventions, pp. 4-5, 14.

12. Pan American Union (hereafter PAU), International Commission of Jurists, Sessions Held in Rio de Janiero, Brazil, 1927, Washington, D.C., 1928, pp. 33-4, 55; PAU, Sixth International Conference of American States: Final Act. Havana, 1928, pp. 20, 69, 135, 166-70; PAU, Diario de la sexta conferencia internacional americana, no. 10 (25 January de 1928) pp.81-3, 486-505, 523-40; PAU, Human Rights in the American States (Washington, D.C.: PAU, 1960), pp. 32-3; Atle Grahl-Madsen, Territorial Asylum (New York: Oceana, 1980), p. 115

13. For a general review of the Seventh Inter-American Conference see Caicedo Castilla, Sistema interamericano, pp. 59-62.

14. PAU, Documentos oficiales de la VII conferencia internacional americana (C.2 no. 4), Washington, D.C., 1933, pp. 1-4; PAU, Documents for the Use of Delegates to the Seventh International Conference of American States, Washington, D.C., 1933, pp. 22-3

15. PAU, Documentos oficiales, pp. 1-6; Documents, 7th Conference, pp. 26-7; PAU, Treaties and Conventions Signed at the Seventh International Conference of American States, (Law and Treaty Series no. 37), (Washington, D.C.: PAU, 1952), pp. 24-30. In addition, at the closing Plenary Session Resolution XCII recommended to governments that they decree that all political exiles may return, exonorated for all, except public crimes.

16. OAS, Inter-American Treaties and Conventions, pp. 75-77.

17. Carlos Urrutia-Aparicio, Diplomatic Asylum in Latin America (Washington, D.C.: American University Press, 1959), p. 68; Luis Carlos Zarate, El Asilo en el derecho internacional americano, (Bogota: Imprenta Nacional, 1957), pp. 76-82; Grahl-Madsen, Territorial Asylum, pp. 125-27.

18. OAS, UN and Inter-American Instruments, p. 43.

19. Anna Schreiber, The Inter-American Commission on Human Rights (Leyden: Sijthoff, 1970), pp. 18-19; Lawrence LeBlanc, The OAS and the Promotion and Protection of Human Rights (The Hague: Martinus Nijhoff, 1977), pp. 13-18. A 1949 opinion of the Inter-American Juridical Committee concluded, inter alia, that the American Declaration did not create a legal contractual obligation; it lacked the status of positive substantive law. Nevertheless, the definitive status of the American Declaration remains in dispute. See, for example, Buergenthal, who argues that the Protocol of Buenos Aires, which amended the OAS Charter, changed the legal status of the declaration to an instrument that, at the very least, constitutes an authoritative interpretation and definition of the human rights obligations binding on OAS member states under the charter of the organization. Thomas Buergenthal, Robert Norris and Dinah

Shelton, Protecting Human Rights in the Americas: Selected Problems (Kehl: N.P. Engel, 1982), pp. 4-7.

20. ICJ, Application, pp. 51-52; OAS, Inter-American Commission on Human Rights (hereafter IACHR), Report on the Work Accomplished during Its 4th Session (ser. L/V/II.4 doc. 34), April 1962, pp. 12-14.

21. Schreiber, IACHR, pp. 27, 29-30; LeBlanc, OAS, pp. 48, 72. Resolution 8 of the Fifth Meeting of Consultation of Ministers of Foreign Affairs (1959) created the IACHR and charged the Inter-American Juridical Committee with preparing a Draft Convention on Human Rights. The IACHR was created in response to the situation of human rights in Cuba and the Dominican Republic.

22. Schreiber, IACHR, p. 10.

23. Ronald L. Scheman, "The Inter-American Commission on Human Rights," American Jouranl of International Law 59, no. 2 (April 1965): 336-37. Although the enforcement powers of the IACHR were minimal, its activities have long irritated many Latin American governments. For example, in 1976, a year of election of members to the Commission, several individuals involved with the IACHR were threatened. In June 1976, Luis Reque, Executive Secretary of the IACHR, resigned, and Justino Jiminez de Arechaga of Uruguay, Genaro R. Carrio of Argentina, and Robert Woodward of the United States decided not to seek reelection. Jiminez de Arechaga stated that the experience of the commission left him sceptical about the dedication of Latin American countries to human rights, and Carrio concluded that the Chilean case had demonstrated the futility of staying with the commission. Regue resigned due to threats to kidnap his daughter if the commission did not restrict its activities. See ICJ, "The Inter-American Commission on Human Rights," Review of the International Commission of Jurists, 16 (June 1976): 23-24.

24. Jose Carbanes, "The Protection of Human Rights and the Organization of American States," American Journal of International Law 62, no. 4 (October 1968): 894; OAS, IACHR, The Inter-American Commission on Human Rights: Ten Years of Activities 1971-1981, Washington, D.C., 1982, p. 5.

25. OAS, IACHR, Report on the Work Accomplished during Its 13th Session (ser. L/V/II.14 doc. 35), April 1966. For a general review of the strengthening of the IACHR, see Pedro Nikken, "Bases de la progresividad en el regimen internacional de proteccion de los derechos humanos," in IACHR, Derechos Humanos en las Americas (Washington, D.C.: IACHR, 1984), pp. 22-40.

26. OAS, IACHR, Annual Report of the Inter-American Commission on Human Rights 1981-1982 (ser. L/V/II.57 doc. 6/rev. 1), 20 September 1982, p. 5; Caicedo Castilla, Derecho internacional, pp. 100-103; Buergenthal et. al., Protecting Human Rights, pp. 9-10. See OAS Revised charter Articles 51 and 112.

27. Uribe Vargas, Derechos humanos, pp. 281-91. On nonintervention, see UN, Charter, Article 103, OAS Revised Charter Article 137. Diplomatic demands to live up to UN and OAS Charter obligations are not considered interference in the internal affairs of a state. See Buergenthal, Protecting Human Rights, pp. 28-29.

28. Thomas Buergenthal and Robert Norris, eds., Human Rights: The Inter-American System (Dobbs Ferry, N.Y.: Oceana, 1982) pt. 2, p. 56. See also Carlos-Jose Guitierrez, "Balance y relacion entre las garantias nacionales e internacionales para la proteccion de los derechos humanos," in IACHR, Derechos Humanos, pp. 41-53. For discussion of hierarchy in international human rights instruments, see Meron, Theodor. "On a Hierarchy of International Human Rights" American Journal of International Law 80, no. 1 (January 1986): 1-23, especially pp. 3-4.

29. OAS, Inter-American Court of Human Rights, Annual Report of the Inter-American Court of Human Rights to the General Assembly (ser. L/V/III.3 doc. 13/corr. 1), October 1980, pp. 3-4.

30. Ibid., pp. 4-5.

31. OAS, Inter-American Court of Human Rights, Advisory Opinion: Other Treaties Subject to the Advisory Jurisdiction of the Court (ser. B., no. 1 Advisory Opinion OC-1/84), 24 September 1982, pp. 4-7; OAS, Inter-American Court, Annual Report 1980, p. 6. In clarifying this provision in a special advisory opinion, the court determined, first, by unanimous decision, that the advisory jurisdiction can be exercised, in general, with regard to any provision dealing with the protection of human rights set forth in any international treaty applicable in the American states, whatever be the principal purpose of such a treaty and regardless of whether nonmember states of the inter-American system are (or have a right to become) parties thereto. Also by unanimous decision, the court decided that it may decline a request if that request would exceed the limits of the court's advisory jurisdiction, for example, if the issue would deal mainly with international obligations assumed by a non-American state or with the structure or operation of international organs or bodies outside the inter-American system, or if granting the request might have the effect of altering or weakening the system established by the convention in a manner detrimental to the individual human being. In general see Thomas Buergenthal, "Judicial Interpretations of the American Human Rights Convention," in IACHR, Derechos Humanos, pp. 253-60 and "The Advisory Practice of the Inter-American Human Rights Court," American Journal of International Law 79, no. 1 (January 1985): 1-27; Maximo Cisneros Sanchez, "Algunos aspectos de la juridiccion consultiva de la Corte Interamericana de Derechos Humanos," in IACHR, Derechos Humanos, pp. 261-69.

32. OAS, UN and Inter-American Instruments, pp. 37-38, 41. See Articles 8, 17, 20, and 27. The reference to the laws of each country and international agreements should not be construed as restricting the right of asylum, but rather as a recommendation that there should be domestic laws and international agreements to govern the exercise of the right.

33. See American Convention, Articles 2, 20 and 22.

34. OAS, UN and Inter-American Instruments, pp. 48-49; OAS, IACHR, Report on the Work Accomplished during Its 23rd Session (ser. L/V/II.23 doc. 27), April 1970, pp. 8-9, 24, 50-51, 56-58. This broader recognition of *non-refoulement* does not constitute grounds for granting asylum. See American Convention, Articles 20, 22, and 27.

35. OAS, Convencion interamericana sobre extradicion, Law and Treaty Series no. 60 (ser. A/36), Washington, D.C., 1981, p. 9; Tatiana de Maekelt, "Instrumentos regionales de materia de asilo," in Asilo y proteccion internacional de refugiados en America Latina (Mexico City: Universidad Nacional Autonoma de Mexico, 1982), p. 166.

36. See Extradition Convention Articles 4(4), 4(5), and 6 on *non-refoulement.* "Extradition will be denied when from the circumstances of the case, it can be inferred that persecution for reasons of race, religion or nationality are involved, or that the position of the person sought may be prejudiced for any of these reasons."

37. OAS, UN and Inter-American Instruments, p. 40.

38. Grahl-Madsen, Territorial Asylum, pp. 141-143.

39. OAS, Council of the OAS, Decisions Taken at the Meetings (ser. G.III/vols. 10-22), 1957-1970; OAS, IACHR, Report on its 23rd Session, pp. 21-23. Even the long term generation of political refugees from Cuba after 1959 received scant attention from the OAS. The only cases on record that deal specifically with asylum arose in 1967. Several communications were presented to the IACHR, charging that Dominican authorities were violating the right to asylum requested by Haitian nationals.

40. OAS, IACHR, Report on the Work Accomplished during Its 7th Session (ser. L/V/II.8 doc. 35), October 1963, pp. 19-20.

41. OAS, IACHR, Report on the Work Accomplished during Its 8th Session (ser. L/V/II.9 doc. 24), April 1964, pp. 19-24; OAS, IACHR, Report on the Work Accomplished during Its 9th Session (ser. L/V/II.10 doc.21), October 1964, pp. 23-25; OAS, IACHR, Report on the Work Accomplished during Its 10th Session (ser. L/V/II.11 doc. 19), March 1965, pp. 9-10; OAS, IACHR, Annual Report of the Inter-American Commission on Human Rights 1984-1985, pp. 138-39. The Castro regime was no longer seated in the OAS. Hence, Cuban

authorities argued that they had no obligation to cooperate. The commission argued that Cuba was not excluded from the OAS, only the Castro regime. Moreover, the IACHR Statute gave jurisdiction over all member states. However, Cuba has never responded favorably to Commission requests for information or assistance. For the status of Cuba and competency of the IACHR, see Buergenthal et. al., Protecting Human Rights, pp. 51-64.

42. OAS, IACHR, Report on the Work Accomplished during Its 12th Session (ser. L/V/II.13 doc. 26), October 1965. See also Report on Political Refugees in America (ser. L/V/II.11), 1 September 1965, and de Maekelt, "Instrumentos regionales," pp. 166-68. UNHCR had drawn attention to the inadequacies of Latin American states' domestic legislation as early as 1952. In a survey conducted that year, UNHCR found that the states' domestic legislation made no distinction between refugees, immigrants and aliens generally. See UN, General Assembly, 8th sess., Report of the United Nations High Commissioner for Refugees (A/2394), 1953, p. 19.

43. OAS, International Council of Jurists, Extraordinary Meeting of the Inter-American Juridical Committee (ser. I/VI.2 CIJ-85), April 1966, p. 31. See Resolution 21: Asylum for Cuban Refugees, which inculded a statement that "the situation of the Cuban refugees as a result of the exodus brought about by the conditions prevailing in the country has created complex problems which require prompt and effective measures, particularly by the American states, in order to provide asylum to those refugees and guarantee their rights and basic freedoms, at least on par with that provided under the Convention on the Status of Refugees."

44. OAS, IACHR, Inter-American Yearbook on Human Rights 1960-1967. (Washington, D.C.: OAS, 1968), pp. 591-93; OAS, IACHR, Annual Report 1981-1982, p. 130.

45. OAS, International Council of Jurists, Extraordinary Meeting, pp. 35-39, 43-46.

46. OAS, IACHR, Report on the Work Accomplished during Its 16th Session (ser. L/V/II.17 doc. 24), October 1967, pp. 30-32; OAS, IACHR, Report on the Work Accomplished during Its 17th Session (ser. L/V/II.18 doc. 25), April 1968, pp. 29-32.

47. OAS, IACHR, Inter-American Yearbook, pp. 501-09; OAS, IACHR, Report on 23rd Session, p. 27. These conclusions were reiterated in OAS, IACHR, The Progress Achieved in Realizing the Goals Set Forth in the American Declaration of the Rights and Duties of Man, 1969.

48. OAS, IACHR, Report on the Work Accomplished during Its 31st Session (ser. L/V/II.31 doc. 54/rev. 1), October 1973, pp. 13-16, 78; OAS, IACHR, Report on the Work Accomplished during Its 32nd Session (ser. L/V/II.32 doc. 31/rev. 1), April 1974, pp. 35-42; OAS, IACHR, Report on the Work

Accomplished during Its 33rd Session (ser.   L/V/II.33 doc. 15/rev. 1). July-August 1974. pp. 3-4.

49. OAS. IACHR. Annual Report 1981-1982. pp. 128-36.

50. OAS. IACHR. Ten Years of Activities. 1971-1981, 24. pp. 316. 336; OAS. IACHR. Annual Report 1984-1985. pp. 38-41. Recommendation 4; OAS. IACHR. Annual Report of the Inter-American Commission on Human Rights 1983-1984 (ser. AG/DOC 1778/84). pp. 15-18, 136.

51. OAS. IACHR. Annual Report of the Inter-American Commission on Human Rights 1982-1983 (ser. L/V/II.61 doc. 22/rev. 1). 27 September 1983. pp. 148-50.

Chapter Six

The Global Regime and
the Inter-American System

It is important that an effort be made to ensure that the common objective of the global regime and inter-American asylum and human rights standards makes it possible to elaborate and implement a coherent and systematic policy designed to protect individuals against persecution for any political reason or motive, regardless of the commission of an offense.[1] This is of the utmost importance, since the majority of persons in Central America who seek territorial asylum or refuge have not committed any political offense and have not been persecuted.

In Latin America, as in general international law, doctrine and positive law distinguish two categories of asylum: (1) territorial asylum or refuge and (2) diplomatic, or political, asylum. The 1889, 1928, and 1933 conventions concern political asylum; the 1939 Montevideo Treaty on Political Asylum and Refuge is the first to make a precise distinction between these two types of asylum. The 1954 Caracas Conference continued this distinction, with seperate treaties for territorial and diplomatic asylum.[2]

There is no uniformity in terminology between the global refugees regime and inter-American asylum law. In general, inter-American asylum law uses the terms asylum and refuge synonymously to refer to admission and protection of individuals. Although territorial asylum and refuge are absolutely synonymous in inter-American law, they are not identical with the concept of refugee in the 1951 and 1967 global instruments. Under the global regime, admission and legal protection are distinct legal concepts. Asylum as used by the global regime refers only to physical admission to a state. Protection does not automatically accompany asylum; it is dependent upon the determination of refugee status pursuant to the criteria contained in the global 1951 convention. Further, no inter-American instrument defines asylee. Rather, the asylum state determines who qualifies as an asylee by interpreting provisions of relevant inter-American instruments. The global 1951 convention, however, defines who a refugee is. Moreover, no American state is a party to all the relevant inter-American Conventions. (See Table 1 of the appendix) As a result, it is difficult to reach conclusions as to which rule is applicable to a specific case. This demonstrates the deficiencies in the inter-American system so far as territorial asylum is concerned.[3]

Extradition is the cornerstone of the protection of asylees in the inter-American system. All inter-American instruments on asylum contain certain clauses that prohibit extradition of the asylee for political crimes and related common crimes, with the *attentat* clause exception. By granting the unilateral determination of the character of a political offense to asylum states, the principle of *non-refoulement* is recognized.[4] On the other hand, neither the global 1951 Refugees Convention nor the 1977 Draft Convention on Territorial Asylum have clauses prohibiting extradition.

The OAS Subsecretariat for Legal Affairs identified the universal properties of asylum as urgency, the threat of danger, *non-refoulement*, and nonexpulsion. Despite these universal properties, there are substantive differences between the inter-American asylum law and the global refugees regime. Within the UN system, territorial asylum is recognized only by means of a legally not binding General Assembly declaration; there is no legally binding document that governs asylum separately and independently. Consequently, the 1951 and 1967 refugees treaties are the two documents usually associated with asylum. This association stems from the recognition by these instruments of the principles of *non-refoulement* and nonexpulsion as characteristic of and essential to protection of the asylee. Also, the global regime uses the terms refuge and asylum interchangeably.[5]

In Latin America, territorial asylum is governed by a number of inter-American instruments, but the nature and application of territorial asylum under these instruments differ. The American Declaration and the American Convention both recognize asylum as a human right; yet the 1954 Caracas Territorial Asylum Convention recognizes asylum as a right of the state and not the individual. The right of asylum as contained in the American Convention may be upheld by petition to the

IACHR and the Inter-American Court. No similar mechanisms exist for provisions of the 1954 convention. In the global refugees regime, asylum is regarded as a human right; however, there are no mechanisms for protection that can be applied in event of violation of this right. Furthermore, the inter-American instruments do not grant asylum for nonpolitical offenses. The global regime expressly excludes some other types of crimes that have no parallels in the inter-American system: crimes against humanity, crimes against peace, war crimes, and perpetuation of acts contrary to the purposes and principles of the United Nations.[6]

Thus, inter-American instruments on asylum are based exclusively on political grounds. No inter-American convention cites "well-founded fear of persecution" as possible grounds for granting asylum. Moreover, the inter-American notion of asylee is based on an objective persecution that when materialized, causes the individual being persecuted to seek and receive asylum. Under the global refugees regime, mere "fear of persecution" is sufficient for international protection.[7]

In the existing inter-American conventions, territorial asylum is applicable for political offenses or common crimes related to, or connected with, political offenses, but it is not clear whether asylum is applicable for victims of political persecution or persons who are pursued for common crimes, but for political reasons. Furthermore, under inter-American asylum conventions, there is no complete parallel between the cases in which territorial asylum can be granted and the grounds that do not permit of extradition. It is also unclear whether persons pursued for political motives can be recognized as asylees despite the absence of an offense, or whether it is only persons pursued for political offenses and related common crimes who can be so regarded. In the former case, where persecution is politically motivated, but no offense exists there would be no grounds for territorial asylum. Also, the fact of being a political refugee under the global refugees regime does not necessarily exclude the right of a state to request extradition for commission of common crimes or offenses that give rise to extradition.[8]

The fact that a person has been accepted as a territorial asylee does not automatically make that person a refugee for the purposes of the global regime. Conversely, classification as a political refugee according to the global refugee regime does not mean that he is ipso jure to be regarded as a territorial asylee (*asilado*). Still, in practice, with the decline in recourse to the system of territorial asylum, the major issues related to refugees in Latin America are dealt with and resolved through application of the global refugees regime and especially through the activities of the UNHCR.[9]

Under inter-American instruments, asylees have the right not to be surrendered by the authorities of a territorial state to those of another state, except in compliance with the rules governing extradition. Asylees also have the right of freedom of expression and assembly or association, except in cases of specific restrictions resulting from applicable conventions. Furthermore, as a matter of principle, asylees should enjoy all the other rights of individuals, irrespective of whether the individual concerned is a national, citizen, alien or resident. Finally, the 1889 and 1939 treaties specifically state that the grant of refuge does not entail an obligation to shelter the asylee indefinitely.[10]

In the state of refuge, asylees have the duty not to commit acts that might endanger the public peace and not to engage in systematic propaganda urging the use of force or violence against another state. The territorial state has the duty to prevent asylees from committing within its territory acts that might endanger the public peace of the asylee's home state. Arrangements are made for surveillance or internment of asylees who violate these principles.[11]

The principle of *non-refoulement* is expressly upheld by the inter-American instruments but is not consistently interpreted within those instruments. The 1889, 1939, and 1954 instruments do not create any *non-refoulement* obligation for the state of refuge and consequently do not guarantee that the asylee will not be expelled from the state of refuge. However, the American Convention on Human Rights recognizes the principle of *non-refoulement* very broadly, since it applies to aliens in the territory of a state and not only to those enjoying the status of asylee. Since the early 1970s application of this principle has undergone a serious testing. There have been many cases of de facto collaboration between police and security forces for coordinated actions against asylees and refugees in the territory of asylum states.[12]

The 1954 Territorial Asylum Convention makes a distinction between *non-refoulement* and expulsion. Article 3 provides that "no State is under the obligation to surrender to another State or to expel from its territory, persons persecuted for political reasons or offenses." This injunction on expulsion is phrased in negative terms: the state is under no obligation. The global 1951 Refugees Convention positively prohibits *refoulement*, where if another state demands expulsion or surrender, the obligation is not to surrender or expel. No provision is made, however, for cases where the state of refuge decides to expel. Thus, should the state of refuge decide to expel an asylee, there is no guarantee that the expulsion will be carried out in accordance with due process of law as established by Article 32 of the global 1951 Refugees Convention.[13]

A distinction between *non-refoulement* and expulsion is also present in Article 22 of the American Convention which in general corresponds to Article 32(2) of the global 1951 Refugees Convention; that is, expulsion is allowed only through due process of law.   The OAS Legal Subsecretariat concluded that the formulation of the principle of *non-refoulement* is neither standard nor absolute in the inter-American system, except in the case of Article 22(8) of the American Convention.   Moreover, inter-American instruments on territorial asylum do not explicitly include nonrejection at the frontier as part of the concept of *non-refoulement.*   In   contrast,   the   global   refugee   regime incorporates a broad exception to *non-refoulement* through the *ordre public* clause.   There is no exception of this kind, nor has any reservation been made to this effect, in the inter-American system.   As to the relationship between *non-refoulement* and nonextradition, the principle of *non-refoulement* in the inter-American system is fully guaranteed in the case of extradition, with absolute respect for asylum and unilateral determination of the character of the offense by the state of refuge.[14]

While the OAS has taken up the issue of refugees and their mass influx, no substantive results analogous to the global regime have been achieved; that is, there are no minimum standards or explicit reference to legal norms of protection applicable in such cases.   This lack of substantive results undermines the importance of the traditional institution of asylum.   Legal problems arise largely from the failure of Latin American states to adhere to and fully implement the standards of the global refugees regime.   Yet this lack of adherence and effective implementation is sufficient to show that the global refugees regime embodies standards that are not unanimously accepted by all Latin American states.

The effective implementation of regime standards is further hindered by several shortcomings within the inter-American community.   The General Secretariat of the OAS has no competence to implement the 1954 Caracas Territorial Asylum Convention.   Moreover, while the IACHR is to oversee implementation of the American Convention (since this refers to human rights in general), there is no system for specific implementation of the rights of asylees and refugees. Furthermore, as many times stressed by the IACHR, the inter-American system has no mechanisms for considering the situation of refugees after they have been granted asylum.   Under inter-American asylum treaties, the territorial state applies the definition of asylee contained in the relevant instrument, whereas UNHCR supervises the application of the definition of refugee of the global refugee regime.   There is no equivalent institutional body for the inter-American system, and the entire operation of the American system of territorial asylum is weakened by this fact.[15]

As noted in Chapter 4, the global refugees regime includes specific basic and equated rights of refugees.   However, in Latin America territorial asylum is viewed essentially as a phenomenon of concern to an individual. Consequently, inter-American asylum law does not provide for extensive social protection nor regulate matters pertaining to the employment, economic livelihood, social settlement, and cultural problems of territorial asylees.[16] In fact, the 1954 Territorial Asylum Convention includes a statement that that no state is under the obligation to establish in its legislation, or in its regulations or administrative acts applicable to aliens, any distinction solely because they are political asylees or refugees. Hence protection is not required to be uniform. This places the asylees at a definite juridical disadvantage and is inconsistent with the requirements imposed upon domestic legislation by the global 1951 Refugees Convention.

This convention states that the question of personal status is governed by the law of the place of residence, as this provides conditions more favorable to the refugee. The inter-American instruments on asylum contain no provisions pertinent to this. Generally, the Latin American states use the principle of *jus soli* to determine personal status. Still, the matter of a refugee's personal status can pose certain difficulties in Latin America. Domestic laws are not uniform, the law of domicile prevailing in some and the law of nationality in others.[17] While the inter-American asylum conventions do not specifically identify all the rights enjoyed by asylees, a framework of guarantees can be constructed from other relevant instruments to which some Latin American states are parties. The right to security and integrity of one's person is guaranteed by the American Declaration and the American Convention, and a considerable number of Latin American states have incorporated such guarantees in their constitutions. Protection of this right is virtually uniform at the global and inter-American levels. The right to equality before the law is expressed in both the American Declaration and the American Convention, and this principle is also upheld by most Latin American constitutions and laws. Nevertheless, some Latin American states uphold this principle only in relation to nationals. Insofar as aliens are concerned, the principle of equality before the law is not absolute, despite the wording of the American Declaration.[18]

Several inter-American instruments specifically deal with the status of aliens. The 1928 Convention on the Status of Aliens, 1928 Bustamante Code of Private International Law, and 1933 American Convention on the Rights and Duties of States all proscribe national treatment for aliens with regard to individual and civil rights. Essentially, these prescriptions for national treatment are equivalent to the standards expressed by the global refugees regime.[19] The right to protection against arbitrary arrest is guaranteed by the American Declaration and the American Convention. In less detail it is addressed by Article 16 (access to courts) of the global 1951 Refugees Convention. The right to due process of law is also guaranteed by both American instruments, but it is not specifically stated in the global refugees regime. However, it can be inferred from the text of Article 16.[20]

Consequently, the inter-American community should be encouraged to address these inadequacies of general economic, social, and cultural rights as one element of protection to political refugees and asylum seekers. There are no a priori limits and no particular reason why the inter-American community should not concern itself with economic, social, and cultural rights. Moreover, violation or denial of these rights may interfere with the attainment of a durable solution to the plight of the refugee.[21]

The inter-American system, including the OAS, has adopted no convention involving a commitment to the economic, social, and cultural rights listed in Articles 17-24 of the global 1951 Refugees Convention. To strengthen this area, the OAS General Secretariat prepared a draft additional protocol to the American Convention on Human Rights, defining social, economic, and cultural rights. This draft was submitted to the General Assembly of the OAS in 1983 and approved and forwarded to member states, the IACHR, and the Inter-American Court for comments. As of the fifteenth (1985) session, only Ecuador, Venezuela, and the Inter-American Court had presented proposals on the content of the draft.[22]

For its part, the IACHR reviewed a series of international instruments dealing with similar rights: the 1948 Universal Declaration, the Covenant on Economic, Social and Cultural Rights, and the OAS Charter. It then compared the basic set of rights found in these instruments to those contained in the draft protocol. The right to work, to education, to health, and to institutions or groups of persons were regarded as requiring special consideration. This study formed the basis for a draft additional protocol to the American Convention, submitted to the OAS General Assembly in the Commission's 1985-1986 annual report.[23]

For protection of the family, children, and young people, the American Declaration and the draft protocol include guarantees consistent with Recommendation B of the global 1951 Refugees Convention.[24] The right to work was considered together with the rights of fair remuneration, leisure time, hygenic conditions, unemployment insurance, union organizations, and collective bargaining, and also the right to strike. Closely connected with the right to work is the right to social security. The right to work and related rights are covered by the American Declaration, the OAS Charter, and the 1986 Draft Protocol. Social security is recognized in the American Declaration and the draft protocol. Taken collectively, the rights of these and related instruments provide protection and guarantees essentially equivalent to those of Articles 15 (right of association), 17 (right to wage-earning employment), and 24 (right to labor legislation and social security) of the global 1951 Refugees Convention.[25]

It is debatable whether or not the inter-American framework is sufficiently flexible (it is not sufficiently detailed) to incorporate Articles 18 (self-employment) and 19 (liberal professions) of the global 1951 Refugees Convention. Article 6 of the 1986 Draft Protocol states that "everyone shall have the right to work, which includes the right of opportunity to lead a decent life by carrying out an activity which one freely chooses and accepts." No specific mention is made of self-employment or recognition of diplomas or professional certificates. In addition, the subsequent three articles of the draft protocol (7-9) are to be read in conjunction with Article 6. Such a reading of these articles leads one to distinguish those activities of gainful employment which warrant greater priority and protection: just and satisfactory conditions of work, trade union rights, and the right to strike. Moreover, the commission suggests that three rights defined in the draft protocol--trade union rights, the right to strike, and freedom of education--should enjoy the system of protection established by the American Convention: the right of individual petition to the commission, and adjudication, where appropriate, by the court. Emphasis on these three rights under the convention enforcement mechanisms, read strictly, would exclude protection of the rights of self-employment and engagement in liberal professions. Finally, the wording of Articles 18 and 19 of the global 1951 Refugees Convention is such that the draft protocol would incorporate only wage-earners, as expressed in Article 17 of the global instrument.[26]

The right to health and the right to food and decent housing are considered in the American Declaration, the OAS Charter, and the 1986 Draft Protocol. It is not clear whether, collectively, these would incorporate the guarantees of Article 21 (housing) of the global 1951 Refugees Convention, which requires a minimum standard of national treatment regarding public allocation of housing. However, the American Declaration refers to housing as one criterion of a decent standard of living or as a requisite for preservation of health. The draft protocol is vague, referring to the right to a healthful environment. Conceivably a refugee or asylee could secure, or be allocated, decent housing or a healthful residence, yet still be subject to discrimination, that is, less than national treatment, during the allocation process.[27]

The right to education should be accompanied by the right to participate in the cultural life and the right to enjoy the results of artistic or intellectual creation. These rights are addressed by the American Declaration, the OAS Charter, and the 1986 Draft Protocol. Collectively, these guarantees are equivalent to the protections required by Articles 14 (artistic rights and industrial property) and 22 (public education) of the global 1951 Refugees Convention.[28]

At both its 1984 and 1985 plenary sessions, the OAS General Assembly noted that the IACHR reiterated the importance of economic, social, and cultural rights for the development of the individual. An additional draft protocol was submitted to the General Assembly and transmitted to member states for their observations and comments at the sixteenth (1986) regular session.[29]

NOTES

1. This chapter follows closely studies done for UNHCR by the Uruguayan jurist Hector Gros Espiell and the OAS Subsecretariat for Legal Affairs. The study by Gros Espiell was first presented at the 1981 Mexico Colloquium. A revised English draft, used here, later was done under the auspices of UNHCR. The OAS study is the single publicly available document of joint OAS/UNHCR efforts to address the problems of refugees in Central America. Hector Gros Espiell, "American International Law on Territorial Asylum and Extradition as it Relates to the 1951 Convention and the 1967 Protocol Relating to Refugees," (HCR/120/24/81/Rev. 1; Geneva: UNHCR, 1981), p. 24. Gros Espiell uses the term American International Law throughout his work. By this phrase he does not wish to rekindle the old debate on the existence of an American International Law; rather, he uses the phrase to refer, in general, to the international instruments adopted with special effect in the Western Hemisphere in respect of territorial asylum and extradition.

2. Ibid., pp. 2-3; Organization of American States (hereafter OAS), Subsecretariat for Legal Afairrs, A Study Comparing United Nations International Instruments and Inter-American Instruments on Asylum, Refugees and Displaced Persons (SER/ser.D/5.2), 20 September 1984, pp. 39- 40. Title II of the 1889 treaty is headed "On Asylum"; Articles 15 and 16 refer to territorial asylum; and Article 17 to diplomatic asylum. The 1928 Havana Convention, Articles 1-3, regulates diplomatic asylum, but Article 1(3) provides for "refuge in foreign territory" and Article 2(5) may also be regarded as referring to territorial asylum. Chapter 2, Articles 12-15, of the 1939 instrument regulate refuge in a foreign territory, that is, territorial asylum.

3. Gros Espiell, "American International Law," pp. 11-15. Moreover, in the political context of Latin America, and especially the practices of the Southern Cone states from 1973 to 1978, the institution of extradition has been undermined. In too many cases offenders and those politically persecuted have been turned over through measures and procedures adopted by security forces, which have completely bypassed the institution of extradition.

4. OAS, UN and Inter-American Instruments, p. 7-8, 42-43,
83; Gros Espiell, "American International Law," p. 6. Extradition
is used in the following multilateral teaties: 1889 Montevideo
Treaty (Title III, Articles 19-29), 1928 Havana Convention
(Article 1.3), 1928 Bustamante Code (Title III, Articles 344-381),
1933 Montevideo Convention on Extradition, 1940 Montevideo
Treaty on International Penal Law (Title II, Articles 18-49),
Caracas Convention on Diplomatic Asylum (Article 17), Caracas
Convention on Territorial Asylum (Article 4), 1971 Convention to
Prevent and Punish the Acts of Terrorism taking the Form of
Crimes against Persons and Related Extortion that are of
International Significance (Article 2), and the 1981 Caracas
Convention on Extradition; OAS, Convencion Interamericana sobre
Extradicion, Law and Treaty Series no. 60 (ser. A/36),
Washington, D.C., 1981. See for example the 1889 Treaty on
International Penal Law, Articles 16 and 23. The second
paragraph of Article 23 recognizes the principle of *non-refoulement*
by providing for unilateral determination of the character of the
offense by the requested state. See also the 1933 Convention on
Extradition, Article 3; 1939 Treaty on Political Asylum and
Refuge, Articles 2, 3 and 11; 1940 Treaty on International Penal
Law, Articles 20(d-f) and 23; and 1981 Caracas Convention on
Extradition, Articles 4 and 6.

5. OAS, UN and Inter-American Instruments, pp. 77-78. In
view of this dichotomy, the OAS Subsecretariat for Legal Affairs
has suggested that states parties to instruments whose
interpretation of this question differs, should abide by the most
recent text that the state in question has ratified, thereby applying
the general principle of law *lex posterior derogat priori*; that is,
subsequent law abrogates the preceeding law. A definitive legal
opinion, however, must come from the Inter-American Court for
Human Rights.

6. Ibid., pp. 80-81; Gros Espiell, "American International
Law," pp. 8-10.

7. OAS, UN and Inter-American Instruments, pp. 79-80.

8. Gros Espiell, "American International Law," pp. 25-26,
28.

9. Ibid., p. 28; OAS, UN and Inter-American Instruments,
p. 1.

10. Ibid., p. 30; OAS, UN and Inter-American Instruments,
p. 43.

11. Gros Espiell, "American International Law," p.   30;
OAS, UN and Inter-American Instruments, p. 44.

12. See Article 22 of the American Convention. Ibid., pp.
31- 32; OAS, UN and Inter-American Instruments, pp. 87-88.

13. OAS, UN and Inter-American Instruments, pp. 87-89.

14. Ibid., pp.   89, 94-95.   See Article 33(2) of the 1951
Refugees Convention for the *ordre public* clause.   On

non-refoulement, see Article 6 of the 1981 Convention on Extradition, which states that "no provision of this Convention may be interpreted as a limitation on the right to asylum when its exercise is appropriate." It should be noted, however, that Article 22(8) of the American Convention, which establishes the principle of *non-refoulement*, prohibits expulsion.

15. Gros Espiell, "American International Law," pp. 33-36.

16. Ibid., pp. 30-31.

17. OAS, UN and Inter-American Instruments, pp. 131-33.

18. Ibid., pp. 101-03.

19. Article 5, 1928 Convention; Article 9, 1933 Convention; compare to Articles 8 (exemption from exception measures) and 31 (nondiscrimination) of the 1951 Refugees Convention.

20. OAS, UN and Inter-American Instruments, pp. 104-10. See Article 26 of the American Declaration and Article 8 of the American Convention.

21. "Refugee Rights Human Rights," Refugees, no. 38 (February 1987): p. 5.

22. OAS, UN and Inter-American Instruments, pp. 114-19, Resolution 657 (XII- O/83); OAS, IACHR, Annual Report of the Inter-American Commission on Human Rights 1985-1986 (ser. L/V/II.68 doc. 8/rev. 1), 26 September 1986, pp. 21-22.

23. OAS, IACHR, Annual Report of the IACHR, 1984-1985 (ser. L/V/II.66 doc. 10/rev. 1), October 1985, pp. 172-74; OAS, IACHR, Annual Report 1985-1986, pp. 195-211.

24. United Nations (hereafter UN), Human Rights: A Compilation of International Instruments (ST/HR/1/rev. 1; New York: UN, 1978), pp. 86-93, 1951 Refugees Convention. See Articles 6-7 of the American Declaration, 17-18 of the 1986 draft protocol.

25. OAS, IACHR, Annual Report 1984-1985, pp. 172-74; UN, Human Rights, p. 5. For the right to work and related rights, see American Declaration, Articles 14-15; OAS Charter, Articles 31(g) and 43(b- c); and 1986 Draft Protocol. Articles 6-9. On social security, see American Declaration, Article 16, and 1986 Draft Protocol Article 10.

26. OAS, IACHR, Annual Report 1985-1986, pp. 198-200; UN, Human Rights, pp. 86-94.

27. Ibid. pp. 206-07; UN, Human Rights, pp. 88-89. See American Declaration Article 11, OAS Charter, Article 31(i-k) and 1986 Draft Protocol. Articles 11-13.

28. See American Declaration, Articles 12-13; OAS, Charter, Article 47; OAS Draft Protocol Articles 14-16.

29. OAS, IACHR, Annual Report 1985-1986, pp. 21-22; OAS, IACHR, Annual Report of the Inter-American Commission on Human Rights 1986-1987 (ser. L/V/II.71 doc. 9/rev. 1), 22 September 1987, pp. 11, 18-19.

Chapter Seven

The South American States

As suggested by the title, this chapter reviews the asylum and refugees policies of the South American states. Separate chapters for the South and Central American states are warranted, because the two geographic areas have experienced different refugee problems. The refugee problems most often associated with South American states, especially the so-called Southern Cone states of Argentina and Chile, have resulted from military coups and extended military rule. For this reason, in its review of these states' national policies toward asylum and refugees, this chapter starts with Brazil and the Southern Cone states before moving northward from Bolivia to Venezuela.

BRAZIL

Brazil announced an open door policy toward refugees in 1954 with the creation of the National Institute of Immigration and Colonization.[1] Unexpectedly soon thereafter, however, this open door policy, including visa issuance for stateless persons, was suspended pending government review of immigration policy and selection procedures. Although this sudden shift of policy was not clearly explained, difficulties experienced in developing the Brazilian economy seem to have been the greatest single factor determining the policy change. Rather than acceptance of new refugees, the focus shifted to family reunion and select sponsorship of skilled individuals. Individual refugees seeking admission to Brazil needed receipt of prior approval from Brazilian authorities.[2] Individual application was discouraged in preference to group entry under colonization schemes. Classification of refugees under colonization schemes placed the refugees under the procedures and guidelines of general immigration and aliens laws. As will be discussed in this section, this restrictive admission practice toward individual refugees was not relaxed until 1986.

Nevertheless, Brazil has been a consistently strong supporter of the UN High Commissioner for Refugees (UNHCR) and a member of its Executive Committee (EXCOM) since inception. As part of its support for the 1959 World Refugeee Year, it ratified the 1951 Refugees Convention in 1960. Although the geographic limitation was invoked with deposit of the instrument of ratification, the Brazilian delegate to the EXCOM assured its members that liberal asylum practices would continue.[3] Also during the World Refugee Year, Brazil made available to UNHCR 700 visas for refugees from the Far East.

Brazil adhered to the 1967 protocol in 1972, again invoking the geographic limitation. Numerous attempts by UNHCR to persuade Brazil to abandon the geographic limitation have been unsuccessful. UNHCR persuasion was renewed with the return of civilian political administration in 1984, which ended 20 years of military rule. Although discussions for removal of the geographic limitation continued through 1986, the civilian administration has given no indication of a change in policy.[4]

The Brazilian rules covering refugees were revised in 1964, 1969-70, and 1980 to afford protection to political refugees consistent with the 1951 Refugees Convention. Refugees in Brazil were granted permanent asylum and protection from extradition. Otherwise, they were subject to all laws applicable to aliens and foreign visitors.[5] All individuals seeking refugee or *asilado* status in Brazil are required to enter under normal visa procedures. Upon entry, asylum seekers declare their status and apply for a permanent visa. The regulations state that no person may be deported for remaining beyond the expiration date of a visa if such deportation amounts to impermissible extradition. In effect, this recognizes the principle of *non-refoulement.*

If asylum is granted, an identification card is issued, but restrictions may be placed on residence and movement. For *asilados,* travel outside Brazil is by permission only. Failure to obtain permission for travel constitutes a waiver of asylum. Those registered as political refugees receive a Brazilian passport, subject only to the travel restrictions faced by any Brazilian national. Four years of residency, knowledge of Portuguese, the ability of self or family support, no record of political denunciation of Brazilian policies and no conviction of a crime carrying a penalty of more than one year in prison are required for naturalization.

Unlike its Southern Cone neighbors, the period of military rule saw the selective, not massive, exile of political opponents. From 1969 to 1979, an estimated 10,000 Brazilians were in exile. Probably half fled to Europe; the others to Latin American states, especially Chile under the Allende regime. The Brazilian government denied passports to all exiles and their children and refused all assistance or protection in their countries of residence. In some cases the Brazilian security police openly acted against members of the Brazilian opposition, as following the coups in Uruguay and Chile.[6]

A political amnesty was announced in 1979, and Brazil returned to civilian rule in 1984. During these years, the great majority of exiles returned; however, their reintegration into Brazilian society was impeded by continual economic crises. Nevertheless, the return to civilian rule has resulted in a general liberalization of Brazilian society. This liberalization has had consequences for the treatment of refugees as well; from a country of transit for most refugees, Brazil is changing to a country of permanent asylum. In large measure this change is attributed to the reduction of refugees in Brazil: from a population of several thousand, today only several hundred remain as groups of Argentines, Uruguayans and Bolivians have repatriated. Also in 1984, UNHCR attained the status of an international organization. Previously UNHCR activities in Brazil had been under the aegis of the UN Development Program.[7]

In 1984 the Brazilian authorities agreed to allow refugees recognized by UNHCR to remain in the country until finally resettled or repatriated. In 1985 refugees and their families were extended national treatment with regard to the right to education. Moreover, in August 1986 the National Council for Immigration began to issue work permits for refugees. Cumulatively, these policy changes now give individual asylum seekers a status similar to that of immigrants legally established in the country.[8]

Finally, although Brazil has shown no indication of removing its geographic limitation to the global refugees regime, exceptional action by its executive has been used to extend regime guarantees to refugees beyond Brazil's treaty obligations. For example, by presidential decree in 1986, 50 Iranian refugee families were accepted for resettlement, with their refugee status explicitly recognized.[9]

Brazil is not a party to the American Convention on Human Rights and has never expressed recognition of the competency of either the IACHR or the Inter-American Court. However, it remains party to the 1928, 1933, and 1954 inter-American asylum conventions. Additional rights and guarantees for *asilados* are contained in the Brazilian constitution.   Since the return to civilian rule, its assembly has been drafting a new constitution. The provisions, if any, applicable to refugees and *asilados* were not know at the time of writing.[10]

Brazilian compliance with the standards of the global refugees regime can be gauged from its treatment of Southern Cone refugees from the early 1970s.   Following military coups in Uruguay, Chile, and Argentina in the 1970s, Brazilian authorities were reluctant to grant even temporary asylum.   Because of the geographic limitation, Brazil refused them refugee status.   Any application for asylum led to detention for 90 days while the application was considered.   If the application was rejected, the applicant was declared an illegal entrant and automatically expelled.   Those expelled were seldom allowed to choose their country of destination, whereby the prohibition of *non-refoulement* was breached.   An individual with UNHCR recognized refugee status received a 90-day visa, renewable upon request, while resettlement to a third country was sought.   The right to work was not recognized, nor access to public schools or universities. Consequently, it remained preferable for individual refugees to seek immigrant or UNHCR-sponsored resettlement status for entry into Brazil.[11]

CHILE

In Chile, the numbers and types of entrants are controlled by the Standing Immigration Board.   In 1955 the Directorate of Immigration of the Ministry of Foreign Affairs expressed willingness to work through UNHCR and voluntary agencies for admission of select cases of refugees. Agricultural settlers were preferred.   By decree in 1956, Chile agreed to issue refugees resident in Chile travel documents consistent with provisions of the 1951 Refugees Convention.[12]

The global 1951 Refugees Convention was submitted to the Chilean Parliament in 1958, but Chile did not become a party to the global refugees regime until 1972, when it ratified both the 1951 convention and 1967 protocol.[13]   Chile is not a party to the American Convention or either of the 1954 American asylum conventions.   However, the 1928 and 1933 American asylum conventions remain in force.

In 1973 a military coup overthrew the constitutionally elected government of Salvador Allende.   Immediately after the coup, four distinct categories of persons were involved with questions of asylum or refuge.   In the first category were some 10,000 to 12,000 persons not of Chilean nationality who had sought refuge in Chile before the coup in the wake of political persecution in their own countries.   6,000-7,000 of them were from other Latin American states (Boliva, Brazil, and Uruguay), and the remainder were from European countries.   Directly after the coup many of them, suspected generally of engaging in left-wing activities or having sympathies of a left-wing nature, were sought by the police and military authorities.   At least 700 were detained, and some unknown number murdered, in the days after the coup.[14] The second category was Chilean nationals who sought and obtained diplomatic asylum in foreign embassies or special places reserved for this purpose.   The third was Chilean nationals detained pursuant to the declared state of siege to whom the military junta offered freedom if they left Chile.   Those leaving were prohibited from reentry without authorization, under pain of severe penal sanctions. Small numbers of individuals have been so banished from Chile each year since 1973. Although these were not initially cases of refugees or asylum, their failure to obtain permission for reentry has created several thousand de facto stateless persons.   The fourth category was Chilean nationals who were abroad at the time of the coup or who subsequently left Chile by their own means for whom Chilean consular authorities refused to renew passports.   This generated refugees with a legal status equivalent to that of stateless persons.[15]

Following the coup, the UNHCR cabled the Chilean Foreign Ministry, reminding it of obligations under the 1951 and 1967 refugee instruments and requesting a personal visit.   As UNHCR did not have a permanent presence in Chile, a representative was sent immediately from the Buenos Aires office, and three staff members were sent from UNHCR headquarters in Geneva.   Until the   UNHCR   personnel   established   a   coordinated   effort, representatives   of   the   United   Nations   Development   Program (UNDP)   helped   to   negotiate   guarantees   for   refugees.   Once established, UNHCR secured the services of a Chilean lawyer to provide, when possible, due process.   In the first weeks following the coup, UNHCR was unable to obtain any clarification of alleged government offenses against refugees.[16] On 17 October 1973, the UNHCR executive committee cabled Chile, requesting continued   cooperation   and   conformity   with   international conventions.   Chilean authorities responded on 26 October 1973, stating that they were "most anxious to find a rapid and effective solution."[17] Also, the Chilean Ambassador to the United Nations sent a letter to the UN secretary-general clarifying the situation of foreign refugees in Chile.   If they had not transgressed the law, they had nothing to fear.   If they had entered irregularly, they would be offered the necessary facilities to normalize their status in Chile.   Foreign refugees who had committed crimes would be tried in Chile.   If the punishment imposed was expulsion, they would be returned to their country of origin only if they so requested; otherwise they would have the opportunity to choose

their destination.   Chilean authorities remained in contact with
UNHCR, and an official statement of intent had been declared
fully satisfactory by UNHCR.   Finally, the Chilean Ambassador
reiterated that Chile maintained total adherence to the legal norms
of the 1967 Protocol.[18]

To meet the needs of protection and movement of refugees,
the National Committee for Assistance to Refugees (CONAR) was
formed on 24 September 1973.   Its members were representatives
of the Christian churches in Chile, International Committee of the
Red Cross (ICRC), InterGovernmental Committee on European
Migration (ICEM), World Council of Churches (WCC), Caritas,
and World Lutheran Aid.   CONAR was to aid in the departure of
refugees, mediate with the authorities, and provide legal
assistance.   A decree issued in October 1973 authorized the
functioning of CONAR "for a maximum period of three months."
It was permitted to establish centers offering information about
the work of the committee and the rights of refugees and centers
of reception and accommodation, to receive refugees who are
staying in the country illegally or who wished to leave the
country.[19]

In light of the chaotic situation following the coup, UNHCR
instituted an innovation in the practice of asylum by establishing
"safe havens," places where foreigners who wished to or had to
leave the country could receive shelter, assistance and protection
before their departure.   Owing to the efforts of UNHCR, 240
Latin American refugees were subsequently transferred from
military custody to such centers.   During 1974, six "safe havens"
were operating with the agreement of the military junta.
Generally they were respected as places of asylum by the police
and the armed forces.   Between September 1973 and March
1974, 3,400 Latin American refugees, the majority being
Bolivians, Brazilians, and Uruguayans, applied for protection at
these "safe havens."[20]

In addition, safe-conduct for 500 of 1,500 diplomatic asylees
was secured in September 1973.   The remaining 1,000 were
allowed safe-conduct when the authorities determined that none
were suspected of committing common crimes.   In March 1974
UNHCR declared that the resettlement crisis had ended and began
to focus on family reunion.[21]

In August 1975, UNHCR closed the last "safe haven" and
the Social Aid Foundation of the Christian Churches (Fundacion
de Ayuda Social de las Iglesias Cristianas, FASIC)   assumed
control of the UNHCR refugee projects, with government consent.
Approximately 1,500 persons remained under FASIC care, all
awaiting family reunification.   Up to August 1975, not including
those finding temporary asylum in Peru or Argentina, UNHCR
resettled 4,482 refugees to third countries and assisted in the
resettlement of about 15,000 Chilean nationals who had to leave

the country but did not fall strictly under the competence of UNHCR. As a consequence of the Chilean coup, a permanent UNHCR presence was estalished in Santiago, the presence in Buenos Aires was expanded, and a new office was established in Lima in 1975.[22]

Overall, the military junta was credited by UNHCR and independent observers to have generally complied with its international obligations toward refugees. An April 1974 International Commission of Jurists (ICJ) report stated that "the Chilean government appears to have made good its undertaking to fulfill its obligations under the various international conventions governing the right of asylum to which it is a party."[23]

While UNHCR was able to assist non-Chilean refugees and diplomatic asylees leave Chile, Chilean nationals of left-wing sympathies were not at liberty to seek asylum or leave the country. However, the UNHCR estimated that 30,000 Chilean nationals eventually made their way to Spain following the coup. As of July 1985, 25,000 had acquired naturalized Spanish citizenship.[24]

From 1973 through 1981, the junta issued a variety of decrees that allowed state authorities to banish or expel Chilean nationals with no right of free return.[25] Eligibility to receive permission to return, whether for those expelled by decree or for Chilean nationals abroad at the time of the coup, was determined by the nationals' behavior toward the military regime while abroad. By Decree Law 81, of December 1973, the Minister of the Interior was given unilateral power to revoke the passports of and deny entry to nationals considered guilty of damaging state interests or national security. This law was not communicated to Chileans abroad, so exile communities initially had no knowledge of the conduct considered inappropriate by the junta.[26]

The effect of this policy was to make stateless those Chilean nationals who either had their nationality revoked or were unable to have their papers renewed, even if not subject to a specific order revoking their nationality. Also, Chilean courts could offer expulsion as an alternative sentence to imprisonment. Military courts were empowered to unilaterally change imprisonment sentences to exile. If a sentence was so changed, reentry without expressed permission was prohibited.[27]

The Chilean military authorities introduced new legal norms regulating the status of foreigners in Chile. These norms entrusted the Ministry of the Interior, in conjunction with the Foreign Ministry, with regulating the conduct of foreigners. Aliens could be prohibited from entry on grounds of public order and national security. Chileans exiled or forced to abandon the country by decree were prohibited from reentry. Political asylum or refuge was recognized for those who presented themselves and a formal written request for asylum to the proper authorities within 10 days of arrival on the national territory. The Ministry of the Interior was empowered to hold applicants for up to 15 days, pending verification of documentation. *Asilado* status was granted for a maximum of two years, after which permanent residency could be applied for. Travel outside the country required permission from the Ministry of the Interior, and travel for more than 15 days would not be permitted. For an individual to be recognized as a refugee under the standards of the global regime, the circumstances of that individual had to conform to subscribed international conventions. The right to work was granted to all *asilados* and refugees. *Asilado* and refugee status could be revoked for reasons of public order and national security. Once status and authorization were revoked, the individuals concerned had 72 hours to leave Chile.[28]

With the decline of pressure for immediate resettlement of refugees in Chile after 1975, UN and Inter-American agencies focused their attention on the practice and effects of expulsion. While the number of Chileans expelled for political reasons each year has declined since 1975, the basic policy has not changed. Thus, in effect Chile continues to generate a small number of stateless persons each year. In 1976 an ad hoc working group of the UN Commission on Human Rights began a study of Chile's practices of denial of nationality and arbitrary expulsion. The court system was judged ineffective in providing due process against such abuses. Challenges to expulsion orders based on the Covenant on Civil and Political Rights were dismissed by the Chilean Supreme Court in a decision on 25 August 1976, even though Chile had declared the provisions of the covenant in force on 23 March 1976. The court ruled that the covenant was not law in the republic and hence provided no grounds for challenging the expulsion provisions of Decree Law 81.[29]

The Chilean policy of expulsion was denounced by resolutions of the General Assembly (UNGA 31/124 of 16 December 1976) and challenged by members of the UNHCR executive committee. The Chilean representatives to both the UN Commission on Human Rights and the executive committee expressed indignation and suprise at this continued harsh criticism. Apparently in an effort to lessen such criticism, a limited amnesty for exiles was announced on 20 April 1978.[30] It applied to all persons directly or indirectly involved in unlawful conduct from 11 September 1973 until 10 March 1978, so long as they had not stood trial or been convicted, and to all convicted by military courts since the coup. Chileans remaining abroad covered who were by the amnesty were required to obtain permission of the Ministry of the Interior if they desired to return. This amnesty had no effect; in 1979 and 1980 the UN Commission on Human Rights found that the Ministry of the Interior had denied the reentry visas. Apparently the Chilean authorities established no linkage between the amnesty and regulations governing the return of exiles.[31]

In 1977-84 the IACHR was repeatedly involved in interceding for Chileans petitioning for the right of reentry. As of 14 February 1978, it recorded that 109 Chileans had been allowed to return, 44 had been denied reentry, and 38 cases remained pending. In 1980 series of mass petitions for return submitted by exiles, and supported by the IACHR, were denied by decree.[32] By Resolution 24/82 in 1982, the IACHR denounced the continued Chilean practice of expulsion as a violation of Article 8 of the American Declaration of Human Rights. Since Chile is not a party to the American Convention, the competency of the IACHR to criticize Chilean policy is of doubtful validity. This lack of explicit jurisdiction, and hence legitimacy, of the IACHR has led the Chilean authorities to refuse to cooperate with IACHR investigations and requests; hence IACHR inquiries since 6 May 1981 have been ignored by the Chilean authorities.[33]

In its 1982-1983 annual report, the IACHR noted that 3,090 previously exiled Chileans had been declared free to return, but that expulsions continued; 10 expulsions were recorded for 1984. Yet over the years the Chilean government has continued to reduce the number of Chileans deprived of their right to return and reside in the country. The latest list presented by IACHR (as of the end of 1986) contained 3,717 names of persons still prohibited from return or reentry.[34] Moreover, those exiles who have returned report that employment is difficult to find and that their children have difficulty in adjusting to Chile. Despite government guarantees of no harassment of the returnees, social workers report that the government is more concerned with the returnees' political behavior than with aiding their struggle to readjust.[35]

The new Chilean Constitution of 1981 contains no mention of refuge or asylum. Since the provisions of this constitution do not take full effect until 1989, the military continues to rule through the broad powers conferred by the 18th Transitory Provision of the Constitution. Hence, the restrictions imposed for the return of Chilean exiles remain in force.[36]

Under the provisions of this constitution, the military junta has continued to rule. The political conditions in Chile have remained highly volatile, requiring frequent resort to declarations of a state of seige or state of emergency. As of the summer of 1987, the latest state of seige had been lifted in April. Under the provisions of the constitution governing a state of seige, the authorities retained broad powers of expulsion from the national territory and prohibition of reentry of exiled Chilean nationals.[37]

ARGENTINA

During the first three postwar decades, Argentina accepted only limited numbers of refugees, selected by skill criteria. Every refugee had to have a private sponsor and a work contract outside of Buenos Aires.[38]

No discrimination between aliens and nationals is contained in the amended versions of the 1853 Constitution, but neither is there any mention of asylum or refuge. The constitution stated that aliens enjoy the same civil rights as nationals; were permitted to own property, work, or exercise a profession; and were not obliged to seek citizenship. Naturalization was possible after two years of uninterrupted residence. All inhabitants were equal before the law and for purposes of taxation. Article 25, however, expressly limited immigration to Europeans. Special favorable treatment was foreseen for aliens who were obviously useful to the development of the nation.[39]

Following a military coup in Paraguay in 1954, Argentina was faced with the problem of illegal entry of Paraguayan nationals seeking asylum. In response, a decree in 1956 established procedures to legalize the status of Paraguayan nationals who entered illegally.[40] Further normalization of *asilados* was accomplished in 1957 by extending the facilities for residence and registration under Argentine legislation for those coming from countries signatory to the Montevideo Convention of 1889.[41]

Argentina adhered to the 1951 Refugees Convention in 1961, subject to the geographic limitation. Domestic legislation to implement provisions of the convention was enacted in 1963, and regulations were adopted in 1965 that established procedures for admission, permanent residence, and expulsion of aliens. The National Directorate of Immigration (DNM) was given authority to permit and regulate entry and residence.[42]

The 1965 Regulations recognized refugees as foreigners with permanent residence status. The directorate controlled the entry of those fleeing for political, religious, or moral reasons, preferably those assisted by national and international organizations. For an individual lacking full documentation, a residence permit would be granted, since that individual was seen as subject to exceptional circumstances. *Asilados* were defined by the Montevideo Convention of 1889 and classified as nonpermanent residents. They could engage in temporary employment only. A provisional residence document would be issued until the Ministries of the Interior and Foreign Affairs determined the case. Residence and movement restrictions could be imposed. Recognized *asilados* were required to report to the police every 30 days, and their status was reviewed every six months. Failure to meet any of these conditions or restrictions led to loss of their status. In October 1967, Argentina adhered to the global 1967 Protocol. The geographic limitation was reiterated.[43]

Granting of convention refugee status remained conditioned by the geographic limitation clause. The Foreign Ministry was reluctant to withdraw this limitation, fearing greater obligations on the part of Argentina. The Ministry of the Interior favored removal of the limitation, since this would provide greater ministry involvement in determination of refugee status.[44]

Little information is found on Argentine participation in, or support of, inter-American human rights initiatives. Given the political difficulties in Argentina for the last 30 years, such lack of information is not surprising. Only after the return to civilian rule in 1984 did Argentina ratify the American Convention.[45] Argentina is a party to the 1954 Caracas Territorial Asylum Convention, but a reservation states that Article 7 does not give due consideration to, nor satisfactorily resolve, problems arising from the exercise on the part of a political asylee of the right of freedom of expression.[46] Also, the 1889 Treaty on International Penal Law and the 1933 Montevideo Extradition Treaty remain in force.

In 1955-73 the country went through a constitutional upheaval and was governed, with a few brief exceptions, by de facto military regimes. During those years, Argentina received a number of refugees from neighboring states, following military coups: Paraguay (1954), Brazil (1964), Bolivia (1971), and Uruguay (1973) and Chile (1973). While an estimated 500,000 persons fled to Argentina, only 300 were formally granted political asylum.[47]

Beginning in June 1973, Argentina experienced a political and economic crisis and an unprecedented escalation of violence. An estimated 15,000 Argentines fled to Chile, and another 5,000-6,000 dispersed to Bolivia, Brazil, Paraguay and Uruguay. Few registered as refugees.[48] In this already highly convulsive situation, a massive number of political exiles from Chile arrived in the wake of the September anti-Allende coup. Between September 1973 and July 1974, an estimated 15,000 refugees arrived from Chile and some 5,000-6,000 more from the other neighboring states (Bolivia, Brazil, Paraguay, and Uruguay). By a decree in 1973, the Federal Police were empowered to issue travel documents to persons lawfully on Argentine territory who had global refugee or stateless persons status. The travel document would comply with the provisions of the global refugees regime, valid for one year with two six-month extensions possible.[49] During this time, the Argentine authorities enabled some 3,500 individuals to regularize their status. A decree of January 1974 regularized the residence and employment status of illegal entrants from neighboring states who had arrived in the country before 1 January 1974. In particular, permanent residence was granted to refugees of Chilean origin and in some cases to refugees who had arrived in Argentina directly from their home country. In general, however, non-Chilean nationals, and those for whom Argentina was a second country of refuge, had to seek resettlement in other countries.[50]

To handle the influx of Chileans, the Coordinating Commission of Social Action (Comision Coordinadora de Accion Social, CCAS) was recognized by the government on 26 April 1974. Immigration authorities would be presented with the registration list so that appropriate travel and identity documents could be issued. The UNHCR would be notified of those refused asylum status, which allowed for UNHCR intervention for reconsideration. Of the estimated 15,000 Chileans who had entered the country by July 1974, a little more than half had registered with CCAS.[51]

While favorable treatment was extended to Chilean refugees, Uruguayans fleeing to Argentina were subject to harsh treatment. Argentine courts granted recognition of extraterritorial criminal charges, and Uruguayan nationals were tried in Argentine courts for offenses allegedly committed in Uruguay. Numerous cases of *refoulement* of Uruguayans and reports of operation of Uruguayan security forces on Argentine territory were documented in 1973.[52]

After the death of Peron in 1974, the government changed its policy of permanently accepting a large number of refugees from neighboring states. Instead, the authorities sought their resettlement abroad with the cooperation of other bodies, particularly UNHCR. Only temporary asylum was henceforth recognized, and all refugees were considered to be in transit. Under this change of policy, the CCAS centers in Buenos Aires and Mendoza were the only mechanisms available to determine refugee status. Those granted temporary asylum were not eligible for work permits. Combined with the overall political climate, the change in policy increased the difficulties of refugees in Argentina.[53]

By September 1975, the UNHCR controlled six refugee centers in Buenos Aires and fifteen in Mendoza, accommodating some 2,000 refugees. Of the 10,000 officially registered refugees, 4,500 were classed as cases for urgent resettlement. An estimated 10,000-11,000 unregistered refugees remained in Argentina. By December 1976 the caseload of refugees of concern to UNHCR remained steady at 12,000, with 973 cases classified as urgent.[54]

A law enacted in 1978 revised the procedures for naturalization. An individual was required to be fluent in Spanish, to have resided uninterrupted in the territory for two years, to have a means of livelihood, and to infringe on none of the exceptions of public order or national security. Loss of nationality could occur for offenses against the symbols of

nationality, reasons of public order, or national security.   No
special provisions or waivers for refugees or *asilados* were
included.[55]

Following the military coup of 1975, expulsion of Argentine
nationals was frequently used as a juridical sentence.   Those
expelled for political or security reasons were not permitted to
reenter unless specific permission from the regime was granted.
The Argentine communities in other Latin American states were
inhibited in aiding resettlement of expellees; the Argentine
communities in Mexico and Venezuela helped with obtaining visas,
but due to job competition, borders were tightened in these
countries in 1978. Brazil was willing to accept Argentine nationals
only in transit to third countries.   In general, Argentine nationals
seeking asylum were hampered by the lack of a specific
international program aimed at their resettlement.[56]

From 1975 to 1979, the international community strongly
criticized the human rights violations of Argentina, which included
expulsion of nationals and failure to provide international
protection to recognized refugees.   In August 1979 Argentina
agreed to accept 1,000 Indochinese, mostly Lao, families for
resettlement. A selection commission and reception and assistance
centers were established.   After years of criticism for violation of
human rights and failure to guarantee refugee protection,
resettlement of Indochinese during the height of the "boat crisis"
did much to silence the international community.[57]

Argentina returned to civilian rule in December 1983, and
the new civilian government issued an amnesty for irregular
immigrants.   A mission was sent to Europe in April 1984 to
encourage the return of Argentine exiles. The National
Commission for the Return of Argentinians Abroad was formed by
decree on 11 June 1984.   By the end of the year 11,500 had
returned, 4,280 with UNHCR assistance.[58]

The Argentine parliament abolished the geographic restriction
for both the 1951 and 1967 global refugee instruments in
September 1984.   Since 1985, as a result of growing social
unrest in Chile, Chilean refugee arrivals in Argentina again have
been on the increase, reaching an average of some 100 persons
per month.   With the civilian government's removal of the
geographic limitation, these latest Chilean arrivals are considered
refugees.   They are registered and invited to appear before the
Eligibility Commission for Refugees (Comision de Elegibilidad
para los Refugiados, CEPARE) which determines refugee status.
It is composed of representatives from the Ministries of the
Interior and Foreign Affairs. UNHCR participates as an observer.
If status is granted, refugees are authorized to live, work, or
study in Argentina until conditions in Chile permit voluntary
repatriation.   From January to May 1986, 360 Chilean asylum
seekers arrived; 107 were granted refugee status.[59]

By Resolution 528 (1986), the Human Rights Secretariat of the Ministry of the Interior became the competent appeals authority for rejection of refugee status. Negative decisions for recognition of refugee status must be appealled within ten days. Either the applicant or UNHCR can submit such an appeal.[60]

PARAGUAY

Paraguay is a party to both the 1951 and 1967 global refugee instruments; the geographic limitation has been invoked for both instruments.   Most of the refugees in Paraguay arrived as part of IRO resettlement schemes and are of European origin. However, there remain a small number of refugees from neighboring Bolivia and Brazil.[61] Paraguay is not a party to the American Convention, but it is a party to all (1928, 1933, and both 1954) inter-American asylum conventions.

There has been no change of legislation or mechanisms dealing with refugees from the IRO period.   Jurisdiction over refugees is in the hands of the Institute of Agrarian Reform, and legal guidance for refugee questions remains under the general immigration laws.[62] While Paraguay has accepted refugees in colonization schemes, for the last 25 years Paraguay is most often associated with generation of small numbers of refugees; especially as a result of a policy of selective expulsion of political dissidents.   In a 1978 country study, expulsion cases for 1974-77 were presented to the Paraguayan authorities by IACHR. Follow-up reports in 1980 and 1987 indicated no change in the policy of expulsion. Efforts to secure the return of those exiled have been generally unsuccessful.[63] In 1984 the Paraguayan government issued a decree allowing selective return of exiles. Guarantees of free movement, entry, exit, and return have not been honored.   The general conditions imposed on returnees are such as to force many back into exile.[64]

URUGUAY

Uruguay has a long tradition of adherence to principles of international law and of strengthening the promotion and protection of human rights.   As one example of this strong human rights position, in 1950 Uruguay argued unsuccessfully for inclusion of the right of asylum in Article 14 of the Universal Declaration.   In the same year, the Uruguayan delegation to the General Assembly supported the right of individuals to petition UN human rights bodies and suggested creation of a High

Commissioner for Human Rights.[65] This tradition was clearly expressed at the early assemblies of the inter-American system, the UN, and the OAS. Interrupted by a decade of military rule from 1973 to 1983, the return to constitutional government has heralded a revival of Uruguay's human rights and international law orientation.

As a small and relatively densely populated state, Uruguay is not in a position to accept more than a small number of select refugees. Despite this, Uruguay is a party without reservation to both the 1951 and the 1967 global refugees regime instruments. Uruguay deposited its instrument of ratification to the American Convention in 1985. It expressed recognition of the competence of the IACHR for an indefinite period and of the Inter-American Court in all matters relating to the interpretation or application of the convention, on condition of reciprocity.[66] Uruguay is a party to all the inter-American asylum conventions (1928, 1933, and both 1954).

Despite its small size and high population density, Uruguay has offered asylum to many Latin American exiles. Decrees in 1949 and 1952 provided for registration of movement of Bolivian *asilados* and residence of Argentine *asilados*. European refugees accepted in the 1950s had to obtain a sponsor or demonstrate special skills.[67] In the 1971-72 UNHCR annual report, it was noted that Uruguay was considering issuing travel documents in accordance with the global regime,[68] but no additional information is found to indicate whether this intention was ever implemented. In any event, the military coup of 1973 created unfavorable conditions for receipt or transit of refugees. Although in the past Uruguay had been a country of refuge for Brazilians, Argentines, Paraguayans, and Bolivians, virtually all left following the imposition of military rule.[69]

Difficult economic conditions and the military coup of 1973 led to the departure of thousands of Uruguayans from the country. Many left for economic reasons, most going to Argentina and Mexico, but sizable numbers went to Canada and Australia as well. In addition, throughout the 1970s a steady flow of political refugees fed Argentina. About 2,000 Uruguayan nationals found refuge in Chile but were forced to flee after the 1973 anti-Allende coup.

It is impossible to say how many Uruguayan political refugees were in Argentina during the military regime. Free movement between the countries was possible without a passport, and many refugees did not register with the Argentine authorities. According to November 1974 figures from the Argentine Immigration Office, 400,000 Uruguayans, both economic migrants and political refugees, had sought permanent residence status in Argentina.

Civilian constitutional rule returned with the presidential and legislative elections in 1984, and an amnesty law in 1985 allowed the return of all exiles. All pending criminal proceedings were dismissed and warrants for arrest cancelled. The law applied to all acts committed after January 1962. UNHCR and the InterGovernmental Committee on Migration (ICM) were contacted to facilitate a program of return and repatriation; this process was underway by July 1985. Returnees were assisted by the Ecumenical Reintegration Service (Servicio Ecumenico de Reintegracion, SER) an umbrella group of ecumenical organizations, and the govenment appointed National Repatriation Commission.[70]

Less than one year after the return to constitutional rule, 20,000 Uruguayans had returned; among these, 7,000 were former refugees. The majority of those who returned did so in the few weeks preceding the elections of November 1984.[71]

BOLIVIA

Prior to Bolivia's becoming a party to the global refugees regime, entry of refugees and *asilados* and determination of their status was governed by decree laws passed between 1926 and 1938.[72] A National Council of Immigration (CONAIN) was created under the Ministry of Interior, but no specific provisions for *asilados* or refugees were included in this law.[73] Bolivia adopted constitutions in 1967 and 1978, yet only the 1978 Constitution gave expressed recognition to the right of asylum on Bolivian territory.[74]

The political chaos in Bolivia in the period 1966-71 created an unknown number of Bolivian refugees who fled to neighboring states. Investigation of these by the IACHR found conflicting statistics. Their motives for flight were mixed, and not all could be considered either refugees or *asilados*. Many Bolivians who left the country following the 1971 coup eventually settled in Argentina. Initially most had gone to Chile but were forced to flee to Argentina following the 1973 anti-Allende Chilean coup. Also, numerous Bolivians were expelled from Paraguay to Argentina.[75]

It was not until elections were held in early 1980 that Bolivia was returned to civilian rule. However, a coup replaced the elected president that July. In response to an IACHR inquiry on 14 November 1980 expressing concern over expulsion and political asylees, the authorities guaranteed safe-conduct to all those seeking asylum. Also, the IACHR had evidence that contrary to the constitution, which prohibited exile during a state of siege, exiles' passports were being stamped with an expressed prohibition to reenter. An IACHR request for an on-site inspection in February 1982 received no reply. The IACHR and the private Bolivian Permanent Assembly for Human Rights pressured the military regime for amnesty and free return for all those in self-imposed or forced exile, but to no effect.[76]

A UN Commission on Human Rights special envoy visited Bolivia in late 1981 to investigate reports of continued circumvention of constitutional guarantees and expulsion of political undesirables. The special envoy received reassurances that expulsions had ceased as of 4 September 1981, but that reentry of exiles could not be permitted, as all those exiled or expelled required a reentry visa.[77]

When Bolivia returned to civilian rule in 1982, among the first acts of the new civilian government was contacting the UNHCR to arrange for the return of all Bolivian exiles. Also in 1982, Bolivia acceded to the 1951 and 1967 global regime instruments without reservations. Aid to refugees and returnees was handled by the Secretariat of Social Studies of the Bolivian Episcopal Conference (Conferencia Episcopal Boliviana, CEB) and asylum monitored by the CEB and the Evangelical Methodist Church.[78]

Domestic legislation was brought into conformity with the provisions of the global refugee regime in 1983 with the creation of the National Refugee Commission. The NRC is composed of delegates from the Ministry of Foreign Relations and Culture and the Ministry of Labor and Development, the church, the Permanent Assembly on Human Rights, UNHCR, and the head of the Faculty of Law of the University of San Andres.[79]

While these decrees and laws provide an adequate legal and constitutional basis for protection, they are too recent for an analysis of their development and implementation. At a 1983 UNHCR-sponsored seminar in La Paz, Bolivian jurists expressed scepticism. Because the political history of Bolivia has been so unstable and violent, these jurists did not expect long-term survival and enforcement of these laws.[80]

Bolivia is not a party to either 1954 inter-American asylum convention, but the 1889 and 1911 extradition agreements and the 1928 Asylum Convention remain in force. By a decree of 1977, Bolivia adhered to the American Convention without reservation, but it has not recognized the competency of the IACHR or the jurisdiction of the Inter-American Court in any capacity.[81]

In 1984 a joint ILO-UNHCR survey of the refugee population in Bolivia was conducted. Two distinct refugee groups were identified: those from the Southern Cone states and those from Central America, particularly Guatemala. Southern Cone refugees were concentrated near and in La Paz and had arrived in a steady stream throughout the 1970s and early 1980s. By 1983 most had resettled to third countries. In the early 1980s the number of refugees increased as a few Chileans, but mostly

Uruguayans from Europe, came to Bolivia to await the return of civilian rule in Uruguay.[82]

Of the Bolivian refugee population, 71 percent is of Central American origin. Less than 1 percent is a combination of Cuban, Mexican, and Ecuadoran refugees. The 109 Central American refugees are overwhelmingly agriculturalists and are centered around the city of Santa Cruz. They have arrived since 1983, after conflict with the Honduran authorities.[83] In 1985 the Bolivian government made known its willingness to agree to family reunification in the case of up to 50 more Guatemalans.[84]

PERU

Little information from any source is available for Peru, and the UNHCR Country File is incomplete. Although Peru expressed interest in refugee questions, most especially for select resettlement, because of unfavorable experience with IRO plans, Peruvian interest waned in the 1960s. The 1951 Refugees Convention was acceded to in 1963 and the geographic limitation invoked.[85] Measures to fully implement the provisions of the global refugees regime were not emplaced until 1982.

Peru is a party to all (1928, 1933, and both 1954) inter-American asylum conventions. In 1978, the Peruvian Constituent Assembly drafted a new constitution, approved by plebiscite in July 1980. Under this constitution, the provisions of the American Convention are declared part of the internal law. The competence of the IACHR is recognized for an indefinite period, subject to reciprocity. The jurisdiction of the Inter-American Court is accepted without special arrangement.[86]

Peru had begun to issue convention travel documents to its small number of refugees in 1969, and on various occasions it has received political exiles from Bolivia. However, the first massive influx of refugees took place after the Chilean coup of 1973. It was estimated that some 2,800 refugees arrived in Peru immediately following the coup. They were mostly Chilean nationals, but also others who had sought refuge in Chile. They received only temporary asylum, and travel documents and work permits were denied to them.[87]

The influx of refugees from Chile was not short-lived, as originally anticipated. Nor had resettlement from Peru gone as rapidly as expected. In 1974, to curb refugee entry into Peru, the authorities arrested a number of refugees for illegal entry, but after UNHCR intervention all the detained refugees were released. Beginning in 1974, refugee concerns in Peru became the responsibility of the Ecumenical Committee of Social Assistance (Comite Ecumenico de Asistencia Social, CEDAS). This responsibility was terminated in 1980 when resettlement had sufficiently reduced the Chilean caseload.[88]

From 1979, political unrest in Bolivia brought additional Bolivian refugees to Peru. In April 1980, events at the Peruvian Embassy in Havana created a pool of 400 Cubans whom Peru agreed to resettle as refugees. Eventually a total of 492 Cubans were accepted. By the end of 1980, residence permits had also been issued to approximately 620 Bolivians.[89]

The return to democratic government in 1980 established conditions for more liberal refugee treatment. The Permanent Ad-Hoc Committee on Refugees, created by decree in 1982, is now responsible for determination of refugee status. Regulation of the legal status of refugees and political asylees is provided by a 1985 Presidential Decree.[90]

ECUADOR

Ecuador is not a party to the 1951 Refugees Convention but did accede to the 1967 Protocol in 1968. UNHCR reports indicate, however, that recognition of convention refugee status began only in 1979. The American Convention was ratified and declared part of the internal law of the republic in 1977. Its provisions are enforceable under Section 7 of the 1978 Constitution.[91] Ecuador is a party to all (1928, 1933, and both 1954) inter-American asylum conventions, and it recognizes the competency and jurisdiction of both the Inter-American Commission and the Inter-American Court. The constitutions of 1967 and 1978 have both expressly recognized the right of asylum for those persecuted for other than common crimes.[92]

Given its small geographic size and developing economic status, Ecuador has not generated or received large numbers of refugees. When approached by UNHCR to accept refugees for resettlement, Ecuador agreed to accept only small numbers of select individuals, usually with skills in agriculture, industry, or fishing.[93]

As of December 1984, the Law and Regulations on the Status of Aliens of 1971 continued to be in force. The provisions of this law deal only with *asilados*. Those displaced as a consequence of wars or political persecution in their country of origin would be admitted as *asilados*. If conventions were deficient in covering certain cases or circumstances, then the provisions of domestic law would be applied. Competency for determining their status resided with the Ministry of Foreign Affairs.[94] The applicant had to express the fear of persecution and other acts that motivated the seeking of asylum. The evidence presented, as well as a personal history of political acts, had to be verifiable by the Ecuadoran authorities. If status was granted, restrictions on personal activities were imposed. Leaving the country without express permission was prohibited, and a periodic renewal of status was conducted. Violation of these restrictions would leave an *asilado* subject to expulsion or deportation.[95]

Other protections contained in the global regime and applicable to refugees and *asilados* in Ecuador are found in Ecuadoran social legislation. Thus in 1972 a new social security code was introduced that provides protection to all inhabitants of Ecuador without distinction as to nationality. Legally there is no discrimination in obtaining work permits, but in practice refugees have found it difficult to obtain employment.[96]

Refugees receive a blue "passport." Information available through UNHCR indicates that border posts attach less value to the blue passport than to other travel documents. It is not clear whether this attitude is due to ignorance on the part of the border personnel or to instructions for a more thorough check of refugees, many of whom came from Communist-bloc states.[97]

Naturalization is governed by a law of 1976. To obtain a naturalization document, individuals must have legal capacity; show means of independent support, have five years' continuous residence in Ecuador, display irreproachable conduct, demonstrate general knowledge of Ecuadoran history and geography and the Ecuadoran Constitution, and be able to speak and write Spanish.[98]

COLOMBIA

In conjunction with the 1959 World Refugee Year, Colombia ratified the global 1951 Refugees Convention invoking the geographical restriction. In accordance with provisions of this convention travel documents were issued beginning in 1964.[99] The 1967 Protocol was ratified in 1980. There is no record or indication that the geographic limitation was again invoked.[100] Colombia is a party to all (1928, 1933, and both 1954) inter-American asylum conventions. Also a party to the American Convention, Colombia recognizes the competence of the IACHR and, subject to reciprocity, the competence and jurisdiction of the Inter-American Court.[101]

Colombian involvement with refugee questions has been rather limited. During the 1950s Colombia argued that its low level of economic development and small absorptive capacity did not enable it to become actively involved with refugees.[102] However, even prior to accession to the global refugees regime, Colombia had agreed to issue a special travel document to resident refugees and stateless persons. [103] And during the March 1956 visit by the High Commissioner to Latin America, Colombia agreed to a standing quota of 100 visas a month for refugees. Placement in a residence and an occupation was guaranteed by the Colombian Immigration Committee.[104] As a consequence of the success of the Cuban Revolution of 1959, however, the Colombian authorities have recognized the increasing difficulty of granting asylum, given the rise of revolutionary movements in general and continued guerrilla activities in Colombia in particular.[105]

Residence permits for refugees and *asilados*, permits that are consistent with provisions of the global refugees regime, were created by decree in 1980. The Ministry of Foreign Relations was granted sole authority for issuance of such permits and determination of status. The Aliens Department of the Security Administration can determine prohibited zones of residence for refugees and *asilados*. Procedures for determining refugee status was entrusted to an Advisory Committee in 1984. Recommendation is made by this Committee to the Minister of Foreign Affairs, who makes final determination.[106] With regard to other equated and basic rights afforded by the global refugees regime, little information is available. The substantive and procedural regulations of the 1968 Colombian Labor Code (still in force as of 1986) contain no mention of refugees or *asilados*.[107] Thus it is uncertain that the right to additional labor and social security rights of the global regime are reflected in Colombian domestic law.

VENEZUELA

In 1986 Venezuela became a party to the global refugees regime through adherence to the 1967 Protocol.[108] As of mid-1987, action taken, if any, to bring Venezuelan domestic law into conformity with the standards of the global refugees regime was not known.

Venezuela ratified the American Convention in June 1977. It recognizes, without reciprocity and for an indefinite period, the competence of the IACHR to receive and examine communications. The competence and jurisdiction of the Inter-American Court is recognized, subject to reciprocity. Venezuela is party to both 1954 inter-American asylum conventions. Venezuela has operated under two constitutions in the postwar period. The 1953 Constitution contained no mention of refugees, asylum, or nonextradition for political offenses. The 1961 Constitution contains general protections for all aliens and expressly recognizes asylum.[109]

According to UNHCR files, the Aliens Law of 1936 remains the basic domestic legislation governing refugee and *asilado* status in Venezuela.[110] Under this law, foreigners are guaranteed the same civil rights as nationals. No specific provisions of the law address *asilados* or refugees; however, the Ministry of the Interior is empowered to review applications and make a determination on a case-by-case basis. The principle of *non-refoulement* is not specifically cited.

The resettlement schemes that recruited European refugees were continued after the creation of the UNHCR. The National Agrarian Institute remained the responsible Venezuelan agency. In 1954 refugees seeking resettlement in Venezuela had to obtain private sponsors or have sufficient capital on hand before a visa would be issued.[111] To provide for more effective legal, administrative and material support for refugees, in 1955 the government established an independent refugee office.[112]

Throughout the 1960s Venezuela was concerned with the steady flow of Cubans seeking asylum. However, it was only in 1966 that Venezuelan delegates to the UNHCR Executive Committee expressed their government's concerns on this matter. Further, the Venezuelan delegate explained that while Venezuelan domestic legislation made no distinction between refugees and other immigrants, Venezuela was prepared to adopt a liberal policy toward the Cubans seeking refuge.[113]

In 1984 a joint ILO-UNHCR survey investigated the issue of refugees in Venezuela. For the European refugees who had resettled during the 1940s and 1950s, Venezuela had been the country of second choice. Refugees arriving as part of a resettlement scheme were more rapidly assimilated than those who arrived individually. Individuals arriving with a tourist visa were impeded in engaging in economic activities until formal recognition of *asilado* or refugee status was given. For psychological reasons, there was extreme reluctance on the part of European refugees to undertake the naturalization process.[114]

In the 1970s Venezuela accepted refugees from the Southern Cone and Nicaragua, but since 1980 most refugees arriving in Venezuela have been Cubans and Haitians. All of the Nicaraguan refugees were under 30 years of age. The highest concentration was of men between 16 and 18. With the fall of Somoza in 1978, most of the Nicaraguans were repatriated. The Haitians have been single men or young boys with little education and no work skills. The oldest group of refugees are the Cubans, most over 30 years of age and with a mixture of skills although peasants are among them. By 1982 most of the Bolivians, who had begun arriving in the mid-1960s, had been repatriated, and beginning in 1984, the Argentines, who had fled or been expelled from Argentina by the 1975-83 military government, also began to return home.[115]

NOTES

1. United Nations (hereafter UN), General Assembly, 8th sess., Report of the United Nations High Commissioner for Refugees (A/2394), 1953, p. 20; UN, General Assembly, 9th Session, Report of the United Nations High Commissioner for Refugees (A/2648/add. 1/add. 2), 1954, p. 17.

2. UN, General Assembly, 10th sess., Report of the United Nations High Commissioner for Refugees (A/2902/add. 1), 1955, pp. 10, 16.

3. UN, General Assembly, 15th sess., Report of the Economic and Social Council (A/4415), 1960, pp. 54-55; UN, General Assembly, 16th sess., Report of the United Nations High Commissioner for Refugees (A/471/rev. 1), 1961, p. 12; UNHCR, 8th sess., Executive Committee (hereafter EXCOM), Summary Record of the 64-68th Meetings (A/AC.96/SR 64-68), 6 March 1963, p. 41.

4. UN, General Assembly, 28th sess., Report of the United Nations High Commissioner for Refugees (A/9012), 1973, p. 4; UNHCR, 29th sess., EXCOM, Summary Record of the 302nd Meeting (A/AC.96/SR 302), 13 October 1978, p. 7; interview: UNHCR protection officer, July 1985.

5. Brazil, Law 941, 6 November 1970. The latest regulations available from UNHCR were for the 1970 revisions. The 1980 Aliens Act was available in Portuguese only. Article 115 of the 1970 regulations defined political crimes not subject to extradition. Assassination of the chief of state or of persons in the position of authority, anarchy, terrorism, sabotoge, distribution of war propaganda, and any other acts against the political or social order were not considered political crimes. Determination of a political offense was the responsibility of the Supreme Federal Tribunal. Article 119 of the regulations governs extradition of *asilados* and global regime refugees. Upon an extradition request from the Supreme Federal Tribunal, the Ministry of Foreign Affairs delivers the person to be extradited to the Ministry of Justice. While said person is in custody, the Ministry of Justice may hold (imprison) the individual for not more than 90 days (Article 139). The president of the republic may grant relief by using a decree revoking the expulsion order (Article 102), but such relief does not state whether the decree grants asylum or simply places the person in status quo ante.

6. Herbert d'Souza, "Return Ticket to Brazil," Third World Quarterly 9, no. 1 (January 1987): 203-09.

7. "Liberalization: A New Era May 1987," Refugees, no. 41 (May 1987): 33.

8. Ibid.

9. Ibid.

10. Pan American Union (hereafter PAU), Constitution of the United States of Brazil (1946, as amended 1956) Law and Treaty Series no. 36, (Washington, D.C.: PAU, 1958); Organization of American States (hereafter OAS), Constitution of the United States of Brazil (1967, as amended 1969).

11. UNHCR, Report on the Regional Seminar on Protection of Refugees in Latin America. Mexico City 20-24 August 1979 (Geneva: UNHCR, 1979), p. 9; interview, Sr. Alejandro Artucio, ICJ, July 1985.

12. UN, General Assembly, Report of UNHCR, 1955, p. 16; UN, General Assembly, 12th sess., Report of the United Nations High Commissioner for Refugees (A/3585/rev. 1), 1957, p. 9; UN, General Assembly, Report of UNHCR, 1961, p. 12.

13. UN, General Assembly, 14th sess., Report of the United Nations High Commissioner for Refugees (A/4104/rev. 1), 1959, p. 15; UN, General Assembly, 27th sess., Report of the United Nations High Commissioner for Refugees (A/8712), 1972, p. 5; UN, General Assembly, 28th sess., Report of the United Nations High Commissioner for Refugees (A/9012), 1973, p. 9.

14. Amnesty International, Chile: Un Informe de Amnestia Internacional (London: AI), 1974, pp. 70-71; U.S. Congress, House, Refugee and Humanitarian Problems in Chile: Subcommittee to Investigate Problems Connected with Refugees and Escapees, 93rd cong., 1st sess., 28 September 1973, pp. 207-08. Refugees from other Latin American states had been labeled by the military authorities as extremists come to kill Chileans.

15. International Commission of Jurists (hereafter ICJ), An Application in Latin America of International Declarations and Conventions Relating to Asylum. (Geneva: ICJ, 1975), pp. 23-24. No statistics are available on the numbers of such refugees.

16. Amnesty International, Chile, p. 71; U.S. Congress, Refugee and Humanitarian Problems, pp. 55-6, 92-3.

17. UN, UNHCR, Press release (ref. 1154), 17 October 1973; UN, UNHCR, Press release (ref 1157), 26 October 1973.

18. U.S. Congress, Refugee and Humanitarian Problems, pp. 30-31, 42, 61.

19. Chile, Decree 1308 of 3 October 1973 (Geneva: UNHCR, 1973) (free translation to English by UNHCR). Decree 1880 extended the operating period of CONAR to 3 February 1974.

20. UNHCR, El Refugio: Refugees from Chile, (Geneva: UNHCR, 1975), p. 9; UN, ECOSOC, Commission on Human Rights, 37th sess., Study on Human Rights and Massive Exoduses (E/CN.4/1503/), 31 December 1981, pp. 9-11. In operating these havens, ICRC and CONAR were of essential aid. CONAR operated fifteen centers in Santiago and eleven in other provinces of Chile.

21. UNHCR, Refugio, pp. 17-20; U.S. Congress, Refugee and Humanitarian Problems, pp. 32-33.

22. UN, UNHCR, 26th sess., Report on UNHCR Assistance Activities for 1975-1976 (A/AC.96/526), 16 August 1976, pp. 85-87. UNHCR activities for Chileans in Peru and Argentina continued beyond 1975. The WCC was of great assistance in aiding the small flow of Chileans to these two countries in subsequent years.

23. U.S. Congress, House of Representatives, Foreign Affairs Committee, Human Rights in Chile, 93rd cong., 2nd sess., December 1973-June 1974, pp. 13-14.

24. Interview, UNHCR assistance personnel, July 1985.

25. Chile, Decreto-ley 81 de 1973, State Security; UN, General Assembly, 34th sess., Protection of Human Rights in Chile (A/34/583), 21 November 1979, pp. 114-15. Decree Law 81 empowered the authorities to cancel Chilean passports for reasons of state security (Article 1). And in accordance with state-of-war provisions, the authorities were able to force citizens to abandon the country in the interests of national security. Free choice of destination for those expelled was allowed (Article 2). All those expelled under provisions of Article 2 were prohibited from reentry without permission from the Ministry of the Interior. And those so expelled had their passports stamped with "L" so that detection of attempted reentry would be easily made.

26. OAS, IACHR, Third Report on the Situation of Human Rights in Chile (ser. L/V/II.40 doc. 10), February 1977, pp. 77-81, Decree 175 of 3 December 1973. Standards of political conduct for Chileans living abroad were further clarified by Decree Law 604 of 9 August 1974. Revoking nationality is a violation of Article 12(h) of the Covenant of Civil and Political Rights, to which Chile is a party.

27. OAS, Inter-American Commission on Human Rights: Ten Years of Activities 1971-1981. (Washington, D.C.: OAS, 1982), pp. 261-62. Decree Law 1504 of 30 April 1975. Permission for reentry was conditioned by the standards contained in Decrees 175 and 604.

28. Chile, Decreto-ley 1094 de 19-7-1975. Estableco normas sobre extranjeros en Chile. Refugees and asilados are governed by Title II of this decree. Decreto-ley 1306 de 27-10-1975: Reglamento de extranjeria. Refugees and asilados are governed by Title II of this decree. Expulsion of foreigners is the responsibility of the Servicio de Investigaciones of the Ministry of the Interior.

29. UN, ECOSOC, Commission on Human Rights, 33rd sess., Report of the Ad-Hoc Working Group Established under Resolution 8 (XXXI) of the Commission on Human Rights to Inquire into the Present Situation of Human Rights in Chile (E/CN.4/1221), 10 February 1977, pp. 59, 62-68. All these

practices violated Articles 9 and 12 of the Covenant on Civil and
Political Rights.   See also OAS, IACHR, Annual Report of the
Inter-American Commission on Human Rights 1985-1986 (ser.
L/V/II.68 doc. 8/rev. 1), 26 September 1986, pp. 132-34.   In
its 1987 annual report, the IACHR concluded that the Chilean
court system remained generally ineffectual in providing relief for
nationals denied the right of reentry. OAS, IACHR, Annual
Report of the Inter-American Commission on Human Rights
1986-1987 (ser. L/V/II.71 doc. 9/rev. 1), 22 September 1987, pp.
213-14.
        30. UN, UNHCR, 28th sess., EXCOM, Summary Record of
the 289th Meeting (A/AC.96/SR 289), 7 October 1977, p. 4;
Chile, Amnesty Law of 1978, free translation of UNHCR,
Document 634, CHL.
        31. UN, ECOSOC, Commission on Human Rights, 35th
sess., Report of the Ad-Hoc Working Group Established under
Resolution 8 (XXXI) of the Commission on Human Rights to
Inquire into the Present Situation of Human Rights in Chile
(E/CN.4/1310), 2 January 1979, pp. 22-23; 39; 47-49; annex 12,
p. 12; UN, General Assembly, Protection of Human Rights in
Chile, 1979 pp. 110-11; UN, ECOSOC, Commission on Human
Rights. 36th sess., Report Prepared by the Special Rapporteur on
the Situation of Human Rights in Chile, Pursuant to Commission
on Human Rights Resolution 11 (XXXV) (E/CN.4/1313), 29
January 1980, pp. 6-8. On 12 March 1986, the UN Committee
on Human Rights received a report on Chile from Special
Rapporteur Fernando Volio of Costa Rica.   This report again
found that expulsion, banishment, and denial of return to Chilean
exiles was continuing. Chilean Foreign Minister Jaime del Valle
Alliende responded to the report, saying that Chile would not be
cornered by its enemies and would continue to do things its own
way. See "Pinochet's Long-Term Prospects in Question," Christian
Science Monitor, 18 March 1986, pp. 11, 18.
        32. OAS, IACHR, Annual Report of the Inter-American
Commission on Human Rights 1977 (ser.   L/V/II.43 doc. 21),
March 1978, pp.   86-88; OAS, IACHR, Annual Report of the
Inter-American Commission on Human Rights 1979-1980 (ser.
L/V/II.50 doc. 13/rev. 1), October 1980, p. 107. As recorded in
the 1979-80 annual report. Decree 78 of 2 April 1980 rejected
152 applications; Decree 86 of 3 June 1980 rejected 176; and
Decree 92 of 3 July 1980 rejected 126.
        33. OAS, IACHR, Annual Report of the Inter-American
Commission on Human Rights 1981-1982 (ser. L/V/II.57 doc.
6/rev. 1), 20 September 1982, pp.   112-15; OAS, IACHR,
Annual Report 1985-1986, p. 145.   For analysis of the role of
political exiles under the Pinochet regime .see Alan Angell and
Susan Carstairs, "The Exile Question in Chilean Politics," Third
World Quarterly 9, no. 1 (January 1987): 148-67.

34. OAS, IACHR, <u>Annual Report of the Inter-American</u> Commission on Human Rights 1982-1983 (ser. L/V/II.61 doc. 22/rev. 1), 27 September 1983, p. 15; OAS, IACHR, <u>Annual Report of the Inter-American Commission on Human Rights 1984-1985</u> (ser. L/V/II.66 doc. 10/rev. 1), October 1985, pp. 34-43; UN, ECOSOC, Commission on Human Rights, 40th sess., <u>Women's International Democratic Foundation</u> (E/CN.4/1985/NGO/11), 8 February 1985, p. 2; OAS, IACHR, <u>Annual Report 1986-1987</u>, p. 214.

35. "Returning Chilean Exiles Find It Tough to Readjust," <u>Christian Science Monitor</u>, 17 April 1986, p. 15.

36. Chile, SANT 319-630 CHL-640 CHL of 4 May 1981: Decree Law Authorizing Expulsion of Foreigners.

37. OAS, IACHR, <u>Annual Report 1985-86</u>, p. 145.

38. UN, General Assembly, <u>Report of UNHCR</u>, 1955, pp. 15-16; OAS, IACHR, <u>Inter-American Yearbook on Human Rights 1960-1967</u> (Washington, D.C.: OAS, 1968), p. 511.

39. PAU, <u>Constitution of Argentina</u> (1853 as amended 1860, 1866, 1898 and 1957) (Washington, D.C.: PAU, 1968); UN, UNHCR, <u>Report on the Constitution of the Republic of Argentina</u>, Buenos Aires, 13 May 1964. Nationality was further defined in 1954. After five years of residency, nationality was automatic unless a declaration to the contrary was made. This law was repealed in 1956 and a commission to draft a new nationality law established. See UN, <u>Yearbook on Human Rights for 1954</u> (New York: UN, 1956), pp. 5-7 and <u>Yearbook on Human Rights for 1956</u> (New York: UN, 1958), pp. 10-11. Act 14354 of 28 September 1954, Decree 14194/56 of 1956.

40. UN, General Assembly, <u>Report of UNHCR</u>, 1957, p. 7. Also, the University of Buenos Aires agreed to recognize the validity of professional diplomas held by *asilados*. If normal authentification were lacking, a statement sworn before a Court would suffice.

41. UN, General Assembly, 13th sess., <u>Report of the United Nations High Commissioner for Refugees</u> (A/3828/rev. 1), 1958, p. 7.

42. UN, General Assembly, 17th sess., <u>Report of the United Nations High Commissioner for Refugees</u> (A/52ll/rev. 1), 1962, p. 2; Argentina, Ley 15,869 de 2-11-1961: Adhesion to 1951 Refugees Convention, Decreto Ley 4805 de 17-6-1963: Admission, residence and Expulsion of Aliens.

43. Argentina, Ley 17,468 de 3-11-1967: Adhesion to 1967 Protocol; Argentina, Decreto 4418, Reglamento de migracion. Theoretically, an *asilado* card provided equality of status, but access to employment and access to education and other social services remained difficult. If permanent residence were granted, movement was restricted to a 20-kilometer radius from the place of residence. Failure to observe such restrictions could lead to withdrawal of status. See UNHCR, <u>Regional Seminar</u>, pp. 8-9.

44. UNHCR, Regional Seminar, p. 25, note 10. The
Argentine immigration law was revised in 1981 by Law 22.439 on
27 March 1981. Territorial asylum was regulated by the
provisions of Chapter III. Determination of status was under the
jurisdiction of the Ministry of the Interior, with advice from the
Ministry of Foreign Affairs. If granted refugee status, immigrants
were subject to a special regime dictated by the executive and
subordinate to the following guidelines: a fixed place of
residence, determination of places not available for residence and
movement, determination of activities and functions prohibited to
refugees, and determination of consequences for breach of
conditions and actions to be taken pending cancellation of asylum
(Article 25). There were no provisions for obtaining a work
permit or exceptions for irregular or illegal entry (Articles 26-39).
If status were denied, the applicant had ten days from notification
to appeal to the Ministry of the Interior, which was required to
respond within 30 days (Articles 73-82). See Argentina, Ley
22.439 de 27-3-1981: General Law on Migration.

45. OAS, Inter-American Court of Human Rights, Annual
Report of the Inter-American Court of Human Rights 1984 (ser.
L/V/III.10 doc. 13), 5 August 1984, p. 66.

46. OAS, Convention on Territorial Asylum (ser. A/10A
Sep F), Law and Treaty Series no. 19, Washington, D.C., 1954;
For Argentine ratification of the American Convention, see
IACHR, Annual Report 1985-86.

47. ICJ, Application, p. 19; AI. Report of an Amnesty
International Mission to Argentina 6-15 November 1976
(Middlesex, U.K.: AI, 1977), p. 40.

48. Ibid., pp. 19-21.

49. Argentina, Decree 978 of 31 December 1973: Issuance
of Convention Travel Documents, English version and Decreto
1093 de 5 Abril 1974: Travel Documents.

50. Argentina, Decree 87 of 11 January 1974: Illegal Entry
of Foreigners, English version. Article 1 granted an alien, native
of a bordering country and resident in Argentina before 1 January
1974, permission of permanent residence regardless of manner of
entry and circumstances of entry. To benefit, an applicant had
180 days to apply to the DNM or equivalent provincial authorities
(Articles 2-5). Upon recognition of permanent residence status,
an appropriate identity card would be issued. Fees for an
identity card were waived (Articles 6, 9).

51. UN, General Assembly, 30th sess., Report of the
United Nations High Commissioner for Refugees (A/10012), 1975,
p. 4; ICJ, Application, p. 20; "Argentina Faces Influx of
Refugees from Chile," UNHCR, no. 2 (May 1974): 1-2.

52. AI, Mission to Argentina, pp. 43-47. See Annex III,
pp. 56-59 for activities of security forces operating in Argentina
and pp. 60-62 for cases of refoulement; 30 cases of refoulement

were recorded for June and July alone and another 70 following
the declaration of a state of seige in Uruguay in December.

53. UN, General Assembly, 31st sess., Report of the United
Nations High Commissioner for Refugees (A/31/12), 1976, pp. 9,
11; UN, UNHCR, Assistance 1975-1976, pp. 80-84.

54. AI, Mission to Argentina, pp. 11-12, 40-41; OAS,
IACHR, Report of the Situation of Human Rights in the Republic
of Argentina (ser. L/V/II.49 doc. 19/corr. 1), June 1980, pp.
14-15, 19.

55. UNHCR, 29th sess., EXCOM, Summary Record of the
295th Meeting (A/AC.96/SR 295), 10 October 1978, pp. 10-11;
Argentina, Ley 21,795 de 18-5-1978: Ley de nacionalidad y
ciudadania.

56. U.S. Congress, Senate, Committee on the Judiciary,
World Refugee Crisis: The International Community's Response.
(Washington, D.C.: Congressional Research Service, 1979), p.
200.

57. Argentina, Decree 2073 of 29 August 1979: Indochinese
Resettlement; Interview, UNHCR assistance personnel, July 1985.
As later studies indicated, however, the resettlement was
unsuccessful. The plans were hastily drawn; no attempt was
made to match refugee skill with available employment and little
was done to aid integration or prepare the refugees for culture
shock.

58. Argentina, Decreto 780/84 de 12-3-1984: Decreto de
amnistia. To be eligible, applicants were required to present
accredited identity papers with documentation, evidence of an
accredited residence while the documentation was being processed,
a declaration of any judicial sentence longer than three years, and
a medical certificate from an approved health official (Article 2).
Article 4 defined accredited documentation as a passport, a
certificate of identity or similar validated document from the
country of origin, or a certificate of nationality from the country
of origin. Asilados were defined and recognized pursuant to the
criteria of the 1889 Montevideo Convention. No expressed
recognition of refugees was included. Jurisdiction was given to
the DNM, which also acted as the appeals body for denial of
amnesty. Until the law entered into force, the expulsion of
foreigners was suspended. See "Interview: Dante Caputo, Minister
of Foreign Affairs," Refugees, no. 4 (April 1984): 43; UN,
UNHCR, 35th sess., Report on UNHCR Assistance Activities for
1984-1985 (A/AC.96/657), 5 August 1985, p. 220. Some
Argentine nationals abroad decided not to return for economic or
family reasons. Also, lack of funding from Argentina and the
international community had slowed the return. UNHCR aid
funds for repatriation were to be phased out by mid-1986. This is
common UNHCR practice; the cessation clause of the 1951
Convention is normally invoked one year after a fundamental

change of domestic circumstances. See "Returnees and Refugees in Argentina and Uruguay," Refugees, no. 25 (January 1986): 20.

59. "Returnees and Refugees," p. 22. In 1985 1,075 were recognized as refugees.

60. UN, UNHCR, 38th sess. Note on Procedures for the Determination of Refugee Status Under International Instruments (A/AC.96/INF.152/), 24 July 1987, p. 2.

61. ICJ, Application, p. 26. The ICJ has estimated that up to 800,000 Paraguayans reside in Argentina, for a mixture of motives.

62. UN, General Assembly, Report of UNHCR, 1953, p. 20; UN, General Assembly, Report of UNHCR, 1954, p. 18.

63. OAS, Inter-American Yearbook 1960-1967, pp. 519-20; OAS, IACHR, Informe sobre la situacion de los derechos humanos en Paraguay (ser. L/V/II.43 doc. 13/corr. 1), 31 January 1978; OAS, IACHR, Ten Years of Activities 1971-1981, pp. 295-296; OAS, IACHR, Annual Report 1981-1982, pp. 122-123. In response to IACHR criticisms, the authorities pointed to the qualifications of Article 10 of the American Declaration of Human Rights; OAS, IACHR, Report on the Situation of Human Rights in Paraguay (ser. L/V/II.71 doc. 19/rev. 1), 28 September 1987, pp. 6, 22.

64. OAS, IACHR, Annual Report of the Inter-American Commission on Human Rights 1983-1984 (ser. P/AG doc 1778/84), 5 October 1984, pp. 123-24; OAS, IACHR, Paraguay, 1987, pp. 56-61.

65. Uruguayan Institute of International Law, Uruguay and the United Nations (New York: Manhatten Publications, 1958), pp. 28-29, 44-53, 74-80; German Cavelier, La Politica internacional de Colombia. Vol. 4, El Asilo Diplomatico (Bogota: Imprenta Nacional, 1960), p. 64.

66. OAS, IACHR, Annual Report 1983-1984, p. 137.

67. OAS, IACHR, Inter-American Yearbook 1960-1967. pp. 512-13; UN, General Assembly, Report of UNHCR, 1954, p. 18; UN, General Assembly, Report of UNHCR, 1955, p. 16; UN, General Assembly, Report of UNHCR, 1957, p. 23; UN, General Assembly, Report of UNHCR, 1958, p. 8.

68. UN, General Assembly, Report of UNHCR, 1972, p. 10.

69. ICJ, Application, pp. 28-29.

70. ICJ, "Uruguay Returning to Democracy," Review of the International Commission of Jurists 34 (June 1985): pp. 20, 23, 27; "Exiles, Welcome Home--A One-Way Ticket from Geneva to Montevideo." Refugees, no. 19 (July 1985): pp. 31-33. Of those Uruguayans in exile, an estimated 80,000 made their way to Spain. Of these only 800 had achieved a recognized or legalized status before the 1984 Uruguayan elections. Interview, Sr. Alejandro Artucio, ICJ, July 1985.

71. "Homecoming in Uruguay," Refugees, no. 25 (January 1986): pp. 28-29, 43. On 7 November 1985, UNHCR announced that restoration of constitutional rule in Uruguay, and the issuance of the political amnesty, were considered events that required invoking the cessation clauses of the global refugee regime. Uruguayan returnees seeking UNHCR aid were required to register by 31 January 1986. See "News in Brief," Refugees, no. 24 (December 1985): p. 7.

72. Jacques Vernant, The Refugee in the Post-War World (London: Allen and Unwin, 1953), p. 609. The anti-Jewish decrees of this period were repealed by Decree on 3 March 1950. The office of Director General of Immigration and Colonization was established on 28 December 1951, and the Ministry of Interior, Justice, and Immigration was given jurisdiction. All entrants to Bolivia were required to have sponsors willing to find them employment and provide for their essential needs. No specific provisions for *asilados* or refugees were included in the 1951 decree.

73. Susana Torrado, "International Migration Policies in Latin America," International Migration Review 13, no. 47 (1979): 430-31; UN, ILO, Migraciones laborales e integracion del refugiado en Bolivia (RLA/83/VAROV), Buenos Aires, May 1984, pp. iv, 48.

74. UN, Yearbook on Human Rights for 1967 (New York: UN, 1969), pp. 13-20; Bolivia, "Constitucion politica del estado," (La Paz: Gaceta oficial de Bolivia), 1978.

75. ICJ, Application, p. 21.

76. OAS, IACHR, Report on the Situation of Human Rights in the Republic of Bolivia (ser. L/V/II.53 doc. 6), 13 October 1981, p. 4-5, 7-8, 15, 63, 107-08, 117; UN, ECOSOC, Commission on Human Rights, 37th sess., Report on the Situation of Human Rights in Bolivia (E/CN.4/1500), 31 December 1981, pp. 18-20; see also OAS, IACHR, Ten Years of Activities 1971-1981, pp. 299-301; and OAS, IACHR, Annual Report 1981-1982, p. 108.

77. UN, ECOSOC, Commission on Human Rights, 37th sess., Report on the Situation of Human Rights in Bolivia (E/CN.4/1500 add. 1), 22 February 1982, pp. 1-8; The Ministry of Interior had expelled another twenty eight persons on 13 August 1981.

78. UN, ECOSOC, Report on Bolivia, 1982, pp. 10-12, 20, 32-34, 42; UN, General Assembly, 37th sess., Report of the United Nations High Commissioner for Refugees (A/37/12), 1982, pp. 11-13; UN, General Assembly, 38th sess., Report of the United Nations High Commissioner for Refugees (A/38/12), 1983, p. 20; UN, UNHCR, 33rd sess., Report on UNHCR Assistance Activities for 1982-1983 (A/AC.96/620), 1 August 1983, pp. 278-286; Mohammed Benamar, "Comentos," in Asilo politico y

situacion del refugiado (La Paz, Bolivia: Ministerio de relaciones exteriores, 1983), p. 11.

79. Anexo VIII, Asilo politico, pp. 186-90; UN, ILO, Bolivia, pp. iv, 50-52; UN, UNHCR, Assistance 1982-1983, 5, 8. Decree 19640 (see Anexo) gave legal effect to the refugee instruments. Article 1 contained the 1951 Convention definition of refugee and Article 2 the broadened criteria found in the OAU Refugee Convention. Cooperation with UNHCR and voluntary agencies for determination of status and provision of aid is required by Article 7. The Ministry of Foreign Affairs has jurisdiction. An applicant who is denied refugee status has 30 days to request reconsideration. UNHCR is advised of all negative decisions. If refugee status is granted, a residence permit, identity card, and travel document are issued. *Non-refoulement* is guaranteed by Article 5.

80. Marcelo Hurtado Villa, Jaime Prudencio Cossio and Reyanaldo Peters Arzabe, "Pautas para una legislacion Boliviana sobre el refugiado," in Asilo politico, pp. 96-98, 102-03; UN, ILO, Bolivia, p. 52.

81. OAS, Human Rights: The Inter-American System, part 2, Legislative History of the American Convention (Washington, D.C.: OAS, 1970), p. 24. As of 1985, no legislation or decrees existed to incorporate provisions of the American Convention into domestic law.

82. UN, ILO, Bolivia, pp. iii-iv, 33-34. As of mid-1984, only 270 Southern Cone refugees were registered with UNHCR. The survey suggested, however, that larger numbers with the appropriate characteristics were resident in Bolivia but had failed to apply or register for refugee status.

83. Ibid., pp. iv-v, 34-35, 38, 40, 44-45, 53-56; UN, UNHCR, Assistance Activities in 1984-1985 (A/AC.96/657), 5 August 1985, p. 271; UN, UNHCR, Fact Sheet no. 12, January 1985.

84. "Guatemalan Refugees Tame the Land," Refugees, no. 24 (December 1985): 15-16.

85. UN, General Assembly, 19th sess., Report of the United Nations High Commissioner for Refugees (A/5811/rev. 1), 1964, p. 4.

86. UN, General Assembly, 34th sess., Report of the United Nations High Commissioner for Refugees (A/34/12), 1979, p. 14; OAS, Inter-American Court of Human Rights, Annual Report of the Inter-American Court of Human Rights to the General Assembly, 1980 (ser. L/V/III.3 doc. 13/rev. 1), p. 56; These commitments to the Inter-American human rights system were reiterated by Bernardo Roca Rey, Peruvian Ambassador to Costa Rica. He placed on record the Peruvian adherence to the principles and norms set forth in the American Convention, pledged irrevocable adherence to the system of international

protection of human rights, and agreed to the binding jurisdiction of the Inter-American Court as recognized and expressed in the Peruvian Constitution. See OAS, Inter-American Court of Human Rights, Advisory Opinion-Other Treaties Subject to the Advisory Jurisdiction of the Court (ser. B., no. 1 advisory opinion OC-1/82), 24 September 1982, pp. 178-80.

87. UN, General Assembly, Report of UNHCR, 1976, pp. 9-11.

88. UN, General Assembly, 30th sess., Report of the United Nations High Commissioner for Refugees (A/10012), 1975, p. 4.; UN, UNHCR, 26th sess., EXCOM, Summary Record of the 267th Meeting (A/AC.96/SR 267), 9 October 1975, p. 124.

89. UN, General Assembly, Report of UNHCR, 1981, p. 35; UN, UNHCR, 30th sess., Report on the UNHCR Assistance Activities for 1979-1980 (A/AC.96/577), 14 August 1980, pp. 125-27. During the airlift from Cuba, the Peruvian Red Cross handled the daily management of refugee concerns. The only agency active in assisting both Bolivian and Cuban refugees was the Comision Catolica Peruana de Migracion, (CCPM).

90. UN, General Assembly, Report of UNHCR, 1983, p. 5. See Presidential Decree no. 1 of 25 January 1985 in UN, UNHCR, Note on Procedures 1987, pp. 24-25.

91. OAS, Human rights: Legislative History, p. 35; see also OAS, IACHR, Annual Report 1985-1986, p. 8; UN, General Assembly, 11th sess., Addenda to the Report of the United Nations High Commissioner for Refugees (A/3123/rev. 1/add. 1/add. 2), 1957, p. 23; UN, General Assembly, 24th sess., Report of the United Nations High Commissioner for Refugees (A/7612), 1969, p. 13; UN, General Assembly, 35th sess., Report of the United Nations High Commissioner for Refugees (A/35/12), 1980, p. 33. During a visit by the High Commissioner in 1956, Ecuador announced the creation of the National Committee on Immigration, charged to study domestic legislation in force and suggest modifications of the law to conform to provisions of the 1951 Refugees Convention. It is difficult to judge how successful this committee was in fullfilling its charge. Immigration and passport laws enacted in subsequent years did contain provisions equivalent to global regime standards, but no references to the committee's functioning or suggestions were found.

92. PAU, Constitution of Ecuador, 1967, Law and Treaty Series no. 36 (Washington, D.C.: PAU, 1968); Ecuador, Constitution of Ecuador 1978, Registro oficial no. 800, 27 March 1979.

93. UN, General Assembly, Report of UNHCR, 1955, p. 16; Louise Holborn, Refugees: A Problem in Our Time, Vol. 1 (Metuchen, N.J.: Scarecrow, 1975), p. 639.

94. UN, General Assembly, Yearbook on Human Rights for 1972 (New York: UN, 1975), pp. 84-86; Ecuador, Ley 1897 de

1984: Ley de extranjeria. Under Article 7, this function is exercised through the Advisory Council on Immigration Policy (Article 8). This council is composed of members from the ministries of Government and Police, Foreign Relations, and National Defense and the National Council of Economic Coordination and Planning. If *asilado* status is granted, the regulations and restrictions applicable to nonimmigrant persons apply (Article 12). See UN, General Assembly, Report of UNHCR, 1955, p. 16.

95. Ley 1899 de 1984: Ley de migracion and reglamento 1900 de 1984: Reglamento de la ley de migracion. This law and its Regulations (1900) became effective on 27 December 1971. The Ministry of Government and Police is responsible for implementation of this law, as exercised through the National Civil Police (Article 3). The Police of the Migration Services are responsible for provisional admission of an *asilado*. They may hold an applicant at the point of entry and conduct interrogation for information required to grant or deny the application for asylum (Articles 5, 15). If deportation is required, the alien is returned to the country of origin or of previous domicile (Article 35). Articles 19-36 of Chapter 5 concern deportation. No specific mention or reference to *non-refoulement* is contained therein.

96. UN, Yearbook for 1972, pp. 83-84.

97. Ecuador, Decreto 1896 de 27-12-1971: Fees for Issuance of Passports.

98. Ecuador, Ley 276 de 14-4-1976: Ley de naturalizacion. See Article 4. As dual nationality is not permitted, renunciation of any previous nationality is required (Article 5). Requests for naturalization are reviewed by the Office of Immigration and Foreigners and the Ministry of Foreign Affairs (Article 4). Nationality may be lost through naturalization by fraud, or for being a disturbing element from a moral, social or political point of view (Article 16).

99. UN, General Assembly, 14th sess., Report of the United Nations High Commissioner for Refugees, (A/4104/rev. 1), 1959, p. 15; UN, General Assembly, 17th sess., Report of the United Nations High Commissioner for Refugees (A/5211/rev. 1), 1962, p. 2; Ley 35 de 12 de Julio de 1961 por la cual se aprueba la convencion sobre estatudo de los refugiados, Anales del Congreso no. 177, 29 July 1961, pp. 2790-96; UN, General Assembly, 20th sess., Report of the United Nations High Commissioner for Refugees (A/60ll/rev. 1), 1965, p. 6.

100. UNHCR, Regional Seminar, p. 26; UN, General Assembly, Report of UNHCR, 1981, p. 33.

101. German Cavelier, La Politica internacional de Colombia, Vol. 4, El Asilo Diplomatico (Bogota: Imprenta Nacional, 1960), pp. 123-127; OAS, IACHR, Annual Report 1985-1986, p. 4.

102. As delegate Santos Motejo explained to the Special Conference on the Problem of Refugees, held in Geneva in 1958, Colombia considered refugee problems from a different perspective than the European states. Colombia had not the same political maturity; the countries of Latin America were still young and consequently had to be more discriminating in their selection of refugees, that is, they had to choose only those who would be able to assimilate. See UN, UNHCR, 4th sess., EXCOM, Summary Record of the 10th Meeting (A/AC.96/SR 10), 15 June 1959, p. 10; UN, UNHCR, 6th sess., EXCOM, Summary Record of the 36th Meeting (A/AC.96/SR 36), 8 February 1961, pp. 5-6; InterGovernmental Committee for European Migration, Reunion especial sobre el problema de los refugiados: Acta resumida de la Primera Sesion. ICEM: Geneva, November 1958, pp. 14-15.

103. UN, General Assembly, Report of UNHCR, 1954, p.8.

104. UN, General Assembly, 11th sess., Report of the United Nations High Commissioner for Refugees (A/3123/rev. 1), 1956, p. 15.

105. Cavelier, La Politica internacional, pp. 123-27.

106. Colombia, Decree 2955 of 5 November 1980: Visas and Control of Foreigners. Under Decree 2817 of 20 November 1984 an applicant can request review of a negative decision before the same authority. After a second negative decision, the applicant may appeal through the Administrative Courts. See UN, UNHCR, Note on Procedures, 1987, pp. 8-9.

107. Colombia, Codigo sustantivo de trabajo (Bogota: Editorial Voluntad, 1968) and Codigo procesal del trabajo (Bogota: Editorial Voluntad, 1968). Under Article 10, all workers are equal before the law and entitled to the same protections and guarantees. Every person has the right to work and liberty to earn (Article 11). Foreign workers, presumably including refugees, are entitled to equal conditions and remuneration, but restrictions on hiring of nonnationals are imposed. All those employing more than 10 workers must have not less than 90 percent ordinary Colombian or 80 percent special qualification Colombian nationals employed (Article 74). Unions must have at least two-thirds Colombian membership before they can legally function. And there is an absolute prohibition against foreigner eligibility for executive director of a union (Part 2, Chapter 6, Article 384).

108. "News in Brief," Refugees, no. 35 (November 1986): p. 7.

109. Thomas Buergenthal and Robert Norris, eds., Human Rights: The Inter-American System (Dobbs Ferry, N.Y.: Oceana, 1982), pp. 54-55; OAS, IACHR, Annual Report 1985-1986, p. 8; PAU, Constitution of the Republic of Venezuela, 1953, Law and Treaty Series no. 36 (Washington, D.C.: PAU, 1954); PAU, The

Constitution of the Republic of of Venezuela, 1961, Law and
Treaty Series no. 36 (Washington, D.C.: PAU, 1968). Under
Article 45, foreigners have the same rights and duties as
nationals. Asylum is recognized by Article 116.

110. Venezuela, Ley de extranjeros y su reglamento,
Caracas: from Editorial. La Torre, 1942. Under Article 2,
admission to Venezuela requires individuals to have a valid
passport and to deposit 500 bolivars. The deposit is returned
upon departure (Articles 6, 11). Aliens are required to maintain
strict neutrality in politics and are prohibited from accepting
public employment, with exceptions reviewed by the executive
branch of the government. Expulsions for reasons of security and
public order are permitted. The principle of *non-refoulement* is
not specifically cited.

111. UN, General Assembly, Report of UNHCR, 1954, p.
18.

112. UN, General Assembly, Report of UNHCR, 1955, p.
8.

113. UN, UNHCR, 15th sess., EXCOM, Summary Record
of the 133rd Meeting (A/AC.96/SR 133), 17 May 1966, p. 22;
UN, UNHCR, 15th sess., EXCOM, Summary Record of the
135th Meeting (A/AC.96/SR 135), 18 May 1966, p. 40.

114. UN, ILO, Venezuela: Informe de avance sobre
migraciones internacionales y empleo (RLA/83/VAROV), Buenos
Aires: 1984, pp. 86, 88.

115. Ibid., pp. 78, 80-82.

Chapter Eight

Mexico, Central America, and the Caribbean

This chapter deals with the national refugee and asylum policies of Mexico, the Central American states, including Panama, and the Latin American Caribbean states. Unlike the states discussed in Chapter 7, the Central American states face an ongoing refugee crisis, a crisis of massive exodus of persons from neighboring states, seeking asylum from civil war or generalized social violence.

May 1986 estimates from UNHCR indicated that at least 1 million, perhaps twice that number, have been displaced by generalized violence in Central America. However, of the estimated refugee population of 320,000, only 120,000 benefit from protection and assistance from UNHCR. Nowhere else in the world does such a wide discrepancy exist; moreover, unlike in the South American states, the political conditions portend an escalation of violence rather than increased accomodation.[1]

MEXICO

Mexico has maintained a low profile regarding both the global refugees regime and regional human rights initiatives, even though it has a tradition of granting asylum on humanitarian grounds to those suffering from political persecution. The vast majority receiving asylum have been of Hispanic background. Contacts with UNHCR over the years have not persuaded Mexico to join the global refugees regime. Disinterest in joining the global refugees regime was most recently reiterated by Under-Secretary of the Interior Jorge Carrillo Olea in October 1986. He stated that Mexico expressed clear solidarity with the sufferings of the refugees and that, consequently, whether or not the 1951 Refugees Convention has been signed in no way alters support and assistance provided to refugees. "The mere signature of a document cannot make a state more generous or more supportive."[2]

Since Mexico is not a party to the global refugees regime, only *asilado*, and not refugee, status is granted. It is determined jointly by the ministries of the interior and foreign affairs. In the 1980s, faced with the mass influx of Guatemalans, who were unable to meet the criteria for *asilado* status, separate administrative procedures were established. It is not clear what protection is enforceable under these procedures; moreover, the available information on Mexican protection and treatment of the Guatemalan refugees is inconsistent and generally unreliable.

Mexico has had little involvement with the UNHCR Executive Committee. The first recorded statements date from 1982. Even during the mid-1960s, when Mexico accepted a substantial number of Cuban refugees, there was no record of a Mexican presence at Executive Committee meetings. Beginning in 1965, Mexico served as a transit point for the Cuban refugees. Aid was channeled through the Comite Evangelico por Refugiados (Evangelical Committee for Refugees), created in May 1965. No work permits were allowed to be issued to the Cubans.[3]

Mexico is a party to the 1954 Caracas Territorial Asylum Convention and adhered to the American Convention on 24 March 1981.[4] It is also party to the 1928 and 1933 inter-American asylum conventions.

Since Mexico is not a party to the global refugees regime, protection for *asilados* and refugees must be sought in the domestic legislation of Mexico. The 1917 Constitution specified broad guarantees to all inhabitants of the territory, such as the freedom to enter and leave the territory and nonextradition for political offenses.[5] Also, all inhabitants are governed by several amendments to the General Laws on Population. Two classes of *asilados* are recognized: foreigners native to the American continent who fled political persecution, and other nationalities accepted according to prior agreements and authorizations. Those native to the American continent are obliged to remain at their point of entry until the Secretary of Interior resolves each case. The secretary may revoke the status of an *asilado* who violates the national law, and deny continued residency in the country. Moreover, the secretary may determine residence restrictions.

Before status is granted, the asylum seeker must explain the motives for persecution and present a chronology of past political activities.[6]

The 1970 federal labor law prohibits all foreigners from participation as directors of unions. Under the 1973 migration law, work permits are not guaranteed for *asilados*. For those exempted from general entry fees, work permits are available for $500 Mexican and renewal of work permits for $100 Mexican. Until 1975 academic and professional credentials obtained outside Mexico were not recognized without extraordinary procedures.[7]

To deal with the mass influx of Guatemalan refugees, the Mexican Commission for Aid to Refugees (Comision Mexicana de Ayuda a Refugiados, COMAR) was created in 1980. The commission, headed by the Secretary of Interior, also has representatives from the Ministry of Foreign Affairs and the Ministry of Labor and Social Welfare. COMAR established the first administrative structure to examine asylum requests.[8]

Government ministries assumed total control of the needs of the refugees. Through 1982, Mexico issued to Guatemalan refugees three-month residence permits that were renewable for up to three years. The refugees were not allowed to seek employment or rent land in Mexico. Nevertheless, in Chiapas State most able-bodied men found seasonal work as day-laborers on local *ejidos*. Such services are in particular demand during the sugarcane harvest, in October-January.[9]

Mexico's policy toward refugees is inconsistent with its professed foreign policy goals in Central America. Mexico does not support the Guatemalan revolutionaries, but providing services to them is seen as complicity with the guerrillas. The Mexican "right" sees the refugees as communists, while the Mexican "left" sees an opportunity for a more radical foreign policy stance. However, reports in 1982, and occasionally thereafter, of intimidation and mass deportation of refugees, are attributable to the actions of particular individuals within the bureaucracy rather than to government policy.[10]

Several times during 1983-84, the Guatemalan military used force against refugee camps in Mexico. Following an attack on El Chupadero in April 1984, Mexico reiterated its guarantee of the rights of life, safety, and subsistence of the Guatemalans fleeing violence. Moreover, they were to be recognized and treated as refugees by COMAR. However, Mexico reserved the right to distinguish a refugee from an economic migrant.[11]

These Guatemalan military attacks showed that the original position of the Guatemalan refugees along the border presented a dangerous security problem. Many of the camps were difficult of access. For these reasons, and in order to to increase the potential for local integration, in mid-1984 the decision was taken to resettle the refugees. El Chupadero camp would be the first moved, to the valley of Ezna in the State of Campeche. Mexican authorities argued that this site provided similar geographic conditions and a low population density. The similarity of geographic conditions, especially climate, is disputed by UNHCR.[12]

Some Guatemalan refugees expressed fear of relocation, since moving from the border decreased the likelihood of their return home. Mexican authorities reiterated that resettlement would not preclude voluntary repatriation, but that repatriation would be possible only when domestic conditions in Guatemala would guarantee the returnees' safety. Furthermore, the refugees would have to express the desire to return, as Mexico would not force them to do so. To ensure humanitarian treatment during the relocation efforts, a coordinating commission for the move to Campeche was established.[13]

The anticipated relocation was preceded by bitter infighting between the Mexican ministries of Interior and Foreign Affairs. The Ministry of Interior was opposed to the relocation, citing increased costs, whereas the Ministry of Foreign Affairs supported the movement as a means of improving relations with Guatemala.[14] Once the moves began, reports surfaced that Mexican authorities were forcing reluctant refugees to relocate.[15] On 12 July 1984, COMAR, through the Mexican Embassy in Washington, D.C., declared such allegations of human rights abuses to be baseless, and UNHCR spokesman in Mexico City agreed with COMAR.[16] By November 1984, 16,500 Guatemalans had been transferred from the border area, and by May their number had increased to 17,300, so that the 99 refugee camps in the State of Chiapas had been reduced to 75. By October 1986, relations between the refugees and COMAR had been restored. Camp numbers were reduced to 64 and all were located at least eight kilometers from the frontier.[17]

At the 1984 UNHCR Executive Committee session, the Director-General of COMAR presented a detailed assessment of Mexican efforts on behalf of the Guatemalan refugees. He stated that the Mexican government would maintain its tradition of asylum on humanitarian grounds but would not allow its territory to be used to sustain violence against Guatemala or any other state.[18]

At the 35th Executive Committee Session, the Mexican observer, Jorge Montano, praised the nonpolitical character of the UNHCR mandate and UNHCR's work in protecting human rights. Subsequently, Mexico accepted *non-refoulement* as a central pillar of the right to asylum as a principle of international law.[19]

Since 1983 the government has not recognized Salvadorans as refugees. Salvadorans, concentrated in urban areas, are seen as economic migrants and must provide documented proof of employment or face deportation. However, Mexican issuance of such documentation, such as a tourist card, has been restricted for all Central Americans. As of May 1987, the Mexican coordinator for Salvadoran refugees estimated that at least 500,000 Salvadorans were residing illegally in Mexico. Young people of urban origin, belonging to the middle classes, largely make up this population. Since they are largely well educated, the Mexican authorities conclude that Salvadorans in Mexico reflect a selected migration. Unable to obtain asylum status or otherwise legalize their presence in Mexico, many Salvadorans prefer to stay underground and blend into the urban environment.[20]

Moreover, funding of refugee aid steadily declined from 1982 to 1985, so it is apparent that the government's treatment of refugees is designed to serve as a deterrent to illegal immigrants. Government officials constantly portray Central Americans as socially undesirable, as political troublemakers, and an as economic burden.[21]

GUATEMALA

Information regarding *asilado* and refugee policy in Guatemala is scant. The country file at UNHCR contains little information. A study conducted by the Refugee Policy Group in March 1984 concluded that Guatemala had no refugee programs.[22] Although Guatemala acceded to both the 1951 and 1967 refugee instruments in 1983, as of late 1985 no implementing legislation had been enacted or was pending.[23] Guatemala is a party to the 1928 and 1933 asylum and 1954 territorial asylum conventions. The American Convention was ratified by a decree in 1978, but Guatemala does not recognize the competence of the IACHR or the Inter-American Court.[24]

The constitutions of 1956 and 1967 recognized the right of asylum for persons persecuted for political reasons and prohibited extradition for political crimes. The 1967 Constitution remained in force until the 1985 civilian elections when a new constitution was approved by the National Assembly.[25] UNHCR protection officers revealed that this new constitution was to contain a section on refugees, including the basic language of the global 1951 Refugees Convention plus the broader definition of refugee contained in the OAU Regional Convention and the Cartagena Declaration. UNHCR gave advice on the wording of this section of the draft. However, no record of such language was reported by the IACHR in its 1985 analysis of this constitution.[26]

In 1983 the Guatemalan military established a policy for repatriation of refugees, linked with development projects. Identification for repatriation of Guatemalan refugees was facilitated by a UNHCR/ICRC census, and the first returnees (53 of them, mostly women and children) arrived in August 1983. Others continued to arrive throughout 1984 and were placed on development projects at the sites of Finca Chacaj, Nenton, and Huehuetanango.[27]

In 1984 the Guatemalan and Mexican foreign ministers discussed further efforts to facilitate the repatriation of Guatemalan refugees, such as creation of a Tripartite Commission to screen refugees in Mexico.[28] A UN Human Rights Commission study of 1984 stated that the return of Guatemalan refugees was preceded by full explanations. Refugees remaining close to the border in Mexico, however, uniformly maintained that they had been ignorant as to the internal conditions in Guatemala.[29] Refugee perceptions and claims had not changed by late 1986. Concerns about internal conditions were reinforced by short-wave radio reports.

Since return to civilian rule in 1986, special attention has been given to encouragement of repatriation. Guatemalans returning from Mexico are met by the Guatemalan Special Committee for Assistance to Returnees. (Comision Especial de Atencion a Repatriados, CEAR), which arranges reception and transport to villages of origin.[30] Further, in a July 1986 letter to President Vinicio Cerezo, Guatemalan refugee representatives from Campeche and Quintana Roo listed their conditions for return: security, justice, and land reform. They also communicated to Raquel Blandon de Cerezo, wife of the president, that they preferred to remain in Mexico because of their fear of the military should they return to Guatemala. The representatives requested that the military be punished for destroying villages and killing of their inhabitants. They stated further that members of religious sects had been arriving at refugee camps and that the Guatemalan government was using these sects to try to convince the refugees to repatriate by offering them land and housing through their sermons. In sum, despite the declared good intentions of the Guatemalan civilian government, a perceptible decline in the observance of human rights occurred immediately after the first months of return to civilian rule.[31]

EL SALVADOR

Little information from any source is available for El Salvador. The country file at UNHCR is incomplete. Prior to the accession of El Salvador to the global refugees regime in 1982, no specific provisions existed pertaining to refugees. Thus, until El Salvador became a party to the global refugees regime, only those general rights and guarantees afforded by the constitution were applicable to refugees or *asilados*. The constitutions of 1950 and 1962 recognized the right of asylum from political persecution.[32]

In June 1978 El Salvador ratified the American Convention. The jurisdiction of the Inter-American Court on a case-by-case basis was recognized.[33] El Salvador is a party to all (1928, 1933, and both 1954) inter-American asylum Conventions.

A general amnesty for all political prisoners and exiles was declared in November 1979. In an effort to normalize relations with Honduras and facilitate cooperative efforts with Salvadoran refugees on Honduran territory, a general treaty of peace between these two countries was signed in October 1980. It provides for free transit of persons between the two territories, and both states pledge to respect the rights essential to the human person and to uphold the rights detailed in the OAS Charter and the American and Universal Declarations of Human Rights.[34] There is no record of legislation adopted to implement provisions of the global refugees regime.

HONDURAS

Prior to the mass influx of Salvadoran refugees beginning in 1980, Honduras had no involvement with the global refugees regime. Despite the continuing influx of refugees to Honduras, that country still has not become a party to the global regime. Consequently, UNHCR presence in Honduras remains at the sufferance of the Honduran government. The protections and guarantees extended to refugees have been minimal and precariously enforced.

Honduras is a party to all (1928, 1933, and both 1954) inter-American asylum conventions, with expressed reservations to the 1954 conventions with respect to those articles opposed to the constitution and the laws of the republic.[35] Honduras signed the American Convention in 1977 and recognized the jurisdiction of the Inter-American Court in 1981.[36]

The constitutions adopted in 1957, 1965, and 1982 all recognized the right of asylum and nonextradition for political offenses.[37] Under the 1970 immigration law, *asilados* are classed as nonimmigrants and regulated as individuals temporarily in the territory. They are allowed to remain for a time judged convenient by the government. If they leave Honduran territory without the expressed permission of the Secretary of Interior and Justice, all their rights to return are lost. There is no specific recognition of *non-refoulement*. Under the 1971 Law on Passports, no mention is made of recognition of refugee travel documents, as issued under the 1951 Convention.[38]

In 1978, refugees from the Nicaraguan civil war fled to

Choluteca and Triunfo districts in eastern Honduras. Estimates of the influx range from 20,000 to 50,000. Honduras requested UNHCR assistance, and an agreement between UNHCR and Honduras was reached in November 1978. All Nicaraguans who entered the country as a result of the events of 1978 were considered refugees; however, no work permits were available. Of those Nicaraguans who fled to Honduras during 1977-79, most had repatriated by early 1980.[39]

As Nicaraguan refugees began to repatriate in 1980, the first mass influx of Salvadorans fleeing civil war arrived on Honduran territory. Due to long-standing animosity between El Salvador and Honduras (they had fought a war in 1969), especially over the undemarcated border areas, Honduras was less than willing to receive large numbers of Salvadorans as refugees. Frequently the Salvadorans were forced to return to their territory by the Honduran army. In order to normalize the border situation and establish a coordinated effort against guerrilla forces operating from Honduran territory, a peace agreement was reached in October 1980. Under this agreement, Honduras recognized Salvadoran nationals as asylees. By decree in 1981, the National Commission for Refugees was established. Identity cards are issued to all UNHCR-assisted Salvadorans in the border area.[40]

In January 1981 the voluntary refugee agencies were informed that supervision of refugee camps would pass to the Honduran military. Since this decision the Honduran Army has retained dominant influence over refugee policy. After being supplanted by the military, voluntary agencies received reports throughout 1981 that registered refugees regularly had their names turned over to Honduran security forces.[41] Furthermore, by a decree in autumn 1981, the location of the Salvadoran refugee camps was restricted to at least 30, but not more than 50, kilometers from the Salvadoran border. The announcement of this border site restriction created grave concern throughout the refugee camps. Salvadorans expressed reluctance to move from immediately astride the border, since this would place them farther from their homes.[42]

The greatest influx of Salvadorans occurred in 1982, with refugees concentrated in the departments of Cabanas and Chalatenango. These camps were to be moved from the border for strategic reasons.[43] Nevertheless, by the end of 1982 there were also heavy concentrations of Salvadoran refugees in Ocotepeque, Lempira, and Intibuca departments, with the largest grouping of refugee camps concentrated near Colomancagua. The military exercised especially strict control over the refugee concentrations near Colomancagua. No movement outside the camp was permitted without special permission. A state of emergency was imposed between 6 P.M. and 6 A.M.; however, by April 1983 inland resettlement had significantly reduced the concentration of refugees at Colomancagua.[44]

Salvadoran refugees established in the Western regions of Honduras were also subject to relocation. Refugee headquarters for the western region is located at San Marcos de Ocotepeque, with camps at Virgina Mapulaca, Guarita, San Marcos, San Francisco, La Virtud, and Mercedes. In this western sector the refugees are highly resented by the local population.[45] Mesa Grande, forty kilometers from the Salvadoran border, was selected as a resettlement site in 1982, and refugees were moved from the camps of La Virtud, Mapulaca, and Mercedes. The region is extremely mountanious and not suitable for agricultural activities. No infrastructure development had been undertaken in anticipation of the resettlement. Military control of the resettlement remained strict. The overall unsuitability of the site soon led to suggestions of another resettlement, to sites further inland that could support self-sufficiency activities.[46]

Since 1982, attempts by the Sandinista regime to consolidate its control over the Atlantic region have created frequent mass flights of Miskitu and Sumo Indians to Honduras. The first influx was of about 15,000 predominantly aged or adolescent Indians.[47] Ethnic and cultural identity with the Honduran Indians sped assimilation of the Nicaraguan refugees, but the remoteness of the region made the logistics difficult for UNHCR. The Honduran authorities, including the military, do not exercise effective control over this area. In May 1983, Honduras and UNHCR relocated Miskitu and Sumo refugees to camps at Rio Patuca, Rio Mocoron, and Rio Warunta. All camps for Nicaraguan Indian refugees were located in the Gracias a Dios Department of Honduras. Renewed mass influx of Indians occurred during March-April of 1986, ending hopes for early repatriation. Nearly 10,000 fled to camps at Morocon and Tapamlaya.[48]

Following the Sandinista victory in 1978, remnants of the former regime, Nicaraguan Ladinos, also sought refuge in southeastern Honduras. In December 1982, when the Honduran authorities judged that their influx had essentially ceased, official refugee status was granted to these Ladino refugees by Honduras. They are concentrated in the Nueva Segovia and Jintega departments.[49] Since 1982 the guerrilla war waged against the Sandinista regime by the predominantly Ladino Nicaraguan "contras" has kept the Southern border of Honduras in a state of constant tension. When Sandinista forces engaged these irregulars on Honduran territory in May 1985, the Honduran military interceded. In July 1985, 1,200 Ladino refugees started on foot to seek entry into the United States. When they were stopped at the Guatemalan border for lacking visas and documents, UNHCR shipped them back to Honduran camps.[50]

Presumably the contra forces were disarmed and moved from the border area. However, the intensity of armed attacks between the contras and the Sandinista forces increased throughout

1986-87. This renewed fighting generated a slow, steady flow of Ladinos seeking refuge in Honduras. By late 1987 the increased Ladino population strained both available resources and the goodwill of local Hondurans. Complaints from local Hondurans about Ladino refugees have revived the possibility of a massive relocation to the interior.[51] Also, through 1987 the Honduran government continued to claim absolute neutrality in the Nicaraguan civil war; that is, Honduras did not lend its territory for attacks on Nicaragua.[52]

A third refugee community in Honduras is composed of Guatemalan refugees fleeing from the counterinsurgency activity of the Guatemalan army. This group began arriving in Northwestern Honduras in 1981. Most of them settled with Honduran families and in the UNHCR camp at El Tesoro, in Santa Rosa del Copan Department. For security reasons, the Honduran military maintains tight control over this camp.[53]

To improve the prospects of agricultural self-sufficiency for both Guatemalan and Salvadoran refugees, Honduras drafted plans for resettlement to Yoro Department in 1983. By February 1984, 18,000 Salvadorans and 500 Guatemalans were scheduled to be relocated to the site of Olanchito. This resettlement was thwarted due to resistance by refugees and strong protests from voluntary agencies. Consequently, in November 1984 the Honduran government reversed its decision to relocate,[54] but resettlement plans were revived in January 1985, and a Honduran delegation led by the Minister of Interior and Justice met with the High Commissioner in Geneva. No information is obtainable on the content of this meeting, or the reaching of an acceptable resettlement plan.

Pressures to repatriate Salvadoran refugees increased beginning in late 1984, when the Honduran National Security Council made known its intention to seek repatriation of Salvadorans. A tripartite commission was established to screen those desiring to return. UNHCR participated on this commission, but it is not clear whether its participation was designed to ensure upholding of *non-refoulement* or was a response to political pressure from Honduras. Throughout 1984 the UNHCR representative in Honduras did not encourage repatriation, since the necessary conditions did not exist in El Salvador.[55] Honduras reiterated its commitment to voluntary repatriation at the thirty-seventh (1986) meeting of the Executive Committee.[56] However, through 1986 the Salvadoran refugee population remained relatively constant. The slow repatriation was at least matched by continued small numbers of new arrivals.[57]

On 28 August 1985, the Honduran Army entered the camps at Colomoncagua, killing 2 refugees, wounding 28 and detaining 11. This was the latest in a series of military attacks on Salvadoran refugee camps. Repeated UNHCR intervention with the Honduran authorities could not stop these military actions; apparently the military intends to instill sufficient fear among the refugees to ease the government problems of control. By late 1987 this continued military intimidation of Salvadoran refugees led over 4000 Salvadorans to choose repatriation, despite the continuing civil war.[58]

The treatment in Honduras of the three refugee groups-- Salvadoran, Guatemalan, and Nicaraguan--is generally consistent with Honduran foreign policy goals. The refugee camps are isolated from the local inhabitants, and despite the formation of a Refugee Commission, there are no formal procedures to determine refugee status. The provisions of domestic legislation are applied with an ideological bias. Sympathy and what might be termed preferential treatment is accorded to ideologically compatible groups, namely Ladinos and Sumo and Miskitu Indian refugees from Nicaragua. In comparison, Salvadoran and Guatemalan nationals are granted asylum, but not refugee status. These groups are also denied freedom of movement, employment, and the right to naturalization. This preferential treatment was denied by Honduran President Azcona Hoyo at a May 1986 UNHCR seminar held in Tegucigalpa.[59]

Still, whatever the preferential treatment, the Honduran government is offering protection and safety even to groups it opposes. This is most remarkable, as Honduras is not a party to the global refugees regime.[60] Claims that global regime standards were implemented by Honduras were reiterated by President Azcona Hoyo at the May 1986 UNHCR seminar.[61]

NICARAGUA

The 1950 Constitution of Nicaragua, in force at the time of creation of the global refugees regime, was redrafted in 1974. Both versions recognized the right to asylum and nonextradition for political offenses.[62] No record of Nicaraguan involvement with the global regime prior to the 1978 Sandinista victory can be found. With the formation of the Government of National Reconstruction, however, the new regime became actively involved in refugee affairs and promotion of human rights in general.[63]

Immediately after the Sandinista victory, the new regime was faced with massive repatriation of Nicaraguans exiled during the war years. Those with middle class families, relatives, and means of support, that is, the traditional *asilados*, did not report to refugee centers. The returnees were assisted by international aid donations, channeled through the Instituto Nicaraguense de Reforma Agraria and the Comision de Ayuda Hospitalaria.[64]

Nicaragua acceded to both the 1951 and 1967 refugee

instruments without reservations in 1980. It ratified the American Convention in 1979, and by decree, its provisions were incorporated as part of Nicaraguan domestic law. Under the Somoza regime Nicaragua had been party to the 1928 and 1933 inter-American asylum conventions. No information can be found indicating that the Sandinista regime has denounced either convention; they are assumed to be still in effect. Both the Statute of the Rights of Nicaraguans and its replacement, the 1987 Constitution, express recognition of human rights as stated in international instruments, such as the Universal and American declarations and the American Convention.[65]

One of the first acts of the Sandinista government was to grant priority aid to Salvadoran refugees, 700 of whom settled in the cities of Managua, Leon, Chinandenga, Esteli, Rivas, and Nueva Guinea in 1980. Initially, legal protection and determination of refugee status were entrusted to the National Office of Refugees, under the Ministry of Social Welfare. This office was restructured in 1982, and refugee affairs became the responsibility of the Nicaraguan Institute of Social Security and Welfare. In cooperation with the Directorate of Migration and Foreigners, the National Refugee Office determines the condition of the refugees in the country, decides on termination or cancellation of their status, and acts as the forum for appeal for reconsideration of status. The directorate is responsible for issuing temporary residence permits. Refugee status is terminated when the conditions in the 1951 Convention are met or if an individual is declared a threat to national security or public order. The principle of *non-refoulement* is expressly recognized.[66]

Legislation dealing with aliens, migration, and nationality was enacted during 1981-82. The 1981 Law of Nationality guarantees equality before the law, regardless of origin, to all inhabitants, with naturalization possible after two years' permanent residency. The 1982 Law of Migration places immigration control under the Ministry of the Interior. Persons identified as refugees are permitted to work anywhere in the country and considered temporary residents. They will be provided with documents of identity and travel if unable to obtain a visa.[67]

The 1982, 1983, and 1984 reviews by international agencies and UNHCR of Nicaraguan handling of refugees have been uniformly favorable. The speed and spontaneity of refugee integration with local populations is seen as a key success, given the continued violence throughout Central America. A UNHCR reporter observed in August 1982 that the freedom accorded refugees to reside, travel, and work in Nicaragua was without parallel in any other asylum country in the region.[68] While only 700 refugees were in Nicaragua in 1980, by February 1983, 22,000 Salvadorans had sought refuge there. An estimated 650 Guatemalan refugees were in Nicaragua in 1983, but only 117

were registered with UNHCR.   By April 1984, the number of
refugees in Nicaragua had been reduced to 17,000 and by
mid-1984 only 1,000 refugees remained under the auspices of the
National Refugee Office.[69] Estimates from May 1986 indicated
that 17,000 Salvadoran and 1,000 Guatemalan refugees remained
in Nicaragua.   The majority were considered integrated into the
social fabric of the country.   Tensions between refugees and local
populations have rarely surfaced.[70]

In late 1985, 298 Miskitu and Sumo Indians from the
camps of Tapamlaya and Musawas in Honduras were repatriated
to Nicaragua under UNHCR auspices. Some 500 additional
Indians in Honduras were registered for repatriation as of
November 1985, so that altogether 531 of them repatriated during
1985. A small but steady flow of Indians continued to repatraite
from Honduras and Costa Rica through mid-1987.[71]

It is argued by Ferris that two factors fundamentally shaped
the liberal refugee policies of the Sandinista regime.[72] First,
friendly treatment had been accorded Nicaraguan exiles and
refugees by other states during the civil war. Secondly, support
for refugees provides ideological identification for the Sandinista
regime.   By recognizing and providing liberal treatment to
refugees, Nicaragua encourages countries still at civil war in
Central America to embrace a Sandinista-style system.
Consequently, these liberal practices have made Nicaragua the
most favored destination for Guatemalans and Salvadorans.
Seeking refuge in Nicaragua, however, will most likely limit the
possibility of repatriation by confirming suspicion of subversive
activities held by the refugees' country of origin.

COSTA RICA

There is no record of Costa Rica ever attending sessions of
the UNHCR Executive Committee.   Attention to refugee matters
was not required until a mass influx of Nicaraguans occurred
during 1978.   The UNHCR Regional Office in San Jose,
established to handle Chilean refugees in the region, was ill
prepared for this mass influx.[73]

In 1978 Costa Rica acceded to both the 1951 and 1967
global instruments without reservations, apparently in response to
the increasing number of Nicaraguan refugees in its territory.
Provisions of the global regime were not applied beyond the
"special case" of the Nicaraguans.   All other asylees in Costa
Rica have remained subject to the more strict *asilado* status and
have to prove that they had suffered political persecution in their
country of origin. Nicaraguans, however, were granted tourist and
special displaced persons cards (*boleta de desplazado*), which
entitled them to residence and work permits as well.[74]

Within the Inter-American system, Costa Rica has long been recognized as an island of stability. It is noted for its consistent support of human rights. It is a party to all (1928, 1933, and both 1954) inter-American asylum conventions. In 1977 it ratified the American Convention and recognized the competence of the IACHR and the obligatory jurisdiction of the Inter-American Court.[75]

The first procedures for determination of refugee status were instituted in 1979 and modified in 1982 and 1983. With the latest revision, the Director General of the Department of Immigration is designated as the authority competent to determine refugee status. Applicants can make their initial appeal either at their point of entry or in San Jose, and a lawyer from the Refugee Department then makes a recommendation on the request. If the appeal is rejected, the applicant has several levels of appeal, first to the Department of Immigration, then to the Ministry of the Interior, and finally through the domestic court system, in accordance with the general administrative law. UNHCR is advised of all decisions and may submit opinions during review and appeal. If refugee status is granted, a *carnet de refugiado* is issued that serves as a residence permit, work permit, and convention travel document and permits access to the Costa Rican educational system. Once refugee status is obtained, an individual falls under the jurisdiction of the National Commission for Refugees (Comision Nacional para Refugiados, CONAPARE) the which was created in 1980.[76]

In 1981 a decree revised the general regulation of visas. Articles concerning *asilados* and refugees were revised to reflect the standards of the global refugee regime and recently created administrative procedures. Both categories were defined according to relevant international instruments and laws of the country.[77] Recognized refugees in Costa Rica receive all the social benifits and privileges accorded nationals, including free schooling and medical care. Although a 1960 law prohibits all forms of discrimination in employment, the general lack of available employment means that few refugees are able to obtain work permits. Rather, they are encouraged to participate in self-help programs.[78]

Despite efforts to normalize refugee status and provide a measure of self-sufficiency through economic projects, continued deterioration of political conditions in Central America has perpetuated the influx of Nicaraguan refugees to Costa Rica. In fact, by mid-1985 Costa Rica had become so swamped with refugees that President Louis Alberto Monge referred to this continued influx and its impact on a homogeneous society as a migratory "time bomb." This steady flow of Nicaraguans continued through 1986.[79]

One result of this "time bomb" has been increased tensions

between refugees and local populations.   On 9 December 1985, members of the Costa Rican *Guardia Civil* entered the Limon camp for Nicaraguan refugees and detained more than 130 suspected of not being refugees, or of having committed common crimes.   This action culminated a long series of incidents and disputes between some residents of the camp and residents of local communities.   The Limon camp was originally established in 1983 as a reception center for Nicaraguan refugees.   As no alternative camp had been constructed, many refugees had been in Limon for almost three years.   The camp population grew to 1,265 in September 1985, mostly of black or Indian Nicaraguans from the Atlantic coast.   Relations between some of the refugees and neighboring communities had been tense, . mostly over questions of employment. The camp offered no opportunities for wage employment.   Consequently, the refugees had to compete in the local labor market, which was already experiencing high unemployment.   Only about 150 refugees had been able to find work and few had the required work permits. To resolve the problem would have required relocation of most of the refugees at Limon.[80]

Playa Blanca, a site on the south Pacific coast on the Osa peninsula, was planned to accommodate 100 refugee families from Limon sometime in 1987.   National treatment with regard to health and social services and education was expected to be extended to those resettled here.[81]

As a result of the intervention at Limon, the camp was placed under the direction of the Center for Sociopolitical Analysis in January 1986.   Food distribution was reorganized to curtail corruption, and camp security was tightened by introducing strict regulations governing entry and exit permits.   Also, issuance of work permits by the Costa Rican government did improve in 1986, when nearly 800 were delivered.   Only 260 were available in 1985.[82]

PANAMA

Information on Panamanian participation in the global refugees regime is limited.   The country file available at UNHCR is incomplete.   There is no record of Panama having participated in the UNHCR Executive Committee.

Until 1977 Panama would grant asylum and *asilado* status on the basis of actual or anticipated persecution. However, with the influx of refugees from Nicaragua beginning in September 1977, the Panamanian government applied the global regime definition of refugee.[83]   The 1951 and 1967 global refugee instruments were ratified only in May 1978, but the 1979-1980

UNHCR Assistance Activities report noted that Panama did not make work permits available to Salvadoran refugees.[84] Full implementation of the global regime did not occur until 1984, with publication of regulations for the National Office for Refugees (Organizacion Nacional para la Atencion de los Refugiados, ONPAR). Earlier, by decree in 1981, a transitory Refugee Commission (La Comision para el tratamiento del problema de los refugiados) was created. This commission studied the problems of refugees in Panama and recommend policies, was responsible for the determination of refugee status, administered refugee projects and aid funds, and determined laws and regulations for the treatment of refugees.[85]

Panama is a party to the American Convention but has not recognized the jurisdiction of the IACHR and the Inter-American Court. It is a party, however, to all (1928, 1933, and both 1954) inter-American asylum conventions.

Prior to accession to the global regime, refugees and *asilados* were governed by provisions of the Panamanian Constitution, domestic legislation, and the 1954 Caracas Asylum Conventions. The 1972 Constitution contains no specific mention of refugees, asylum, or related categories. Protection applicable to refugees is governed by several articles.[86]

CUBA

Cuba is not a party to instruments of the global refugees regime. However, the 1928 and 1933 inter-American asylum conventions remain in force. Information on refugees in Cuba and Cuban policy prior to the 1959 revolution is equally scant, although the Constitutional Law and a decree in 1955 regulated, *inter alia*, aliens who sought refuge or asylum in Cuba for political reasons.[87]

With the chaos of revolution in the late 1950s through early 1960s, many Cuban nationals sought asylum and refuge on the premises of diplomatic representatives in Havana. Numerous incidents were recorded indicating that the revolutionary authorities frequently violated the immunity of diplomatic grounds to arrest asylees. Cuban nationals removed from these grounds were usually charged with counterrevolutionary crimes under the Code of Civil Defense. While not defined, counterrevolutionary crimes were not treated as political crimes. With this determination, revolutionary authorities could argue that those seeking asylum were not political refugees but common criminals.[88]

Since the establishment of the Castro regime in 1959, Cuba has both accepted for settlement and generated large numbers of Latin American refugees. Information to determine either Cuban refugee policy or the status of political refugees resettled in Cuba is difficult to obtain. Since 1963 Cuban authorities have been unwilling to provide information to the IACHR concerning, *inter alia*, political refugees. The material available to UNHCR is also scant, and discussions with UNHCR's Americas Section Protection Officers indicated that field agents were unable to add substantially to this information. The greatest number of political refugees accepted for resettlement resulted from the anti-Allende Chilean coup of 1973. Interviews with protection officers and members of the International Commission of Jurists disclose that there is no knowledge or evidence that refugees accepted by Cuba for resettlement are first subjected to ideological criteria or examination. Nor was there evidence indicating that ideological standards were being applied to any other Latin American refugees accepted for resettlement. Refugees in Cuba have come from Bolivia, Uruguay, and Argentina as well as Chile. There are no Brazilian refugees in Cuba.[89]

Since the Communist revolution, Cuban refugees have fled in waves: directly after the revolution, in the period between the Bay of Pigs and the Cuban missile crisis, in a government-sponsored airlift between 1966 and 1973 and in the Mariel exodus of 1980. Spain has accepted the largest number of Cuban refugees, either in transit or for resettlement, with most Cubans seeking resettlement in the United States. However, strict limitations on U.S. entry have created a backlog of cases.[90] Smaller numbers of Cubans sought refuge in Latin American states. By mid-1962 an estimated 20,000-30,000 had sought refuge. UNHCR "good offices" facilitated reception of these Cuban refugees. The largest number settled in Venezuela, with smaller numbers settling in Costa Rica, Colombia, Mexico, Nicaragua, and Panama.[91]

With the international community focusing on the flow of Cuban refugees to Spain, Cuba sent observers to UNHCR's Executive Committee Sessions in 1962, 1966, and 1968-69. While the Cuban observer expressed interest and willingness to cooperate with UNHCR, he maintained that the Cubans arriving in Spain were not refugees and that they had adequate funds and travel documents and were able to travel openly, that they had left Cuba and abandoned property of their own free will and consequently should be treated as ordinary immigrants and not under the UNHCR Mandate. Moreover, the delegates continued, the Spanish press consistently and openly encouraged Cubans to flee and go to Spain and to carry on counterrevolutionary activities.[92]

In 1980 several thousand Cubans entered and refused to leave the Peruvian and Venezuelan legations in Havana. A resettlement agreement with the ANDEAN Pact states was reached on 9 April 1980, whereby the Cubans at the Peruvian embassy would be transferred to Lima. Costa Rica agreed to act as a base for their resettlement.   An airlift to San Jose began but was abruptly cancelled in May 1980 as the Cuban response to bad press from Costa Rican newspapers.   Subsequent mass departures were channelled through the port of Mariel. In addition to those Cubans initially on legation grounds, the Cuban authorities selectively expelled undesirable nationals.   Cuban government actions throughout clearly demonstrated direct initiation and complicity in generating a mass exodus of refugees.[93] Consistent with earlier policy pronouncements on persons fleeing Cuba as refugees, in 1981 the Cuban observer to the UNHCR Executive Committee stated that the Cuban nationals fleeing in 1980 had not been refugees, but individuals who had left of their own free will.[94]

The Constitution of the Republic adopted in 1976 contains no mention of refugees, asylum, or related categories.   Chapter 12, Section 2 of the Penal Code of 1979 contains provisions for illegal departure from the territory.   According to Article 242(1), those leaving, or attempting to leave, the territory without fullfilling all of the legal requirements are subject to deprivation of liberty for up to six years.   Part of the legal formalities required to leave is expressing the reason for leaving. Individuals subject to, or fearing, persecution thus must declare this fear or attempt clandestine departure.   In effect, this law makes it impossible for a genuine refugee to leave legally.[95]

DOMINICAN REPUBLIC

There is no country file for the Dominican Republic at UNHCR.   Information obtained for this section is derived from various sources.

In 1978 the Dominican Republic acceded without reservation to both the 1951 and 1967 global refugee regime instruments. Implementation of standards of the global refugee regime has been slow.   A UNHCR seminar on refugees held in Santo Domingo in 1983 urged the government to establish a commission for implementation of the provisions of the global regime.[96] This was done by decree in 1983, when the National Commission for Refugees (Comision Nacional para el Refugiado) was created, designed to collaborate with UNHCR in drafting regulations and establish criteria for determination of refugee status and procedures for determination, cessation, exclusion, and expulsion.   It is also responsible for issuing all necessary documentation.   All refugees in the Dominican Republic under UNHCR auspices during the previous ten years were recognized as refugees (an improvement for those Haitians recognized only as *asilados*).[97]

Constant tensions with Haiti and a slow influx of Haitian refugees led to the denouncement of the 1928, 1933, and 1954 inter-American territorial asylum Conventions in early 1966 when several hundred Haitian refugees were subjected to *refoulement*.[98]

The Dominican Republic ratified the American Convention in 1978. The instrument of ratification contained no statement regarding recognition of the competency of the IACHR or the jurisdiction of the Inter-American Court. No information exists to indicate that provisions of the American Convention have been incorporated into domestic law.[99] A 1950 law states simply that those granted asylum must respect the national sovereignty and laws. The constitutions of 1955, 1963, and 1966 contain no mention of asylum, refuge, or related categories.[100] The Act of Dominican Reconciliation of 1965, which ended the civil war, contains general guarantees and protections found also in the global refugees regime.[101]

Prior to accession to the global refugees regime, Dominican authorities had occasionally cooperated with UNHCR on a humanitarian basis. As reported by UNHCR in 1955, the Dominican Republic had agreed to receive under the UNHCR Mandate several refugees who could not obtain asylum in other countries.[102] Between 1970 and 1975 the Dominican Republic acknowledged receipt of some 360 Haitians seeking asylum. They enjoyed access to employment, health care, and freedom of movement under the same conditions as nationals. Their admission gave no rise to questions of public order.

A complicating factor in dealing with the majority of refugees in Dominican territory is that they have the same origin as illegal migrants and residents: since the mid-1960s refugees in the Dominican Republic have been exclusively Haitian.[103] The sugar harvest creates a strong demand for migrant labor, mostly Haitian. Three classes of Haitians participate in this harvest: those with a signed labor agreement; annual illegal migrants; and illegal residents. This latter class is normally tolerated, as it is composed of subsistence peasants or urban poor. The labor conditions of the migrants create constant controversy. Moreover, the low wages of the migrants exacerbate the cyclical swing of the Dominican labor market.[104] Also, Haitian political refugees have a different socioeconomic backgound and different motivations for remaining in the Dominican Republic. In general they tend to be urban in origin, middle-class, and older, and they arrive in family groups and experience high unemployment because their skills compete in an already saturated market.[105] A major barrier to providing protections to Haitian refugees is the fact that Dominican employers do not distinguish them from the illegal migrants, and the middle class status of the refugees increases the competition with Dominican nationals of equal competence.[106]

Refugee flows to the Dominican Republic have been highly irregular, reflecting the degree of political instability in Haiti at the time. The influx began in the 1950s, with 1962, 1964, and 1965 as years of many arrivals. However, since 1974 there has been only a slight increase in arrivals.[107] Since the fall of President Francois Duvalier on 7 February 1986, some of the estimated .5 million exiles have returned to Haiti. However, no program for mass repatriation has been established by UNHCR or any voluntary agencies.[108]

CONCLUSIONS

The treatment of refugees in Mexico and Central America is a study in contrasts. Mexico and Honduras, the states hosting the largest numbers of refugees, are not parties to the global regime. Their treatment of refugees on their territory is sometimes questionable. Nicaragua is judged to have the most comprehensive refugee policies in the region, but the increasing level of violence has driven most refugees from its territory. However, the important point is the response by states of the region that are not parties to the global regime. Strictly speaking, the global 1951 Convention is ill-suited for mass exodus situations. General guidance from the UNHCR Executive Committee has a more direct bearing on such situations. This reflects the evolutionary nature of the global refugees regime, especially the Office of the High Commissioner. It is appropriate, then, to lastly inquire whether the experience of mass exodus in Central America has had any impact on inter-American regional institutions.

NOTES

1. "Refugees in Central America: What Lies Ahead?" Refugees, no. 31 (July 1986): 19; "Dossier: Refugees, A 1986 Overview," Refugees, no. 36 (December 1986): 21.
2. "Interview: Jorge Carrillo Olea," Refugees, no. 34 (October 1986): 31.
3. Francis Stanley, The New World Refugee: The Cuban Exodus (Church World Service, 1966), pp. 37-39.
4. Organization of American States (hereafter OAS), Convention on Territorial Asylum (A/10 Sep F) Law and Treaty Series no. 19, Washington, D.C., 1954; Thomas Burgenthal and Robert Norris, eds., Human Rights: The Inter-American System. (Dobbs Ferry, N.Y.: Oceana, 1982), pp. 46-48. Mexico

expressed reservations to Articles 9 and 10 "because they are contrary to the individual guarantees enjoyed by all inhabitants of the Republic of Mexico in accordance with the Political Constitution of Mexico."

5. Rodolfo Bravo Caro, Guia del extranjero (Mexico City: Imprenta Nacional, 1979), pp. 17, 37, 101-04. Under the 6 June 1952 version, the secretary of government is responsible for *asilados*. They are not obliged to sign the National Registry of Foreigners within thirty days, as is required of aliens generally. In order to engage in activities other than specifically authorized, an *asilado* must receive permission from the secretary. Upon change of address, the National Registry of Foreigners must be notified. Expulsion is permitted for reasons of public order. There were no specific or indirect references to *non-refoulement* in this legislation.

6. Rafael de Pina, Estatuto legal de los extranjeros (Mexico City: Imprenta Nacional, 1953); Mexico, Consejo Nacional de Poblacion, Ley general de poblacion (1952), Reglamento de la ley general de poblacion (1952) and Reglamento de la ley general de poblacion (1976). In 1976 a minor modification of this law was passed that strengthened the background information required from asylum seekers before status would be granted. For a more recent review of Mexican domestic legislation pertaining to asylees and refugees see Joan Friedland and Jesus Rodriguez y Rodriguez, Seeking Safe Ground, Mexico-U.S. Law Institute, University of San Diego Law School, 1987.

7. Mexico, Consejo Nacional de Poblacion, Ley de impuestos de migracion (1973); Mexico, Convenio colectivo de trabajo de la UNAM (1-11-1978 a 31-10-1980). These same conditions were contained in the Collective Work Agreement for the National University (effective November 1970-October 1980). Under Clause 7, all service workers were to be Mexican nationals. Provisional services of foreigners were permitted when no Mexican nationals were able to fill the positions. In no case could foreign nationals exceed 5% of the work force, but this ceiling could be modified for cases of *asilados*, with agreement between the university and the union; they were designated as category FM-10 workers. The initial authorization fee was $500, renewal was $100 Mexican. Mexico, Articulos de la ley Federal del trabajo sobre extranjeros (1970); Mexico, Decreto de 29-7-1975: Promulgacion el convenio regional de convalidacion de estudios, titulos y diplomas de educacion superior en America Latina y el Caribe; Mexico, Decreto de 18-10-1975 por el que los asilados politicos y sus familiares en Mexico podran obtener la revalidacion de estudios o certificacion de conocimientos. Immediate recognition of studies, diplomas and certificates of academics and professionals is required. Revalidation of studies or certificates of study for political refugees of any nationality or country of origin is provided for by the decree of 18 October 1976.

8. Mexico, Decreto de 4-7-1980: Comision Mexicana de Ayuda a Refugiados; UN, Genereal Assembly, 36th sess., Report of the United Nations High Commissioner for Refugees (A/36/12), 1981, pp. 5, 33. It is charged with the study of the needs of foreign refugees on Mexican territory, and is supposed to act as liaison with agencies that help refugees, approve refugee-oriented projects and seek permanent solutions. The president of the Commission calls sessions when necessary. Interested representatives, including UNHCR, are invited to attend.

9. UN, Report on UNHCR Assistance Activities for 1982-1983 (A/AC.96/620), 1 August 1983, pp. 235-38. The Education Ministry distributed textbooks; Health provided 10,000 doses of vaccines; Social Security sent teams to evaluate health needs; and COMAR hired six medical personnel. Nutrition centers were established at the camps of Puerto Rico and Chajul and field warehouses at Puerto Rico, Chajul, Boca Lacantun, Flor de Cafe, and Nuevo Huitan.

10. Elizabeth Ferris, "Regional Responses to Central American Refugees: Policy Making in Nicaragua, Honduras and Mexico," in Elizabeth Ferris, ed., Refugees and World Politics (New York: Praeger, 1985), pp. 205-06, 208 and "The Politics of Refuge: National Admissions Policies Toward the Central American Refugees," paper presented at the Annual Meeting of the International Studies Association, Washington, D.C., 9 March 1985, pp. 9-11 (used with permission of the author).

11. OAS, IACHR, Annual Report of the Inter-American Commission on Human Rights 1982-1983 (ser. L/V/II.61 doc. 22/rev. 1), 27 September 1983, p. 153; "Emergency in Southern Mexico," Refugees, no. 15 (March 1983): pp. 1-2; "News in Brief," Refugees, no. 2 (February 1984): p. 7; "Killing Time Which Kills Us," Refugees, no. 6 (June 1984): p. 10; OAS, IACHR, Annual Report of the Inter-American Commission on Human Rights 1983-1984 (ser. P/AG/doc. 1778/84), 5 October 1984, p. 106; Mexico, Secretariat of Governmental Affairs, Press release, 10 May 1984, unofficial English translation by UNHCR, pp. 1-4. On 25 and 26 January 1983, the camps of Sanitago el Ventico and La Hamaca were attacked by Guatemalan troops. Attacks on the camps continued through 1984: on 6 January, Flor de Cafe and Paln de Rio Azul were subject to air bombardment; in April, El Chupadero was attacked. The IACHR denounced the attack on El Chupadero as a violation of the 1949 Geneva Conventions.

12. Interview, UNHCR assistance personnel. July 1985.

13. "Guatemalan Refugee Rights Guaranteed," Refugees, no. 3 (March 1984): 37; "News in Brief," Refugees, no. 7 (July 1984): 7. For a review of conditions at relocation sites and adaptation and self-sufficiency of refugees see "The Relocation Experience: Refugees in Campeche and Quintana Roo,"

Refugees, no. 34 (October 1986):   27-29. Medical teams and social workers accompanied the refugees.   Refugees from the Lacandon and Comitan camps cooperated with relocation through their own elected representatives.

14. "Rumors, Conflicts Complicate Mexico's Relocation of Refugees," Washington Post, 15 July 1984.

15. Amnesty International (hereafter AI), "Mexico: Treatment of Refugees and Camp Workers Questioned," Amnesty Action, October 1984, p.   5.   Amnesty International, among other international humanitarian organizations, continued to raise this concern throughout 1984.

16. Mexico, Ministry of Internal Affairs, press release, 12 July 1984, official English translation. Field visits to China and Hecelchakan sites in Campeche allowed direct UNHCR contact with relocated refugees.   Interviews with refugees relocated from the Puerto Rico camp indicated that those unwilling to relocate had not been moved.

17. UN, UNHCR, Fact Sheet no. 12, January 1985; UN, UNHCR, 35th sess., Report on the UNHCR Assistance Activities for 1984-1985 (A/AC.96/657), 5 August 1985, pp. 8, 246-47. For progress report on refugee camps in Quintana Roo state as of January 1986, see "Guatemalans in Quintana Roo," Refugees, no. 27 (March 1986): 17-18; UN, ECOSOC, Commission on Human Rights, 40th sess., Report on the Situation of Human Rights in Guatemala (E/CN.4/1985/19), 8 February 1985, p.   53; Jeffery Wilkerson, "The Usumacinta River: Troubles on a Wild Frontier," National Geographic 168, no. 4 (October 1985): 531. Of these refugees, 12,300 had been relocated to Campeche State and 5,000 to Quintana Roo State. The refugees were authorized to live and work on rural settlement projects.   Those relocated established the following settlements: in Campeche: Maya Tecun (9,000) and Quetzal Edzana (7,000); in Quintana Roo, Los Lirios (2,000)   and   Los   Ranchos   (6,000).   See   also   "Guatemalan Refugees in Chiapas," Refugees, no. 34 (October 1986): 20.

18. Mexico, Sintesis intervencion representante de Mexico, Jorge Montano, a la XXXV perido de sesiones de Comite Ejecutivo del Alto Comisionado de las Naciones Unidas para los Refugiados, (Washington, D.C.: Embassy of Mexico, 1984): 3-4.

19. Ibid., pp. 6-7.

20. "Central Americans in Mexico," US-Mexico Report 6, no. 6 (June 1987): 20.

21. Patricia Weiss-Fagen, "Refugees and Displaced Persons in Central America," (Washington, D.C.: Refugee Policy Group, 1984), pp.   3-4; U.S. General Accounting Office, Central American Refugees: Regional Conditions and Prospects and Potential Impact on the United States (GAO/NSIAD-84-106; Washington, D.C.: Government Printing Office, 1984), pp. iii, 10, 26 ; "Salvadorans in Mexico," Refugees, no. 34 (October 1986): 30-31.

22. Weiss-Fagen, Refugees and Displaced Peersons, p. 3.

23. UN, General Assembly, 8th sess., Report of the United Nations High Commissioner for Refugees (A/2394), 1953, p. 4; UN, General Assembly, 38th sess., Report of the United Nations High Commissioner for Refugees (A/38/12), 1983, pp. 3-4.

24. Pan-American Union (hereafter PAU), Tenth Inter-American Conference: Final Act (Washington, D.C.: PAU, 1954); OAS, IACHR, Report on the Situation of Human Rights in the Republic of Guatemala 1981, p. 17; Buergenthal and Norris Human Rights, p. 40, with reservations expressed on Articles 3 and 9 of the latter.

25. UN, Yearbook on Human Rights for 1956 (New York: UN, 1958), pp. 90-102; UN, Yearbook on Human Rights for 1963 (New York: UN, 1963), pp. 143-45; OAS, IACHR, Report on the Situation of Human Rights in the Republic of Guatemala, p. 8; Guatemala, Constituction de la Republica de Guatemala (Guatemala: Ministerio de Gobernacion, 1965). Article 61 recognized the right of asylum for political asilados, so long as they respected the sovereignty and laws of the state. Extradition for political crimes was prohibited. If expulsion of an asilado were necessary, it would not be to a country of persecution. Access to the court system for all inhabitants was guaranteed under Article 74.

26. Interview, UNHCR protection officer, July 1985. For commments on Guatemalan constitution see IACHR, Annual Report 1985-86, pp. 156-59.

27. Guatemala, Decreto-ley 56-84 de 15 Junio de 1984; Embassy of Guatemala, Washington, D.C., correspondence with author. This policy was initiated on 11 August 1983 by Decree Law 89-939, which included an amnesty for political exiles. The policy was supplanted by Decree Law 56-84 of 15 June 1984, which extended the amnesty for an additional 90 days. Model development villages were established at Nebaj, San Juan Cotzal, and Chajul in central Quiche Department. These model villages were renamed development poles, established by Decree Law 65-84 on 26 June 1984.

28. Embassy of Guatemala, Washington, D.C., correspondence with author; UN, ECOSOC, Human Rights in Guatemala 1984, p. 37.

29. UN, ECOSOC, Human Rights in Guatemala 1985, pp. 48-49, 53.

30. "Guatemalan Refugees in Chipas," pp. 21-22; "40.000 Refugees in Mexico." US-Mexico Report 5, no. 12 (December 1986): 9.

31. "News in Brief." Refugees, no. 41 (May 1987): 7; OAS, IACHR, Annual Report of the Inter-American Commission on Human Rights 1986-1987 (ser. L/V/II.71 doc. 9/rev. 1), 22 September 1987, pp. 228-29.

32. PAU, Constitution of the Republic of El Salvador, 1950
Law and Treaty Series no. 36 (Washington, D.C.: PAU, 1953);
El Salvador, Constitucion Politica de la Republica de El Salvador,
1962 (San Salvador: Departamento de Relaciones Publicas, 1976);
OAS, IACHR, Report on the Situation of Human Rights in El
Salvador (ser. L/V/II.46 doc. 23/rev. 1), November 1978, pp.
32-35 Under Article 153 of the 1950 Constitution, asylum for
political persecution was recognized; extradition for political
offenses was prohibited.   When the 1950 Constitution was
replaced by the 1962 Constitution, these guarantees were repeated.
33. OAS, IACHR, Human Rights in El Salvador, pp.
48-49; Buergenthal and Norris, Human Rights, pp. 36-38.
Ratification was without prejudice to those provisions of the Pact
that conflict with express provisions of the constitution.
34. OAS, IACHR, Annual Report of the Inter-American
Commission on Human Rights 1979-1980 (ser. L/V/II.50 doc.
13/rev. 1), October 1980, p. 137; El Salvador, Tratado general
de paz entre las republicas de El Salvador y Honduras, San
Salvador, 1981.
35. OAS, Convention on Territorial Asylum. With expressed
reservations to the 1954 Conventions with respect to those articles
opposed to the constitution and the laws of the republic.
36. Buergenthal and Norris, Human rights, pp. 42-44.
37. UN, Yearbook on Human Rights for 1957 (New York:
UN, 1959), pp. 127-37; PAU. Constitution of the Republic of
Honduras, 1965, Law and Treaty Series no. 36 (Washington,
D.C.: PAU, 1966); Honduras. Decreto 131 de 1982:
Constitucion de la Republica.   Under the 1957 document, aliens
were entitled to the same civil rights as nationals, excepting in
questions involving national security.   Extradition for political
offenses was prohibited, and aliens were guaranteed the same
individual rights as nationals (Articles 26, 29, and 31). Under
Article 86, Honduran territory was recognized as an asylum for
cases of political persecution, as governed "in accordance with the
international conventions to which [Honduras] was a party." Free
movement and residence in the territory was extended to all
inhabitants.   Under Article 120, a preference in employment for
Honduran nationals is stated.   The 1965 Constitution used
essentially the same wording and included the same rights and
guarantees (Articles 24-25, 31). Under the 1982 Constitution,
naturalization is possible after three years' consecutive residence
(Article 24).   Aliens are granted the same civil and individual
rights as nationals, have recognized legal personality before the
courts, but are under a total prohibition of political activities
(Articles 30-32).   Article 101 recognizes the right of asylum. If
the status of asilado is revoked or denied, the individual is not to
be sent to the territory of a persecuting state.   Extradition for
political offenses is prohibited.   Under employment, Articles

127-41, while aliens are guaranteed equality of conditions, Honduran nationals are to receive preference in hiring (Article 137).

38. Susana Torrado, "International Migration Policies in Latin America," International Migration Review 13, no. 47 (1979): 431; Honduras, Decreto 124 de 3-1971: Ley de pasaportes.

39. UN, UNHCR, press release Ref 1354, 25 September 1978; UN, UNHCR, press release Ref 1371, 6 November 1978; U.S. Congress, Senate, Committee on the Judiciary, World Refugee Crisis: The International Community's Response (Washington, D.C.,: Congressional Research Service, 1979), pp. 227-28; UN, UNHCR, Report on the Regional Seminar on Protection of Refugees in Latin America, Mexico City, 20-24 August 1979 (Geneva: UNHCR, 1979), pp. 10-11; UN, UNHCR, 30th sess., Report on the UNHCR Assistance Activities for 1979-1980 (A/AC.96/577), 14 August 1980, pp. 118-23; UN, ILO, Migraciones laborales e integraction del refugiado en Honduras (RLA/83/VAROV), Buenos Aires, July 1982, p. 44.

40. Ferris, "Regional Responses," p. 198-200; Honduras, Decreto 14 de 21-1-1981: Comision nacional para refugiados; "The Geography of Refuge," Refugees, no. 2 (February 1982): 5, 7; Americas Watch, Honduras: On the Brink (Washington, D.C.: Americas Watch, 1984), p. 53; UN, General Assembly, 37th sess., Report of the United Nations High Commissioner for Refugees (A/37/12), 1982, pp. 5, 32; Members of the commission were drawn from the ministries of Government and Justice, Foreign Relations, National Defense and Public Security, Public Health and Social Assistance, and Labor and Social Security (Article 2). The commmmission is to function as the organ of communication between the government and the UNHCR, coordinate the activities of established refugee service organizations, and serve as the government representative to national and international humanitarian organizations. Retired Colonel Abraham Turcios was appointed head of the commission.

41. Ferris, "Regional Responses," p. 199; Americas Watch, Honduras, pp. 1-6. Also subsequent to military control of the camps, reports surfaced indicating that the World Vision relief agency had worked actively with security forces in identifying "subversives" among the refugees.

42. Ferris, "Regional Responses," p. 200.

43. UN, ILO, Migraciones en Honduras, pp. 48-50; UN, UNHCR, 32nd sess., Executive Committee (hereafter EXCOM), Summary Record of the 350th Meeting (A/AC.96/SR 350), 15 October 1982, p. 13.

44. "Situation Improves in Honduran Refugee Camps," Refugees, no. 15 (April 1983): 4.

45. "Geography of Refuge," Refugees, no. 2 (February 1982): 5.

46. UN, ILO, Migraciones laborales, pp. 50-53.

47. Ibid., pp. 44-46; Americas Watch, Honduras, pp. 1-6; International Committee of the Red Cross (hereafter ICRC), Red Cross Action in Aid of Refugees (ICRC/LRCS/CD/8/1), Geneva: August 1983, annex c: p. 10.

48. "Dispersal and Self-Sufficiency," Refugees, no. 17 (May 1983): 1, 8; "News in Brief," Refugees, no. 2 (February 1984): 7. By February 1984 the numbers of refugees in the Rio Patuca, Rio Mocoron and Rio Warunta camps were, respectively, 4,000, 3,000, and 3,500. Minor camps had been established at Tapamlaya, Cocobial, and Prunmitara.

49. "Dossier: Central American Refugees," Refugees, no. 31 (July 1986): 27.

50. UN, ILO, Migraciones laborales, pp. 46-48; UN, UNHCR, Assistance 1982-1983, pp. 221-23.

51. UN, ILO, Migraciones laborales, p. 21; "Honduras Disarms Contra Forces," The Guardian (London), 16 May 1985; "Nicaragua Steps Up Raids on Rebels on Honduran Border, US Aides Say," International Herald Tribune, 20 May 1985; "Honduras Puts Controls on Nicaraguan Rebels," International Herald Tribune, 21 May 1985; UN, UNHCR, Assistance 1984-1985, p. 236; "Growing Concerns," Refugees, no. 47 (November 1987): 15-18.

52. "Dossier: Central American Refugees," Refugees, no. 31 (July 1986): 27.

53. UN, ILO, Migraciones laborales, pp. 53-54; "Guatemalan Refugees Arrested by Honduran Army," Refugees Magazine, no. 4 (August 1983): 20. In July 1983 a military sweep through the camp resulted in the arrest of 10 refugees, allegedly for subversive activities. Intervention by UNHCR eventually secured the release of these ten refugees and their resettlement to Bolivia. A total of 106 Guatemalans were similarly resettled in Bolivia.

54. "Health Services Adjust to Miskito Dispersal," Refugees, no. 2 (February 1984): 20; "News in Brief," Refugees, no. 11 (November 1984): 7.

55. "News in Brief," Refugees, no. 10 (October 1984): 7; "Dossier: Central American Refugees," Refugees, no. 31 (July 1986): 21

56. "Dossier: The 37th Session of the EXCOM," Refugees, no. 35 (November 1986): 21.

57. "Dossier: Central American Refugees," Refugees, no. 31 (July 1986): 20.

58. "News in Brief," Refugees, no. 22 (October 1985): 7. For the IACHR investigation of the attack (case 9619) see Resolution 5/87 of 28 March 1987 in OAS, IACHR, Annual Report 1986-1987, pp. 75-88. For Salvadoran repatriation see "Large-Scale Return to El Salvador Unprecidented Operation," Refugees, no. 47 (November 1987): 14.

59. "Dossier: Central American Refugees," Refugees, no. 31 (July 1986): 20.

60. GAO, Central American Refugees, pp. 8-9.

61. "Dossier: Central American Refugees," Refugees, no. 31 (July 1986): 20.

62. PAU, Constitution of the Republic of Nicaragua, 1950, Law and Treaty Series no. 36 (Washington, D.C.: PAU, 1954); OAS, Constitution of the Republic of Nicaragua, 1974, Law and Treaty Series no. 36 (Washington, D.C.: OAS, 1976). Aliens were extended the same rights and guarantees as nationals, but their involvement in politics was prohibited (Article 26). Extradition for political crimes, as defined by treaty, was prohibited. The territory of Nicaragua was recognized as an asylum for those fleeing political persecution (Article 31). If an asilado had to be expelled, it would not be to a persecuting state (Article 55).

63. UN, ECOSOC, Commission on Human Rights, 37th sess., Study on Human Rights and Massive Exoduses (E/CN.4/1503), 31 December 1981, p. 28.

64. UN, General Assembly, 35th sess., Report of the United Nations High Commissioner for Refugees (A/35/12), 1980, p. 33. Figures on those returning can only be estimated, as there are only inaccurate numbers available of those who fled Nicaragua under the Somoza regime.

65. International Commission of Jurists, Human Rights in Nicaragua Yesterday and Today. (Geneva: ICJ), 1980; OAS, IACHR, Report on Nicaragua, pp. 10, 23-24, 29-31; Nicaragua, The Basic Law of 21-8-1979; OAS, IACHR, Annual Report 1986-1987, pp. 249-56. In the new constitution Articles 23 through 91 define rights in detail. Article 42 addresses asylum and Article 43 addresses extradition.

66. UN, ILO, Migraciones laborales e integracion del refugiado en Nicaragua (RLA/83/VAROV), Buenos Aires, May 1984, p. 30, 43-44 UN, General Assembly, Report of UNHCR, 1983, p. 5; Nicaragua, 600 NIC, 28-12-1982: Draft Regulations on the Nicaraguan National Refugee Office. Regulations for the National Office of Refugees were not enacted until April 1984. See Nicaragua, Reglamento de ley creadora de la Oficina Nacional para Refugiados (6-4-1984); "Priority to Rural Integration," Refugees, no. 9 (September 1984): pp. 18-19.

67. Nicaragua, Decreto 867: Ley de Nacionalidad de 19-11-1981 and Decreto 1031 de 4-5-1982: Ley de Migracion; UN, ILO, Migraciones en Nicaragua, pp. 46-47. Under Article 5(c), foreigners, including refugees, must complete two years' residence before being eligible for a residence permit. Permanent residence requires a presence of three years (Article 19). Documents are good for six months and allow only one return trip. While these provisions conform to the travel document

requirements of the global regime, there is no specific mention of the 1951 Convention travel document in this law. *Asilados* and refugees, as temporary residents, are entitled to a corresponding residence permit (Article 34).

68. UN, UNHCR, UNHCR Assistance 1982-1983, p. 246. These observations were reiterated by UN, General Assembly, Annual Report of UNHCR, 1983.

69. UN, UNHCR, UNHCR Assistance 1982-1983, p. 196; UN, ILO, Migraciones en Nicaragua, pp. 30-31; "Agricultural Cooperatives," Refugees, no. 17 (May 1983): 6; "Dossier: Central American Refugees," Refugees, no. 34 (July 1986): 21-22.

70. "Dossier: Central American Refugees," Refugees, no. 31 (July 1986): 21-22.

71. "News in Brief," Refugees, no. 24 (December 1985): 7; IACHR, Annual Report 1986-1987, p. 261.

72. Ferris, "Regional Responses," pp. 195-196.

73. UN, UNHCR, press release no. Ref 1319, 5 December 1977.

74. UN, UNHCR, 31st sess., Note on Procedures for the Determination of Refugee Status under International Instruments (A/AC.96/INF 152/rev. 3), 4 September 1980, pp. 6-7; Costa Rica, Decree 11950-S of 10-10-1980: Determination of Refugee Status; UN, UNHCR, Note on Procedures for the Determination of Refugee Status under International Instruments (A/AC.96/INF 152/rev. 5), 30 October 1981, p. 8; UN, General Assembly, Report of UNHCR, 1981, pp. 5, 11-12; Costa Rica, Decree 11939-P of 7-10-1980: Creation of National Reugee Commission. CONAPARE (Comision Nacional para Refugiados) is a permanent organ, responsible for initiating and coordinating action for refugees in conformity with international instruments and democratic and humanitarian tradition. The commission is composed of representatives from the presidency, UNHCR, the ministries of Foreign Affairs and Labor and Social Security, the private sector (as nominated by the president), and the Costa Rican Red Cross. The commission is convened as circumstances require or by call of the commission president, with three members constituting a quorum.

75. OAS, Human Rights: The Inter-American System, Part 2: Legislative History of the American Convention. (Washington, D.C.: OAS, 1970), p. 31.

76. Costa Rica, Decree 14,155-J of 23-12-1982: CONAPARE. The 1982 decree charged CONAPARE with four functions: to develop policies on refugees as dictated by the National Security Council and fix the necessary policies; to develop programs and projects relating to refugees; to coordinate and supervise those in its charge, between organs of government and national and international benificent agencies; and to maintain coordination with government entities in charge of legal aspects of

refugees (Article 2).   CONAPARE is composed of representatives from the ministries of Justice, Foreign Affairs, Government, Labor and Social Security, and Public Security and Planning, and from the presidency, the Institute of Agrarian Development, the Institute of Combined Social Aid, the National Institute of Apprenticeship, and the Costa Rican Red Cross.   UNHCR and ICM are to provide assistance and have observer status but no voting powers.

77. Costa Rica, Decree 12,903-S of 4-8-1981: Temporary Residence.

78. GAO, Central American Refugees, p.   10; UN, Yearbook on Human Rights for 1962 (New York: UN, 1964), p. 61; UN, UNHCR, UNHCR Assistance 1984-1985, p. 8; "Influx of Refugees from Nicaragua to Costa Rica," Refugees, no. 20 (August 1985): 22.

79. Interview, assistance personnel, July 1985; "Influx of Refugees from Nicaragua to Costa Rica," pp. 20-22.   UNHCR figures chart this influx: 1981, no refugees; 1982, 500 refugees; 1983, 1,850 refugees; 1984, 5,900 refugees; and January-November 1985, 11,600 refugees.   And 50 percent of the 1985 figure were totally dependent on UNHCR aid.   For the latest available figures at this writing see "Dossier: Central American Refugees," p. 20.

80. "Trouble in Limon," Refugees, no. 26 (February 1986): 17-18.

81. "Dossier: Central American Refugees," Refugees, no. 31 (July 1986): 21; "Playa Blanca: A New Settlement for Nicaraguan refugees," Refugees, no. 40 (April 1987): 16-17.

82. "Limon: Under New Management," Refugees, no. 32 (August 1986): 8.

83. UNHCR, Regional Seminar, p.   10

84. Buergenthal and Norris, Human Rights, p. 50; UN, UNHCR, UNHCR Assistance 1979-1980, pp.   118-23.

85. UN, General Assembly, Report of UNHCR, 1982, p. 32; UN, UNHCR, UNHCR Assistance 1979-1980, p. 123; Panama, Decree 100 of 6-7-1981: Creadora de la comision para el tratamiento del problema de los refugiados. The commission is composed of vice-ministers from the Directorate of Migration and Naturalization (under the Ministry of Government and Justice), the Director of External Politics (under the Ministry of Foreign Affairs), the Director General of Labor (under the Ministry of Labor and Social Welfare), a member from G-2 (state security) of the National Guard and a member of the Panamanian Red Cross. Implementation was accomplished through Resolution 461 of 9 October 1984. See Note on Procedures 1978. op. cit.   pp. 23-24.

86. OAS, Constitution of the Republic of Panama, (1972) (Washington, D.C.: OAS, 1974).   Article 14 states that immigration is regulated in accordance with the social, economic,

and demographic interests of the country.   Freedom of movement throughout the territory is guaranteed by Article 26.   Extradition for political offenses is prohibited (Article 23), as is exile as a form of punishment (Article 29).

87. UN, Yearbook on Human Rights for 1952 (New York: UN, 1954), pp. 33-34.   Naturalization required five years of residence and competence in the Spanish language (Article 13). Aliens were extended equal personal and property rights. Asylum for political persecution was recognized (Article 19), and extradition for political offenses was prohibited (Article 31). Cuban citizens by birth were required to constitute the majority of workers in each class of employment (Article 73), yet the Ministry of Labor was empowered to ensure that there was no discrimination in employment (Article 74).   Professional positions were restricted to Cuban nationals (Article 82); UN, Yearbook on Human Rights for 1955 (New York: UN, 1958), p.   40; UN, General Assembly, 12th sess., Report of the United Nations High Commissioner for Refugees (A/3585/Rev.1), 1957, p. 6.

88. UN, Yearbook on Human Rights for 1959 (New York: UN, 1961), pp. 61-73; Jose Agustin Martinez Viademonte, El Derecho de asilo y el regimen internacional de refugiados. (Mexico City: Ediciones Botas, 1961), pp. 67-82, 90-91. Nevertheless, the new Fundamental Law of the Republic, promulgated on 7 February 1959, repeated verbatim the guarantees of asylum contained in the 1952 Constitution.

89. Interviews, UNHCR protection officer and Sr. Alejandro Artucio, ICJ, July 1985.

90. Louise Holborn, Refugees: A Problem in our Time. Vol.1 (Metuchen, N.J.: Scarecrow, 1975), pp.   515-16; U.S. Senate, World Refugee Crisis, pp.   210-15.   An estimated 800,000 Cubans had fled by 1975, and between 10,000 and 20,000 returned between 1959 and 1971.   More current figures were unobtainable.   By October 1961, 5,000 Cuban families had arrived in Spain. Through 1966, between 300 and 450 Cubans continued to arrive each month. From 1964 through December 1970, this backlog was approximately 12,000 cases each year.

91. Holborn, Refugees, pp. 647-48.

92. UN, UNHCR, 7th sess., Executive Committee, Summary Record of the 58th Meeting (A/AC.96/SR 58), 15 May 1962, p. 19; UN, UNHCR, 15th sess., EXCOM, Summary Record of the 140th Meeting (A/AC.96/SR 140), 24 May 1966, p. 99; UN, UNHCR, 19th sess., EXCOM, Summary Record of the 179th Meeting (A/AC.96/SR 179), 22 October 1968, p. 42; UN, UNHCR, 20th sess., EXCOM, Summary Record of the 198th Meeting (A/AC.96/SR 198), 24 October 1969, p. 8.

93. Andean Group, Declaracion del Consejo de Ministros de Relaciones Exteriores del Grupo Andino, Lima: 9 April 1980; Ronald Copeland, and Patricia Weiss-Fagen, "Political Asylum: A

Background Paper on Concepts, Procedures and Problems,"
(Washington, D.C.: Refugee Policy Group, 1982), p. 40.

94. UN, UNHCR, 31st sess., Executive Committee,
Summary Record of the 334th Meeting (A/AC.96/SR 334), 15
October 1981, p. 12; UN, UNHCR, 31st sess., Sub-Committee
on International Protection: Summary Records of the 46th
Meeting (A/SPC/35/SR 46), 1 December 1980, pp. 10-14; UN,
UNHCR, 32nd sess., EXCOM, Summary Record of the 347th
Meeting (A/AC.96/SR 347), 14 October 1982, p. 11.

95. Cuba, Constitucion de la Republica de Cuba (Havana:
Ministerio de Justica, 1976); 1979 Cuban Penal Code, Chapter 12
section 2, UNHCR translation.

96. "Haitians in the Dominican Republic," Refugees, no. 21
(September 1983): 1, 5. This commission is composed of the
Foreign Minister, who acts as president of the commission, the
Minister of Labor, the Attorney General, the Director General of
Migration, and representatives from the National Police, the
Department of National Investigations, and the Judicial Council of
the executive.

97. UN, ILO, Migraciones laborales e integracion del
refugiado en Republica Dominicana (RLA/83/VAROV), Buenos
Aires, July 1984, pp. 85-86, conclusions 12-13. At the
November 1984 meeting of Latin American states in Cartagena,
Colombia, this basic Decree was modified by Decree 2330 of 10
September 1984. No information is available as to the substance
of the modifications. Upon review of the commission framework,
the UNHCR concluded that the Dominican authorities had made a
significant effort to regularize the situation of the foreign
population.

98. Lawrence LeBlanc, The OAS and the Promotion and
Protection of Human Rights (The Hague: Nijhoff, 1977), p. 122;
Tatiana de Maekelt, "Instrumentos regionales de materia de
asilo," in Asilo y proteccion internacional de refugiados en
America Latina (Mexico City: Universidad Autonoma de Mexico,
1982), pp. 150-54; UNHCR, Regional Seminar, p. 10. Between
March and May, 103 Haitian refugees arrived, and another 318
had arrived during September.

99. OAS, Human Rights: Legislative History, p. 39.

100. UN, Yearbook on Human Rights for 1955 (New York:
UN, 1958), pp. 47-52; Dominican Republic, Constitucion de la
Republica Dominicana. (Santo Domingo: Junta Central Electoral,
1966); UN, Yearbook 1963, pp. 90-97. The general guarantees
to aliens included in these constitutions were equal access to the
courts (Article 58, 1963) and freedom of movement throughout
the territory (Article 78, 1963).

101. UN, Yearbook on Human Rights for 1965 (New York:
UN, 168), pp. 72-76. Part 2 of the Act of Dominican
Reconciliation pledges respect and enforcement of those rights

proclaimed in the American and Universal declarations.   Expulsion or deportation must be carried out only by following determined channels. All residents are granted freedom of transit in the national territory.

102. UN, General Assembly, 10th sess., _Report of the United Nations High Commissioner for Refugees_ (A/2902/add. 1), 1955, p.   16; UN, General Assembly, 17th sess., _Report of the United Nations High Commissioner for Refugees_ (A/5211/rev. 1), 1962, p. 16.

103. UN, ILO, _Migraciones en Republica Dominica_, pp. 85-86.

104. Ibid., conclusions 5-9.

105. Ibid., p. 68, conclusion 10.

106. Ibid., pp. 73-74.

107. Ibid., pp. 70-72.

108. See special edition of _Refugees_, no. 39 (March 1987) for information on Haitian repatriation.

Chapter Nine

Massive Exodus in Central America: The Prospects of Regime Transformation

The inadequacies in the protection of refugees in Latin America are made markedly clear by the mass exodus of asylees beginning with the Nicaraguan civil war in 1977. Since this event, violence has become generalized in El Salvador, Nicaragua, and until early 1986. Guatemala; a mass movement of persons seeking asylum has been one of the consequences. Apparently the phenomenon of massive exodus of asylees has altered the perceptions of some Latin American states, because Latin American states have joined OAS organs and UNHCR in suggesting changes to the traditional inter-American practice of asylum. These suggestions concern modification not only of existing inter-American asylum conventions, but also of the inter-American human rights system. This chapter discusses the possibility of transformation of inter-American asylum practices in two dimensions, the negotiated and the spontaneous. Specific actions in either dimension could transform the nature of activity of current inter-American asylum practices from concern for individual asylees to concern with massive exodus.

The discussion of the negotiated dimension deals with specific revisions of inter-American asylum conventions, if any and includes suggestions for further improvement, especially enactment of an inter-American refugees convention.   The discussion of the spontaneous dimension will deal with the possibility of using the inter-American human rights system and human rights law as a more immediate complement to the global refugees regime.

TRANSFORMATION OF THE INTER-AMERICAN SYSTEM

Two factors, one legal and the other political, account for the present inadequacies of the inter-American asylum conventions. In legal terms, the concept of political asylee (*asilado*), as defined by inter-American conventions, is more restrictive than the concept of refugee that is used in the global refugees regime.[1] On the political side, the generalized violence in Central America has changed the character of its refugees.[2] Transformation of the existing inter-American practices of asylum so as to provide adequate protection for mass exodus situations requires several initiatives by the Latin American states.   There is a need to revitalize the application of relevant inter-American asylum treaties and to conceive and apply formulas of coordination and cooperation between the global refugees regime and the inter-American human rights system.[3]

A major gap in UNHCR protection in Latin America is the lack of permanent consultative machinery with the OAS or any other interested organizations, including such nongovernmental organizations as the Latin American Bishops Conference and the social science and bar associations. There are also no permanent contacts between the Inter-American Commission on Human Rights (IACHR), the Andean (or Cartagena Group) states, and national, non-official human rights organizations.   Lack of regular contacts with the political and specialized agencies of the OAS has been a constant complaint raised by UNHCR: OAS contacts with UNHCR, either by the secretariat or IACHR, have been intermittent and haphazard.   Repeated calls for standardized machinery and consultations have gone unfullfilled.   The lack of consistent participation by the OAS seems to indicate that OAS member states view refugee problems as essentially of no concern to the organization and assumed that whatever contacts were maintained could be relegated to the usually ignored IACHR.[4]

This lack of sustained or standardized coordination curtails the effective application of the international guidelines of the global refugees regime by inhibiting full use of its compliance mechanisms. International monitoring for compliance with regime guidelines becomes ineffectual.   Lack of coordination implies inconsistent use of mutually recognized means to bring state behavior into accord with global (or regional) standards.   Also, information exchange is not standardized or generally reliable.

This is reflected in IACHR's difficulty in receiving from states repeatedly requested information pertaining to refugees and in the lack of solid data available to UNHCR, at headquarters and also with field agents. Consequently, accurate data can be compiled only by indirect means and after long delay.

Further, the lack of standardized information exchange affects international promotion activities. UNHCR and IACHR, both with scarce resources, may be duplicating efforts on certain issues at the expense of other issues. Or IACHR may be interpreting standards dissimilarly to UNHCR or the EXCOM. Policy coordination also suffers. With no firm data base, useful policy suggestions cannot be forthcoming. This is further evidence of Latin American states in asylee and refugee concerns, shown by their unwillingness to respond to IACHR or UNHCR information requests and also by their failure to draft and approve uniform legislation.

Several initiatives can be made to improve operation of regime compliance mechanisms in Central America. At the global level, supplementing the bibliography prepared by the UN Conference on Territorial Asylum so as to bring up to date the knowledge of territorial asylum and extradition in Latin America can affect both information exchange and coordination mechanisms. A supplementary bibliography would help ensure that regional guidelines are at least as comprehensive as global regime guidelines. And as a consequence, it would be easier to identify gaps between regional and global guidelines and coordinate responses.[5]

A systematic compilation of pertinent domestic legislation could be undertaken, with the goal of preparing draft rules for domestic law. This compilation would be a form of information exchange, used to identify policy areas that fall below global regime standards. Moreover, from a compilation it may be possible to identify common accepted language that encompasses global regime standards and guidelines. Finally, availability to national decision makers of a compilation of domestic legislation could promote regional policy coordination and a broader acceptance and application of global refugee regime standards.

By all means available, UNHCR could encourage further accessions to the 1954 Caracas Territorial Asylum and 1969 American Convention instruments, as well as adherence of Latin American states to the global regime. Promoting broader regime membership would expand the number of states accepting the global refugee regime standards and minimum obligations. Also, expanded regime membership would ease policy coordination as more states became subject to common mimimum obligations.

Finally, and perhaps most importantly, the UNHCR could enter into preliminary contacts with the OAS to determine the scope and limits of cooperation, possibly toward preparing a draft agreement on cooperation between the UNHCR and the OAS. Similar contacts should be made with the IACHR. Formalized cooperative efforts with OAS organs, principally the IACHR, should have spillover effects for the compliance mechanisms of monitoring, information exchange and guideline promotion

At least one of these actions has been taken; as of November 1985 an OAS/UNHCR compilation of national legislation was completed. However, UNHCR personnel had no knowledge of these studies other than that they had been undertaken. Furthermore, in 1985 an assistance officer in the Americas Section dismissed the OAS efforts, describing the OAS as lacking seriousness. The inter-American agencies, according to the interviewee, remain concerned with statements of principle but fail to address concerns of substance.[6] Also, while a compilation of national legislation on asylees and refugees had been completed for select Latin American states, the studies were not available for circulation, as they had yet to be approved by the political organs of the OAS. As of November 1985, it was not known when these studies would be available.[7] On a related point, draft projects for national legislation have been presented to UNHCR, and it is in the process of drafting a model framework for domestic legislation.

One conclusion seems clear from the foregoing: the substantive component of the global refugees regime in Latin America is determined by national decision makers and national standards. This national orientation is clear from the states' unwillingness to cooperate with regional and global international agencies, from their reluctance to exchange and provide adequate and accurate information, and from the difficulty of changing domestic legislation to bring state practice into compliance with global regime obligations and guidelines. Thus, for Central America, national decision making remains the primary, and perhaps only, effective compliance mechanism in operation. This has led to variation in the Central American states' response to massive exodus situations: the Costa Rican response has been generally good, while Mexican and Honduran actions are best explained by national interest, for instance in the movement of asylees from border regions, and their activities are undertaken even if such activities are of questionable compliance with the global refugees regime.

One must conclude that there can be no solution to the problem of Central American massive exodus under the global refugees regime alone. The global regime cannot deal with the political root causes of massive exodus; moreover, the countries that support the greatest number of asylees, Honduras and Mexico, are not party to the global regime. Furthermore, several of the South American states retain the geographical limitation (Peru, Colombia, Brazil) to the global refugees regime. Hence they are not legally obliged to concern themselves with the Central American asylees.[8] Perhaps the only realistic basis for regime transformation, then, is to work within the existing agencies of the inter-American framework and to coordinate their efforts as much as possible with the global refugees regime.[9] It is imperative that such transformation take place. The existing inter-American asylum conventions reflect the norms and practices that prevailed in the nineteenth century. The basic assumption of these conventions is that individuals seek asylum from actual political persecution. With a massive exodus of asylees, however, large groups cross borders to obtain snactuary from generalized violence and social anarchy. This change in the character of asylum seekers has greatly undermined the accepted obligations and norms of the earlier inter-American asylum instruments. These are inadequate to deal with massive exodus.[10] Moreover, there is little point in expecting adoption of an inter-American or regional legal instrument for massive exodus. The 1965 OAS draft refugees convention was designed to accomodate the changed character of asylum seekers in Latin America, but it was rejected in 1967. The current political difficulties in Central America, coupled with poor domestic economic performance, leave Latin American states in a restrictive mood. There is no political will to sustain renewed attempts for a regional refugees instrument. Nor are the states willing, or able, to assume the burden of allocating the resources required to sustain a regional refugees organization.

Nevertheless, efforts to resolve differences between the global regime and inter-American asylum conventions have been undertaken. UNHCR has sponsored several colloquia in Latin America as a means of creating guidelines among Latin American states for transformation of inter-American asylum practices. From these colloquia, and from suggestions by international jurists, agreement has been reached on differences and similarities between inter-American asylum laws and global refugees regime obligations.[11]

Some scholars suggest use of the inter-American human rights regime to compliment UNHCR legal protection activities. One specific activity by which the IACHR could complement UNHCR in providing international protection would be in the area of voluntary repatriation.[12] IACHR could be involved in country surveys, determining the actual conditions facing repatriates and disseminating accurate information to potential repatriates, and in conducting follow-up surveys and investigations to ensure that repatriation agreements were upheld. Such agreements must contain specific provisions granting the IACHR unrestricted access to returnee settlements for a predetermined period, perhaps a minimum of one year. Also, the IACHR could participate in tripartite repatriation commissions, acting as the recognized neutral guarantor for refugees by both home and host states.[13] A potential limitation of this latter suggestion is the very real possibility that the IACHR would be granted less than comprehensive access to resettlement areas in home states. Without unrestricted access, accurate information could not be communicated to potential repatriates.

A second area of IACHR activity could be in a regional eligibility commission that would advise on which individual groups were qualified for refugee (or *asilado*) status under regional and international guidelines. The commission would thus provide a set of standard definitions and procedures. The existing lack of such standards has been continually recognized by both UNHCR and the regional colloquia. Initially established as an advisory body, the commission could be upgraded to the status of a binding authority.[14]

Numerous actions could be undertaken to revise and/or expand coverage of inter-American asylum conventions. A protocol to the 1954 Caracas Territorial Asylum Convention has been suggested as the best means for aligning inter-American asylum practices with the authoritative international obligations of the global refugees regime.[15] This protocol should contain at least the following points. First, there must be an expressed recognition of the principle of unilateral determination of a political crime. Second, a restrictive definition must be derived for the Caracas Convention term "subversive movement." Such a restrictive definition should recognize that the asylum state has the final determination of the veracity of evidence presented to justify declaring asylees' activities subversive. Also, explicit and restrictive conditions must be agreed to before the surveillance and internment provisions of the convention become operative. Finally, the protocol should reinterpret the *non-refoulement* provisions of inter-American asylum conventions so as to create an obligation for the state of refuge; that is, it should adopt the language of Article 33 of the global 1951 Refugees Convention. This interpretation should expressly state that nonrejection at the frontier is part of the principle of *non-refoulement*.[16] Alternatively, the OAS could draft a protocol designed to address the current mass exodus situation in Central America. Its substantive points would include recognition that nonrejection at the frontier is part of the principle of *non-refoulement*, and that *non-refoulement* is an obligation of the state of refuge. Moreover, it should state that persons forming part of a mass influx situation are to be afforded minimum treatment as defined by the UNHCR Executive Committee.[17]

If political considerations within the OAS do not allow for the adoption of either protocol, a declaration of the organization could establish guidelines of conduct. Recently, such guidelines have been recognized. At its fifteenth (1985) regular session, the OAS General Assembly passed consensus resolutions making extensive reference to the Cartagena Declaration. The Cartagena Declaration is a first step to fill a vacuum between the mass influx of refugees in Central America and the applicability of existing refugee instruments. As used in the declaration, the term refugee includes, among others, persons who have fled their country because of generalized violence, foreign aggression, internal conflicts, or massive violation of human rights. Moreover, emphasis is placed upon the humanitarian and nonpolitical character of asylum and refugee status. The widespread recognition and legitimacy of the principles contained in the Cartagena Declaration are reflected in state practice: Costa Rica, Mexico, and Honduras apply the recommendations of the declaration, and draft refugee legislation in El Salvador and Guatemala also contains the Cartagena definition of refugee.[18]

In addition to this action taken by the OAS General Assembly, the IACHR could appeal to the Inter-American Court. Under the provisions of its jurisdiction for the American Convention, an interpretation of Article 22 could be requested, that is, it may be asked to decide whether the provisions of this article incorporate nonrejection in the concept of *non-refoulement*. If the court found for incorporation, the obligation of nonrejection at the frontier would be binding only to those states party to the American Convention that explicitly recognize the court's jurisdiction. In Central America this judgment could have legal effect only for Costa Rica and Honduras. However, should the obligation of nonrejection be perceived as too burdensome, either state could withdraw its expressed recognition of the court's jurisdiction.

Lastly, the OAS Draft Protocol on Economic, Social and Cultural Rights can be expanded to include the protections found in the 1951 Refugees Convention, which are not yet dealt with in the inter-American system. At present, no inter-American convention in force, or the draft protocol, specifically grants protections equivalent to Articles 18 (self-employment) and 19 (liberal professions) of the 1951 Refugees Convention. If expanded, the draft would provide socioeconomic guidelines at least equivalent to those of the global refugees regime. Upon adherence, states would accept its provisions as legally binding.

REGIME TRANSFORMATION: A HUMAN RIGHTS REGIME?

In recent years many scholars have suggested that international human rights law can be used to extend protection to refugees. To cite but one example, in several articles since 1978 Uruguayan jurist Hector Gros Espiell has presented a case for reforming inter-American refugee activities through expanded use of the inter-American human rights system. He argues that there is a need to conceive, conclude, and apply formulas of coordination and cooperation between universal and regional human rights systems. Universal and regional protection of human rights are complementary and coordinated for common objectives. This is especially true where regional efforts focus on a common language and culture, which makes adjustment and adaptation less difficult, as is the case with the inter-American human rights system.[19]

At the global level, Stephen Young has suggested that international human rights law can serve as a complement to, and eventual replacement for, international refugee law. This shift to human rights law should minimize the government failures that provoke mass migrations. Also, the emerging law of human rights provides the rules to extract from governments some solicitude for individuals. Human rights laws conceive of a refugee as an individual and not as a national. Fleeing the national territory breaks the reciprocal relationship between national authority and citizenry. Hence, pertinent questions focus on the status of territorial residents rather than on nationality, nationals, or citizens. Use of such human rights standards would make the problems of defining refugee and stateless person moot.[20]

A regional human rights focus has also often been suggested by the UNHCR, the IACHR and the Inter-American Juridical Committee (IAJC). The inter-American community has well developed structures and substantial precedent for expanding its activities to complement the role of the UNHCR. Unlike the UNHCR, whose presence must be requested, the regional human rights machinery has a capacity for independent investigation.[21] The IACHR, with both convention authority and the prerogatives of a major organ of the OAS, has demonstrated its independence from the member states of the OAS. Thus the IACHR seems well placed to assume this protection role. Moreover, human rights questions have played a part in the development of the inter-American community since its inception at the Congress of Panama, and scholars point to human rights as one of the issue areas where the OAS system retains some potential.[22]

At least two difficulties--one legal, the second institutional-- are faced by those who would make a shift of focus from refugee to human rights law in the Americas. To bring about a change in the law of asylum and refuge in the Americas would require the presentation of human rights as already universally recognized and incorporated into general international law. Some Latin American jurists have argued that Article 29 of the American Convention reflects this recognition and incorporation.[23] Furthermore, the IACHR has expressed similar conclusions. In presenting an advisory opinion to the Inter-American Court in 1982, the president of the commission stated that "the norms of human rights are considered, doctrinally, as norms of *jus cogens*, norms of international public order, norms which limit the contractual authority of the State."[24]

If this assertion in true, then the principle of *non-refoulement*, including nonrejection at the frontier, is applicable to all Latin American states, as an obligation *jus cogens*, without signature to either of the global refugees instruments or the American Convention. In fact, participant states at the 1984 Cartagena colloquium unequivocally stated that nonrejection at the frontier and minimum standards for temporary asylees were part of the body of international humanitarian law, and specifically declared *non-refoulement* as a "norm of international law of an imperative character, that is *jus cogens*, as contained in Articles 53 and 64 of the Vienna Convention on the Law of Treaties."

Thus a consensus seems to have emerged regarding what responsibilities are due refugees under the inte-American human rights system. It is argued by some scholars, however, that human rights norms have not gained the standing of *jus cognes*, and that statements or declarations of regional human rights institutions are insufficient for elevation of such norms to the status of *jus cogens*. As noted by Theodor Meron: "the reach of hierarchically superior [human rights] instruments adopted within a particular regional or specialized institution is limited to the legal system of the parent organization and should not be confused with *jus cogens*."[25]

Since human rights norms are not readily accepted as part of general international law, perhaps a more practicable course would be to interpret *non-refoulement* and nonrejection at the frontier as obligations *erga omnes*. As understood by the International Law Commission, "a number . . . of international obligations which, by reason of the importance of their subject-matter for the international community as a whole, are . . . obligations in whose fullfillment all States have a legal interest."[26] While obligations *erga omnes* have an elevated status in the hierarchy of human rights norms, such obligations do not impose upon states the same stringent conduct required of a peremptory (*jus cogens*) norm.

Interpretation and application of the American Convention as a basis for international legal protection faces a second, or institutional, limitation. Suggestions for an inter-American institution's involvement in refugee questions are numerous. The Inter-American Juridical Committee (IAJC) could play a larger role in the area of refugee law. It could work toward greater collaboration with UNHCR, perhaps by preparing a draft collaboration agreement. Also, the committee could draft a resolution charging the IACHR with responsibility for international protection of refugees in the inter-American system. Further, it has been suggested that the IACHR can be charged with enforcement of the *non-refoulement* obligation of the global refugee instruments and the American Convention and American Declaration. Upon receiving a charge of state violation, the Commission may submit its findings to the Inter-American Court for authoritative judgment of state obligations due, pursuant to Article 8 of the American Declaration and/or Articles 22 and 27 of the American Convention.[27]

Several objections can be raised to using institutions of the OAS human rights system to supplant the global refugees regime. For the IACHR to be involved in international protection of refugees, the American Convention must serve as the juridical and enforceable foundation. One might question, however, the practicability of relying on provisions of a general human rights instrument, regardless of its obligatory provisions, for enforcement of those rights applicable to refugees. Moreover, strong criticism from scholars and political leaders has been leveled at the substance of the American Convention. It has been termed a "dormant instrument" and an "unfulfilled promise."[28] In general, human rights instruments have proven to be ineffectual, because the issue of human rights touches the very foundations of a political regime.[29]

How effective, then, can a general human rights instrument be as a basis for protection of refugees and asylees in the inter-American system? The UNHCR, a global humanitarian agency with high visability and a diverse resource base has achieved mixed success in providing protection to political refugees in Central America. In comparison, the IACHR seems even less well positioned to assume responsibilities associated with provision of international protection. While the American Convention has entered into force, and the IACHR has status of a principal organ of the OAS, the commission is not taken seriously by most American states. The continued rebuffs of the IACHR by Cuba and, since 1981, Chile prove instructive on this point. Moreover, the commission is small; its seven members serve in a part-time capacity. Its secretariat and staff are also limited. This reflects both the small line-item amount it receives as part of the OAS budget and the member states' unwillingness to provide the commission with the means of exercising its responsibilities too well. Adequate fullfillment of the above-mentioned protection responsibilities would require a substantial increase in secretariat staff, quasi-permanent presence at refugee "hot spots," and the full-time attention of the Commission or its selected representatives. There is no indication that the member states are willing to support such institutional capabilities. Nor is it prudent to expect the current capabilities of the Commission to be sufficient to absorb refugee protection responsibilities.

The role and effectiveness of the Inter-American Court on

refugee protection questions could be enhanced through use of its contnetious jurisdiction. For instance, a substantial body of scholarship concludes that on the basis of state practice and the activity of international and regional organizations, temporary asylum (or refuge) has emerged as a customary norm of international law.[30] Thus, relying either on *jus cogens*, or more advisably, custom, creates an opportunity for the Inter-American Court, which could be exploited for the benefit of Central American refugees.   Under the provisions of its jurisdiction for the 1969 American Convention, an interpretation of Article 22 could be requested; that is, determine whether provisions of this Article incorporate nonrejection at the frontier as part of the *non-refoulement* guarantee. Such an interpretation of Article 22 would incorporate as part of treaty obligations the consensus achieved by the Cartegana colloquium in 1984.

Articulation of an authorative complete and coherent doctrine pertaining to asylum or refuge in Central America has the opportunity to effect states' practices. In Central America, Costa Rica and Honduras have recognized the court's jurisdiction. Moreover, while Honduras is not a party to the global refugees regime, it extends temporary asylum to Guatemalan, Salvadoran, and Nicaraguan nationals in its territory. Binding and authoritative minimum standards due asylees, based either on principles of customary international law or the American Convention, could improve conditions of international legal protection for Central American refugees.

Alternatively, the commission could request advisory interpretation from the court. With respect to advisory opinions, the court can consider problems that have arisen in countries that have neither ratified the convention or accepted the court's jurisdiction. In an advisory opinion, specific countries will not be named and the decisions will not have the same binding effect. Thus a general problem like massive exodus and the interpretation of the convention, the American Declaration, or any other treaty concerning human rights in the Americas--which would include any of the refugee instruments--would be well suited to the court's advisory jurisdiction.   Such opinions might increase the weight of moral arguments for states' obligations to refugees and asylees; however, without binding authority, such advice is unlikely to change states' behavior toward refugees and asylees.

An additional danger: If the IACHR or the court should become involved in international protection of refugees, a perceived political or ideological bias could undermine not just the commission and the court's jurisdiction, but the entire inter-American human rights system; their actions must not be perceived as biased by any member state.[31] This is especially important because the OAS General Assembly remains the only means of making the "legal and binding" decisions of the court effective. And although the IACHR has been recognized for its broad and even-handed criticism in the past, polarization within the political bodies of the OAS would prohibit implementation of suggestions from either the commission or the court.

In sum, several key questions remain unanswered by those suggesting that the inter-American human rights system can be used to augment the global refugees regime in its application in Latin America. For instance, would commission competency be limited to the current situation, which concerns mass exoduses and questions of temporary refuge? If it is concerned only with these phenomena, then it seems clear that the perception of the refugee crisis in Central America as transitory persists among the region's political leadership. Perhaps the first step should be to direct all efforts to change this perception and convince the region's leadership that the current refugee "crisis" is probably a permanent one.

For any expansion of the inter-American human rights system to be effective, a substantial commitment by the larger Latin American states is essential. How substantial a commitment can be expected from them? Does Brazil still have a stake in the OAS system? The immediate refugee crisis in Central America is treated in a low-keyed and detached manner by the Brazilian leadership. The concerns of Central America are simply not of fundamental importance to Brazilian policy objectives. Moreover, Brazil was well able to weather the refugee crisis of the Southern Cone states in the 1970s without substantial international involvement. Thus, its most recent experience with refugees would suggest no need for involvement in expanding inter-American capabilities. Similar questions might be regarding Mexico and Venezuela. Their involvement in Central America is conditioned by propinquity to the crisis areas, possible U.S. intervention, and their desire for greater influence in the Caribbean basin. How ready, or "neutral," is either state for expanding the inter-American human rights system to refugees in Central America? For years Mexico has refused to allow UNHCR to take an active role in international protection and assistance to refugees on Mexican territory. What are the chances, then, of the IACHR achieving greater success? Does either state have the capacity to back an expansion of the inter-American human rights system substantially? Both states border on the current crisis area and would be required to expend resources (political and economic) if the undertaking is to be successful. Yet it seems that neither state, especially Mexico, has the capability to back an initiative within the inter-American human rights framework.

Lastly, sustained support for the protection of refugees under provisions of human rights law through the inter-American human rights system presupposes the longevity of democratic regimes in Latin America. True, the last few years have witnessed a "rising tide of democracy" over the Southern continent, engulfing states from Argentina to Guatemala. However, the tradition of regime instability in Latin America, coupled with the region's socioeconomic burdens, seems to make the assumption of longevity of democratic regimes unwarranted.[32]

NOTES

1. Poul Hartling, "Declaracion," in Asilo y proteccion internacional de refugiados en America Latina (Mexico City: Universidad Nacional Autonoma de Mexico, 1982), pp. 21-24; Frank Krenz, "La Definicion del refugiado," in Asilo politico y situacion de refugiado (La Paz, Bolivia: Ministerio de relaciones exteriores, 1983), pp. 35-40

2. Republic of Colombia, Coloquio sobre la proteccion internacional de los refugiados en America Central, Mexico y Panama: Problemas juridicos y humanitarios, (Cartagena, Colombia: Ministerio de relaciones exteriores, 1984), p. 4

3. Hector Gros Espiell, "La Proteccion y asistencia internacional de los refugiados: Posibilidades de cooperacion al respecto entre el sistema de las Naciones Unidas y los regimes regionales de proteccion de los derechos humanos, en especial America Latina," in International Institute of Humanitarian Law, Roundtable on Some Current Problems of Refugee Law, San Remo, Italy, 8-11 May 1978 (Geneva: UNHCR, 1978), pp. 95-96, 98, 100-01.

4. UNHCR, Report on the Regional Seminar on Protection of Refugees in Latin America, Mexico City, 20-24 August 1979. (Geneva: UNHCR, 1979), pp. 27-29. On this last point, however, prospects were not good. The only non-official body with a mandate to promote the observance of human rights was the Brazilian Commission for the Protection of the Rights of the Human Being. And political conditions, that is, government aversion, made the creation of similar bodies in other Latin American states unlikely. The first contacts on record between the UNHCR and the OAS took place in 1964, with the OAS first present at an EXCOM session in 1965. Since then, the OAS has been an observer at EXCOM sessions in 1967, 1970, 1973-75, and 1978-81. Also, since 1973 either the OAS or the IACHR has been mentioned by UNHCR in its Annual Report among the regional organizations and agencies with which it has maintained contact. See UN, UNHCR, 17th sess., Executive Committee (hereafter EXCOM), List of Representatives and Observers (A/AC.96/371), 9 June 1967, p. 9; UN, UNHCR, 17th sess., EXCOM, Summary Record of the 163rd Meeting (A/AC.96/SR 163), 29 May 1967, pp. 108-109; UN, UNHCR, 18th sess.,

EXCOM, Summary Record of the 175th Meeting (A/AC.96/SR 175), 7 November 1967, p. 116; UN, UNHCR, 19th sess., EXCOM, List of Representatives and Observers (A/AC.96/404), 21 November 1968; UN, UNHCR, 20th sess., EXCOM, List of Representatives and Observers (A/AC.96/425), 5 November 1969; UN, UNHCR, 21st sess., EXCOM, List of Representatives and Observers (A/AC.96/445), 16 October 1970; UN, UNHCR, 22nd sess., EXCOM, List of Representatives and Observers (A/AC.96/481), 9 November 1972; UN, UNHCR, 24th sess., EXCOM, List of Representatives and Observers (A/AC.96/501/Rev. 1), 20 February 1974; UN, UNHCR, 25th sess., EXCOM, List of Representatives and Observers (A/AC.96/512), 6 November 1974; UN, UNHCR, 26th sess., EXCOM, List of Representatives and Observers (A/AC.96/522/Corr. 1), 29 December 1975; UN, UNHCR, 27th sess., EXCOM, List of Representatives and Observers (A/AC.96/533), 22 October 1976; UN, UNHCR, 28th sess., EXCOM, List of Representatives and Observers (A/AC.96/548), 27 November 1977; UN, General Assembly, 24th sess., Report of the United Nations High Commissioner for Refugees (A/7612), 1969, p. 8; UN, General Assembly, 25th sess., Report of the United Nations High Commissioner for Refugees (A/8012), 1970, p. 40; UN, General Assembly, 26th sess., Report of the United Nations High Commissioner for Refugees (A/8412), 1971, p. 36; UN, General Assembly, 27th sess., Report of the United Nations High Commissioner for Refugees (A/8712), 1972, p. 36; UN, General Assembly, 29th sess., Report of the United Nations High Commissioner for Refugees (A/9612), 1974, p. 35; UN, General Assembly, 30th sess., Report of the United Nations High Commissioner for Refugees (A/10012), 1975, pp. 42-43; UN, General Assembly, 31st sess., Report of the United Nations High Commissioner for Refugees (A/32/12), 1976, p. 52; UN, General Assembly, 32nd sess., Report of the United Nations High Commissioner for Refugees (A/32/12), 1977, p. 40; UN, General Assembly, 33rd sess., Report of the United Nations High Commissioner for Refugees (A/33/12), 1978, p. 47; UN, General Assembly, 34th sess., Report of the United Nations High Commissioner for Refugees (A/34/12), 1979, p. 48; UN, General Assembly, 35th sess., Report of the United Nations high Commissioner for Refugees (A/35/12), 1980, p. 61.

5. Hector Gros Espiell, "American International Law on Territorial Asylum and Extradition as it Relates to the 1951 Convention and the 1967 Protocol to the Status of Refugees," (HCR/120/24/81/Rev. 1; Geneva: UNHCR, 1984), pp. 41-43.

6. Interviews. Americas-Section protection officer and Americas Section assistance officer, July 1985.

7. Letter 450/85 to author from OAS Subsecretariat for Legal Affairs, Hugo Caminos, Assistant Secretary for Legal

Affairs, 25 October 1985; UN, General Assembly, 37th sess., Report of the United Nations High Commissioner for Refugees (A/37/12), 1982, pp. 14, 58; UN, General Assembly, 38th sess., Report of the United Nations High Commissioner for Refugees (A/38/12), 1983, pp. 14, 34; UN, UNHCR, 34th sess., Report on UNHCR Assistance Activities in 1982-1983 (A/AC.96/620), 1 August 1983, p. xxxviii; UN, UNHCR, 35th sess., Report on UNHCR Assistance Activities for 1984-1985 (A/AC.96/657), 5 August 1985, p. 19.

    8. Hector Gros Espiell, "Communication to the Roundtable on 'Refugees in Orbit'," in International Institute of Humanitarian Law, Roundtable on Refugees in Orbit, San Remo, Italy, May 1979 (HCR/120/27/79), pp. 22-24, 27 and "American International Law," pp. 37-40; Guillerme Da Conha, "Proteccion internacional de los refugiados en America Latina," in Asilo politico, pp. 20-22; Cesar Sepulveda, "El Asilo territorial en el sistema interamericano: Problemas capitales," in Asilo y proteccion internacional, pp. 83-83.

    9. Republic of Colombia, Coloquio sobre la proteccion internacional, p.5; Gros Espiell, "American International Law," pp. 37-40.

    10. Danilo Jimenez Veiga, "Evolucion historica del asilo y necesidad de su compatibilizacion con el estatuto de los refugiados," in Asilo y proteccion internacional, pp. 197-199.

    11. UNHCR, Press release (Ref 836, NY), 12 May 1981; UN, General Assembly, 36th sess., Report of the United Nations High Commissioner for Refugees (A/36/12), 1981, p. 12. From 20 to 24 August 1979, UNHCR sponsored a seminar in Mexico City on the protection of refugees in Latin America. The purposes of this seminar were to identify protection problems and ascertain what concrete plans could be worked out for future. In May 1981 a five-day colloquium on asylum and international protection was held in Mexico City; 15 scholars and 18 representatives of various international organizations participated. See also Republic of Colombia, Coloquio sobre la proteccion internacional, pp. 8-10.

    12. Ibid., pp. 30-33, 35-38.

    13. Ibid., pp. 39-40. These Commissions would have the following objectives:

1. appropriate rules would be developed to ensure voluntary repatriation;

2. domestic legislation would be adjusted pertaining to repatriation and reintegration;

3. information would be obtained on home country conditions by sponsorship of representative group visits prior to return;

4. guarantees would be obtained from the home state that repatriates would not be subject to sanctions for seeking asylum;

5. home states would recognize that UNHCR and voluntary organizations had a role in policing these guarantees;

6. home states would develop projects to assist repatriates reinsertion into society;

7. repatriates would be issued appropriate travel documents and entry permits and provided with transport necessary to return; and

8. legal means would be available for recovery of nationality, by those who returned and also those born while in exile.

14. Atle Grahl-Madsen, "International Refugee law Today and Tomorrow," Archiv des Volkerrechts 20, no. 4, (1982): 432-3 and "Identifying the World's Refugees," in Gilburt Loescher and John Scanlon, eds., The Global Refugee Problem: US and World Response (Beverly Hills: Sage, 1983), p. 22.

15. Republic of Colombia, Coloquio sobre la proteccion internacional, pp. 15-16, 20.

16. Ibid., pp. 23-30; see also UNHCR, Handbook for Emergencies, part 1: Field Operations (Geneva: UNHCR, 1982), pp. 10-11.

17. OAS Subsecretariat for Legal Affairs, A Study Comparing United Nations International Instruments and Inter-American Instruments on Asylum, Refugees and Displaced Persons (SER/ser.D/5.2), 20 September 1984, pp. 26-27. Participants at the Cartagena colloquium declared non-refoulement to be a "norm of international law of an imperative character, that is jus cogens as contained in Articles 53 and 64 of the Vienna Convention on the Law of Treaties." Jus cogens is that body of peremptory norms or principles from which no derogation is permitted. Thus this principle was applicable to Latin American states, as an obligation of customary law, without signature to either of the global refugees instruments or the American Convention.

18. "OAS General Assembly: an inter-American initiative on refugees," Refugees, no. 27, (March 1986): 5.

19. Hector Gros Espiell, "La Proteccion y asistencia internacional," pp. 95-96; "Asylum and Protection in Latin America: the Cartagena Declaration," Refugees, no. 36 (October 1987): 32-33; see also his "Communication to the Roundtable on

'Refugees in Orbit'" and "American International Law"; See also
OAS Resolutions 774 (XV-O/85) Legal Status of Asylees,
Refugees and Displaced Persons in the American Hemisphere and
778 (XV-O/85), Annual Report of the IACHR and Special
Reports, in OAS. IACHR, Annual Report of the Inter-American
Commission on Human Rights 1985-1986 (ser. L/V/II.68 doc.
8/rev. 1), 26 September 1986, pp. 13-15 and 17-19 respectively.
        20. Stephen Young, "Between Sovereigns: A Reexamination
of the Refugee's Status," in Michigan Yearbook of International
Legal Studies: Transnational Legal Problems of Refugees (New
York: Clark Boardman, 1982), pp. 339-42, 351-57.
        21. Telford Georges, "The Scope and Limitations of State
Machinery," in International Commission of Jurists, Seminar on
Human Rights and Their Promotion in the Caribbean (Bridgetown,
Jamaica: ICJ, 1978), p. 49. In addition, as Grahl-Madsen has
observed, refugee protection can be enhanced if provided by an
intergovernmental organization independent of the states exercising
protection.   See Atle Grahl-Madsen, "Refugees and Refugee Law
in a World in Transition," in Michigan Yearbook, pp. 75-76.
        22. Alejandro Orfila, The Americas in the 1980's: An
Agenda for the Decade Ahead. (Lanham, Md.: University Press
of America, 1980), pp.   v-viii, 10, 125-38; Richard Bloomfield,
"The Inter- American System: Does it Have a Future?" in Tom
Farer, ed., The Future of the Inter-American System (New York:
Praeger, 1979), pp.16-17; Tom Farer, "The Changing Context of
Inter-American Relations," in Farer, Future, p. xix.   This
potential is reflected in the changed focus of debate within the
OAS from Communism to human rights and from economics to
North-South issues and the common objective of expansion and
protection of a body of human and economic rights.
        23. Rodolfo E. Piza Escalante and Maximo Cisneros
Sanchez. "Algunas ideas sobre la incorporacion del derecho de
asilo y de refugio al sistema interamericano de derechos
humanos," in Asilo y proteccion internacional, pp.   104-09. Thus
the Inter-American Court could be used to articulate a complete
and coherent doctrine pertaining to asylum and refuge.
        24. OAS, The Effect of Reservations on the Entry into
Force of the American Convention on Human Rights (ser. B. no.
2.   Advisory Opinion OC-8/82), 24 September 1982, p. 100.
        25. Theodor Meron, "On a Hierarchy of International
Human Rights," American Journal of International Law 80, no. 1
(January 1986): 4.
        26. Ibid., p. 1.
        27. Amy Young-Anawaty, "International Human Rights
Forums: A Means of Recourse For Refugees," in Michigan
Yearbook, pp. 451-456; Edmundo Carreno, "El Comite juridico
interamericano y el desarollo del asilo y la proteccion de los
refugiados," in Asilo y proteccion internacional, p. 136.   It is the

consensus of IAJC members that, given the continuing violence in
Central America, the current timing is inappropriate for renewed
attempts at an inter-American convention on refugees.

28. Lloyd Barnett, "Political Implications of Inter-State
Machinery," in ICJ, Seminar, p. 55; Sepulveda, "El Asilo
territorial," pp. 83-84.

29. Tom Farer, "Policy Implications of the Possible Conflict
between Capitalist Development and Human Rights in Developing
Countries," in Farer, Future, p. 115.

30. Michael Heyman, "Redefining Refugee: A Proposal for
Relief for the Victims of Civil Strife," San Diego Law Review 24,
(1987): 476-77; D. Perlus and J. Hartman, "Temporary Refuge:
Emergence of a Customary Norm," Virginia Journal of
International Law 26, no. 3 (1986): pp. 579-600.

31. Orfila, Americas in the 1980s, p. 138.

32. Bloomfield, "Inter-American system," pp. 12-13;
William Rogers, "A Note on the Future of the Inter-American
System," in Farer, Future, pp. 20-29.

APPENDIX

Table 1

Inter-American Asylum and Extradition Conventions

	ARGENTINA	BOLIVA	BRAZIL	CHILE	COLOMBIA	COSTA RICA	CUBA	DOMINICAN REPUBLIC	ECUADOR	EL SALVADOR	GUATEMALA	HONDURAS	MEXICO	NICARAGUA	PANAMA	PARAGUAY	PERU	URUGUAY	VENEZUELA
MONTEVIDEO TREATY, PENAL LAW, 1889	R	R														R	R	R	
BOLIVAR EXTRADITION AGREEMENT, 1911		R			R				R								R		R
HAVANA ASYLUM CONVENTION, 1928		R	R	R	R	R	R		R	R	R	R	R	R	R	R	R	R	
BUSTAMANTE CODE 1928		R	R	R	R	R	R	R	R	R	R	R		R	R		R		R
MONTEVIDEO ASYLUM CONVENTION, 1933					R	R	R		R	R	R	R	R	R	R	R	R		
MONTEVIDEO EXTRADITION CONVENTION, 1933	R		R					R	R	R	R	R	R	R	R	R			
CARACAS TERRITORIAL ASYLUM CONVENTION 1954	R				R	R			R	R	R	R					R	R	R

Source: International Commission of Jurists, An Application in Latin America of International Declarations and Conventions relating to Asylum (Geneva: ICJ, 1975) p. 61.   R = Ratified

TABLE 2

States Party to the Global Refugees Regime

	1951 Convention	1967 Protocol
ARGENTINA	yes	yes
BOLIVIA	yes	yes
BRAZIL	yes[1]	yes[1]
CHILE	yes	yes
COLOMBIA	yes[1]	yes
COSTA RICA	yes	yes
CUBA	no	no
DOMINICAN REPUBLIC	yes	yes
ECUADOR	no	yes
EL SALVADOR	no	yes
GUATEMALA	yes	yes
HONDURAS	no	no
MEXICO	no	no
NICARAGA	yes	yes
PANAMA	yes	yes
PARAGUAY	yes[1]	yes[1]
PERU	yes[1]	no
URUGUAY	yes	yes
VENEZUELA	no	yes

[1]Geographic restriction applies. See: "Protection: Twenty Years after the Protocol," Refugees, no. 46 (October 1987): 22.

TABLE 3

Parties to the American Convention on Human Rights

	Ratified American Convention	Recognizes IACHR competency	Recognizes Court* jurisdiction
ARGENTINA	yes	yes	yes
BOLIVIA	yes	no	no
BRAZIL	no	no	no
CHILE	no	no	no
COLOMBIA	yes	yes	yes
COSTA RICA	yes	yes	yes
CUBA	no	no	no
DOMINICAN REPUBLIC	yes	no	no
ECUADOR	yes	yes	yes
EL SALVADOR	yes	no	no
GUATEMALA	yes	no	yes
HONDURAS	yes	no	yes
MEXICO	yes	no	no
NICARAGUA	yes	no	no
PANAMA	yes	no	no
PARAGUAY	no	no	no
PERU	yes	yes	yes
URUGUAY	yes	yes	yes
VENEZUELA	yes	yes	yes

Source: OAS, IACHR, Annual Report of the Inter-American Commission on Human Rights 1986-1987 (ser. L/V/II.71 doc.9 rev.1), 22 September 1987. * reference to Inter-American Court for Human Rights.

Bibliography

International organization documents are listed in chronological rather than alphabetical order. This was done with hope for more easily finding a source cited. Also, the reader may note extensive citation from Refugees magazine. Refugees is the monthly publication of the Public Information Service of the United Nations High Commissioner for Refugees.

BOOKS

Alfredo Robayo, Luis. Extranjería, inmigración, extradición y naturalización. Quito: Imprenta Nacional, 1949.

Bravo Caro, Rodolfo. Guia del extranjero. Mexico City: Imprenta Nacional, 1979.

Buergenthal, Thomas and Robert Norris eds. Human Rights: The Inter-American System. Dobbs Ferry, N.Y.: Oceana, 1982.

Buergenthal, Thomas, Robert Norris and Dinah Shelton. Protecting Human Rights in the Americas: Selected Problems. Kehl: N. P. Engel, 1982.

Caicedo Castilla, José Joaquín. El Derecho internacional de el sistema interamericano. Madrid: Ediciones Cultura Hispanica, 1970.

Carlos Zarate, Luis. El Asilo en el derecho internacional americano. Bogota, 1957.

Cavelier, German. La Politica internacional de Colombia. Vol. 4. El Asilo Diplomático. Bogotá: Imprenta Nacional, 1960.

de Pina, Rafael. Estatuto legal de los extranjeros. Mexico City: Imprenta Nacional, 1953.

Friedland, Joan and Jesus Rodriguez y Rodriguez. Seeking
Safe Ground.   Mexico-U.S. Law Institute, San Diego:
University of San Diego Law School, 1987.

Goodwin-Gill, Guy. International Law and the Movement of
Persons between States. Oxford: Clarendon Press, 1978.

------. The Refugee in International Law.   Oxford:
Clarendon Press, 1983.

Grahl-Madsen, Atlee. The Status of Refugees in International
Law.   Vol. 2. Leiden, The Netherlands: A. W. Sitjhoff,
1972.

------. Territorial Asylum. New York: Oceana, 1980.

Hellman, Judith. Mexico in Crisis. New York: Holmes and
Meyer, 1978.

Holborn, Louise.   The International Refugee Organization.
Oxford: Oxford University Press, 1956.

-----.   Refugees: A Problem in Our Time.   Vol. 1.
Metuchen, N. J.: Scarecrow, 1975.

International Commission of Jurists. States of Emergency.
Geneva: ICJ, 1983.

International Refugee Organization.   The Facts about Refugees.
Geneva: UN, 1948.

-----. Migration from Europe. Geneva: UN, 1951.

Keohane, Robert, and Joseph Nye.   Power and
Interdependence.   Boston: Little, Brown, 1977.

League of Nations. The Refugees. Geneva: LON, 1938.

LeBlanc, Lawrence.   The OAS and the Promotion and
Protection of Human Rights. The Hague: Nijhoff, 1977.

Lillich, Richard.   The Human Rights of Aliens in
Contemporary International Law.   Manchester, U. K.:
Manchester University Press, 1984.

Macartney, C.A.   Refugees-The Work of the League. London:
League of Nations Union, 1931.

María Yepes, Jesús. Del Congreso de Panama a la Conferencia de Caracas. Caracas: Imprenta Nacional, 1976.

Martínez Viadamonte, José Agustín. El Derecho de asilo y el régimen internacional de refugiados. Mexico City: Ediciones Botas, 1961.

Moreno Arango, Sebastian. Codificacion de las leyes y disposiciones ejecutivas sobre extranjeros. Bogota: Imprenta Nacional, 1929.

Nys, Ernst, ed. De Indis et de Jure Belli Relectiones. New York: Oceana, 1964.

Orfila, Alejandro. The Americas in the 1980's: An Agenda for the Decade Ahead. Lanham, Md.: University Press of America, 1980.

Simpson, John Hope. The Refugee Question. New York: Farrar and Rinehart, 1939

Schreiber, Anna. The Inter-American Commission on Human Rights. Leyden: Sitjhoff, 1970.

Shina, S. Parkash. Asylum and International Law. The Hague: Nijhoff, 1971.

Stanley, Francis. The New World Refugee: The Cuban Exodus. Church World Service, 1966.

Thompson, Dorthy. Refugees: Anarchy or Organization? New York: Random House, 1938.

United Nations Department of Social Affairs. A Study of Statelessness. Lake Success, N. Y.: UN, 1949.

-----. The Impact of the Universal Declaration of Human Rights. New York: UN, 1953.

United Nations High Commissioner for Refugees. Conventions, Agreements and Arrangements concerning Refugees Adopted before the Second World War (HCR/DC/42/1966). Geneva: UNHCR, 1966.

-----. El Refugio: Refugees from Chile. Geneva: UNHCR, 1975.

-----. Report on the Regional Seminar on Protection of Refugees in Latin America, Mexico City, 20-24 August 1979. Geneva: UNHCR, 1979.

------. Handbook for Emergencies. Part One: Field Operations. Geneva: UNHCR, 1982.

United Nations, Office of Public Information. United Nations Action in the Field of Human Rights. New York: UN, 1974.

United Nations. Human Rights: A Compilation of International Instruments. New York: UN, 1978.

-----. Yearbook on Human Rights for 1947. New York: UN, 1949.

-----. Yearbook on Human Rights for 1950. New York: UN, 1952.

-----. Yearbook on Human Rights for 1951. New York: UN, 1953.

-----. Yearbook on Human Rights for 1952. New York: UN, 1954.

-----. Yearbook on Human Rights for 1954. New York: UN, 1956.

-----. Yearbook on Human Rights for 1955. New York: UN, 1958.

-----. Yearbook on Human Rights for 1956. New York: UN, 1958.

-----. Yearbook on Human Rights for 1957. New York: UN, 1959.

-----. Yearbook on Human Rights for 1959. New York: UN, 1961.

-----. Yearbook on Human Rights for 1962. New York: UN, 1964.

-----. Yearbook on Human Rights for 1963. New York: UN, 1963.

-----. Yearbook on Human Rights for 1965. New York: UN, 1968.

-----. Yearbook on Human Rights for 1967. New York: UN, 1969.

-----. Yearbook on Human Rights for 1972. New York: UN, 1975.

Uribe Vargas, Diego. Los Derechos humanos y el sistema inter-americano. Madrid: Ediciones Cultura Hispanica, 1972.

Uruguayan Institute of International Law. Uruguay and the United Nations. New York: Manhattan Publications, 1958.

Urrutia-Aparicio, Carlos. Diplomatic Asylum in Latin America. Washington, DC: American University Press, 1959.

Vernant, Jacques. The Refugee in the Post-War World. London: Allen and Unwin, 1953.

ARTICLES

Angell, Alan, and Susan Carstairs. "The Exile Question in Chilean Politics." Third World Quarterly 9, no. 1 (January 1987): 148-67.

Barnett, Lloyd. "Political Implications of Inter-State Machinery." In International Commission of Jurists. Seminar on Human Rights and Their Promotion in the Caribbean. Bridgetown, Jamaica: ICJ, 1978, pp. 52-9.

Benamar, Mohammed. "Asilo político y situación del refugiado." In Alto Comisionar de Naciones Unidas para Refugiados Coloquio asilo político y situación del refugiado. La Paz, Bolivia: ACNUR, 1983. p. 11.

Bloomfield, Richard. "The Inter-American System: Does it Have a Future?" In Tom Farer, ed. The Future of the Inter-American System. New York: Praeger, 1979, pp. 3-19.

Boczek, Boleslaw. "The Concept of Regime and the Protection and Preservation of the Marine Environment." in Ocean Yearbook. 6 (1986): 271-297.

Buergenthal, Thomas. "Judicial Interpretations of the American Human Rights Convention." In IACHR, Derechos humanos en las Americas. Washington, D.C.: IACHR. 1984, pp. 253-260.

Buergenthal, Thomas. "The Advisory Practice of the Inter-American Human Rights Court." American Journal of International Law 79, no. 1 (January 1985): 1-27.

Carbanes, Jose. "The Protection of Human Rights and the Organization of American States." American Journal of International Law 62, no. 4 (October 1968): 889-908.

Carreno, Edmundo. "El Comite juridico interamericano y e desarollo del asilo y la proteccion de los refugiados." In Asilo y proteccion internacional de refugiados en America Latina. Mexico City: Universidad Nacional Autonama de Mexico. 1982, pp. 113-137.

Cisneros Sanchez, Maximo. "Algunos aspectos de la juridiccion consultiva de la Corte Interamericana de Derechos Humanos." In IACHR. Derechos Humanos en las Americas. Washington, D. C.: IACHR, 1984, pp. 261-69.

Copeland, Ronald, and Patricia Weiss-Fagen. "Political Asylum: A Background Paper on Concepts, Procedures and Problems." Washington, D. C.: Refugee Policy Group, 1982.

Da Conha, Guillerme. "Protección internacional de los refugiados en America Latina." In Asilo político y situación de refugiado. (La Paz. Bolivia: Ministerio de relaciones exteriores, 1983), pp. 18-24.

de Maekelt, Tatiana. "Instrumentos regionales de materia de asilo." In Asilo y proteccion internacional de refugiados en America Latina. Mexico City: Universidad Nacional Autonoma de Mexico, 1982, pp. 162-72.

Donnelly, Jack. "International Human Rights: A Regime Analysis" in International Organization 40, no. 3 (Summer 1986): 599-642.

d'Souza, Herbert. "Return Ticket to Brazil." Third World Quarterly 9, no. 1 (January 1987): 203-11.

Farer, Tom. "The Changing Context of Inter-American Relations." In Tom Farer, ed. The Future of the Inter-American System. New York: Praeger, 1979, pp. xv-xxiii.

------. "Policy Implications of the Possible Conflict between Capitalist Development and Human Rights." In Tom Farer, ed. The Future of the Inter-American System. New York: Praeger, 1979, pp. 115-18.

Ferris, Elizabeth. "The Politics of Refuge: National Admissions Policies toward the Central American Refugees." Paper presented at the annual meeting of the International Studies Association, Washington, D. C., 9 March 1985. Used with permission of the author.

------. "Regional Responses to Central American Refugees: Policy Making in Nicaragua, Honduras and Mexico." In Elizabeth Ferris, ed. Refugees and World Politics. New York: Praeger, 1985, pp. 187-209.

Georges, Telford. "The Scope and Limitations of State Machinery." In International Commission of Jurists. Seminar on Human Rights and Their Promotion in the Caribbean. Bridgetown, Jamaica: ICJ, 1978, pp. 40-51.

Goodwin-Gill, Guy. "Entry and Exclusion of Refugees: The Obligations of States and the Protection Function of the Office of the United Nations High Commissioner for Refugees." In Michigan Yearbook of International Legal Studies: Transnational Legal Problems of Refugees. New York: Clark Boardman, 1982, pp. 291-337.

Grahl-Madsen, Atle. "The Expulsion of Refugees." In Bound Pamphlets on Refugees. UN Library Code, n.d., pp. 99-109.

------. "The League of Nations and the Refugees." Paper presented at Symposium: 60th Anniversary of the Founding of the League of Nations, Geneva, November 1980.

------. "International Refugee Law Today and Tomorrow." Archiv des Volkerrechts 20, no. 4 (1982): 411-67.

------. "Refugees and Refugee Law in a World in Transition." In Michigan Yearbook of International Legal Studies: Transnational Legal Problems of Refugees. New York: Clark Boardman, 1982, pp. 65-88.

------. "Identifying the World's Refugees." In Gilburt Loescher and John Scanlan, eds. The Global Refugee Problem: US and World Response. Beverly Hills: Sage, 1983, pp. 11-23.

Gros Espiell, Hector. "La Protección y asistencia internacional de los refugiados: Posibilidades de cooperación al respecto entre el sistema de las Naciones Unidas y los regimenes regionales de proteccion de los derechos humanos, en especial América Latina." In International Institute of Humanitarian Law. Roundtable on Some Current Problems of Refugee Law. San Remo, Italy, 8-11 May 1978. Geneva: UNHCR, 1978, pp. 93-103.

------. "Communication to the Roundtable on 'Refugees in Orbit'." In International Institute of Humanitarian Law. Roundtable on Refugees in Orbit. San Remo, Italy, May 1979 (HCR/120/27/79), pp. 22-36.

------. "American International Law on Territorial Asylum and Extradition as it Relates to the 1951 Convention and the 1967 Protocol relating to the Status of Refugees" (HCR/120/24/81/Rev.1), Geneva: UNHCR, 1981.

Guitierrez, Carlos-Jose. "Balance y relacion entre las garantias nacionales e internacionales para la proteccion de los derechos humanos." In IACHR, Derechos humanos en las Americas. Washington, D.C.: IACHR, 1984, pp. 41-53.

Hartling, Poul. "Declaration." En Asilo y protección internacional de refugiados en America Latina. Mexico City: Universidad Nacional Autónoma de Mexico, 1982, pp. 21-24.

Hechen, Jorge. "The Argentine Republic." In The Positive Contribution of Immigrants. Paris: UNESCO, 1955, pp. 147-161.

Heyman, Michael. "Redefining Refugee: A Proposal for Relief for the Victims of Civil Strife." San Diego Law Review 24, (1987): 399-484.

Hurtado Villa, Marcelo, Jaime Prudencio Cossio and Reyanaldo Peters Arzabe. "Pautas para una legislación Boliviana sobre el refugiado." In Asilo político y situación del refugiado. La Paz, Bolivia: Ministerio de relaciones exteriores, 1983, pp. 91-103.

Jaeger, Gilbert. "Status and International Protection of Refugees." Geneva: UNHCR, 1980, internal memo.

Jimenez Veiga, Danilo. "Evolución historica del asilo y necesidad de su compatibilizacion con el estatuto de los refugiados." In Asilo y protección internacional de refugiados en América Latina. Mexico City: Universidad Nacional Autónoma de México, 1982, pp. 197-199.

Krasner, Stephen. "Structural Causes and Regime Consequences: Regimes as Intervening Variables." International Organization 36, no. 4 (Spring 1982): 185-205.

Krenz, Frank. "La Definición del refugiado." In Asilo político y situación del refugiado. La Paz, Bolivia: Ministerio de relaciones exteriores, 1983, pp. 35-41.

Landall, M. "The Organization of UNHCR." Geneva: UNHCR, June 1980, internal memo.

Meron, Theodor. "On a Hierarchy of International Human Rights." American Journal of International Law 80, no. 1 (January 1986): 1-23.

Nikken, Pedro. "Bases de la progresividad en el regimen internacional de proteccion de los derechos humanos." In IACHR. Derechos Humanos en las Americas. Washington, D. C.: IACHR, 1984, pp. 22-40.

Perluss, D. and Hartman, J. "Temporary Refuge: Emergence of a Customary Norm." Virginia Journal of International Law 26, no. 3 (1986): 551-626.

Piza Escalante, Rodolfo E. and Maximo Cisneros Sánchez. "Algunas ideas sobre la incorporacion del derecho de asilo y de refugio al sistema interamericano de derechos humanos." In Asilo y protección internacional de refugiados en America Latina. Mexico City: Universidad Nacional Autónoma de México. 1982, pp. 103-111.

Rogers, William. "A Note on the Future of the Inter-American System." In Tom Farer, ed. The Future of the Inter-American System. New York: Praeger, 1979, pp 20-29.

Sassen-Koob, Saskiam. "Economic Growth and Inmigration in Venezuela." International Migration Review 13, no. 47 (1979): 455-474.

Scheman, L. Ronald.   "The Inter-American Commission on Human Rights." American Journal of International Law 59, no. 2 (April 1965): 335-344.

Sepúlveda, Cesar.   "El Asilo territorial en el sistema interamericano: Problemas capitales." In Asilo y protección internacional de refugiados en America Latina.   Mexico City: Universidad Nacional Autónoma de México, 1982, pp. 83-88.

Torrado, Susana.   "International Migration Policies in Latin America."   International Migration Review 13, no. 47 (1979): 428-39.

Vargas Carreno, Edmundo. "El Comité jurídico interamericano y el desarollo del asilo y la protección de los refugiados." In Asilo y protección internacional de refugiados en America Latina.   Mexico City: Universidad Nacional Autónoma de México, 1982, pp. 113-37.

Weis, Paul.   "The Development of Refugee Law."   In Michigan Yearbook of International Legal Studies: Transnational Legal Problems of Refugees.   New York: Clark Boardman, 1982, pp.   27-42.

Weiss-Fagen, Patricia. "Refugees and Displaced Persons in Central America." Washington, D.C.: Refugee Policy Group, March 1984.

Wilkerson, Jeffery.   "The Usumacinta River: Troubles on a Wild Frontier."   National Geographic 168, no. 4 (October 1985): 514-43.

Wood, Bryce.   "Human Rights and the Inter-American System."   In Tom Farer, ed.   The Future of the Inter-American System. New York: Praeger, 1979. pp. 119-152.

Young, Stephen.   "Between Sovereigns: A Reexamination of the Refugee's Status."   In Michigan Yearbook of International Legal Studies: Transnational Legal Problems of Refugees. New York: Clark Boardman. 1982, pp. 339-70.

Young, Oran.   "International Regimes: Problems of Concept Formation."   World Politics 32, no. 3 (April 1980): 331-56.

------. "Regime Dynamics: The Rise and Fall of International Regimes." International Organization 36, no. 4 (Spring 1982): 277-97.

-----. "International Regimes: Toward a New Theory of Institutions." World Politics 39, no. 1 (October 1986): 104-22.

Young-Anawaty, Amy. "International Human Rights Forums: A Means of Recourse for Refugees." In Michigan Yearbook of Internatinal Legal Studies: Transnational Legal Problems of Refugees. New York: Clark Boardman, 1982, pp. 451-76.

GOVERNMENT DOCUMENTS
Andean Group

Declaración del Consejo de Ministros de Relaciones Exteriores del Grupo Andino. Lima, 9 April 1980.

Argentina

Ley 15,869 de 2-11-1961: Adhesion to 1951 Refugees Convention.

Decreto-Ley 4805 de 17-6-1963: Admission, Residence and Expulsion of Aliens.

Decreto 4418 de 4-6-1965: Immigration regulations.

Ley 17,468 de 3-11-1967: Adhesion to 1967 Protocol.

Decreto 978 de 31-12-1973: Issuance of Convention Travel Documents.

Decreto 87 de 11-1-1974: Illegal Entry of Foreigners.

Decreto 1093 de 5-4-1974: Travel Documents.

Resolucion 2,853 de 26-4-1974: Recognition of CCAS.

Ley 21,795 de 18-5-1978: Law of Nationality and Citizenship.

Decreto 2,073 de 29-8-1979: Indochinese Resettlement

Ley 22,439 de 1981: General Law on Migration

Decreto 780/84 de 12-3-1984: Amnesty Decree.

Bolivia

"Constitucion politicia del estado." en (La Paz: Gaceta Oficial de Bolivia), 1978.

Brazil

Law 941 of 6-11-1970: Aliens Act.

Chile

Decreto-Ley 81 de 1973: State Security.

Decreto 1308 de 3-10-1973: Authorization for the Functioning of the National Committee for Assistance to Refugees.

Decreto-Ley 1094 de 19-7-1975: Norms Regulating Foreigners in Chile.

Decreto 1306 de 27-10-1975: Regulations Applying to Foreigners.

5634 CHL (Santiago): Amnesty Law of 1978.

SANT 319 630 CHL-640 CHL of 5-1981: Decree-Law Authorizing Expulsion of Foreigners.

Colombia

Ley 35 de 12 de Julio de 1961 por la cual se aprueba la convención sobre estatuto de los refugiados, Anales del Congreso, no. 177, 29 July 1961: Adherence to 1951 Convention.

Codigo sustantivo de trabajo. Bogotá: Editorial Voluntad, 1968.

Codigo procesal de trabajo. Bogotá: Editorial Voluntad, 1968.

Decree 2,955 of 5 November 1980: Visas and Control of Foreigners.

Coloquio sobre la protección internacional de los refugiados en
America Central, México y Panama: Problemas jurídicos y
humanitarios.   Cartagena: Ministerio   de   relaciones
exteriores, 1984.

Costa Rica

Decree 11,939-P of 7-10-1980:   Creation of National Refugee
Commission.

Decree 12,950-S of 10-10-1980: Determination of Refugee
Status.

Decree 12,903-S of 4-8-1981: Temporary Residence.

Decree 14,155-J of 23-12-1982: Revision of National Refugee
Commission (CONAPARE).

Cuba

Constitución de la República de Cuba.   Havana: Ministerio
de Justicia, 1976.

Cuban Penal Code, 1979. UNHCR translation.

Dominican Republic

Constitución de la República Dominicana.   Santo Domingo:
Junta Central Electoral, 1966.

Ecuador

Decreto 1896 de 27-12-1971: Fees for Issuance of Passports.

Ley 276 de 14-4-1976: Naturalization Law.

Constitution of Ecuador, 1978. Registro oficial, no. 800, 27
March 1979.

Ley 1897 de 1984: Law Regulating Foreigners.

Ley 1899 de 1984: Immigration Law.

Reglamento 1900 de 1984: Regulations for Immigration Law.

El Salvador

Constitución política de la República de el Salvador, 1962
(rev. 1976). San Salvador: Departmento de Relaciones
Públicas, 1976.

Tratado general de paz entre las repúblicas de el Salvador y
Honduras. San Salvador, 1981.

Guatemala

Secretaria de Gobernacion y Justicia. Leyes de inmigración y
extranjería. Guatemala City: Imprenta Nacional, 1931.

Constitución de la República de Guatemala. Guatemala City:
Ministerio de Gobernacion, 1965.

Decreto-ley 89-939 de 11-8-1983. Repatriation and Amnesty
Policy.

Decreto-ley 56-84 de 15 Junio de 1984. Amnesty Extension.

Decreto-ley 65-84 de 26 Junio de 1984. Establishment of
Development Poles.

Honduras

Decreto 95 de 13-3-1946.

Decreto 124 de 3-1971. Law on Passports.

Decreto 14 de 21-1-1981: National Refugee Commission.

Decreto 131 de 1982: Constitution of the Republic.

Mexico

Secretaría de Relaciones Exteriores. Memoria 1928-29, Tomo
I. Mexico City: Imprenta Nacional, 1929.

Consejo Nacional de Población. Ley General de Poblacion.
Mexico City, 1952.

-----. Reglamento de lay ley general de población. Mexico
City, 1952.

-----. Reglamento de la ley federal del trabajo sobre extranjeros. Mexico City, 1970.

-----. Reglamento de la ley general de población. Mexico City, 1976.

-----. Ley de impuestos de migración de 1973. Mexico City, 1973.

Convenio colectivo de trabajo de la UNAM (1-11-1970 a 31-10-1980)

Decreto de 29-7-1975: Promulgación el convenio regional de convalidación de estudios, títulos y diplomas de educacion superior en América Latina y el Caribe.

Decreto de 18-10-1976 por el que los asilados políticos y sus familiares en México, podrán obtener la revalidación de estudios o certificación de conocimientos.

Convenio colectivo de trabaja de la UNAM: 1-11-1978 a 31-10-1980.

Decreto de 4-7-1980: Comisión Mexicana de ayuda a refugiados.

Secretariat of Governmental Affairs. Press Release, 10 May 1984.

Ministry of Internal Affairs. Press Release. 12 July 1984.

Síntesis intervención representante de Mexico, Jorge Montano, a la XXXV periodo de sesiones de Comite Ejecutivo de Naciones Unidas para Refugiados. Washington, D. C.: Embassy of Mexico, 1984.

Intervención del embajador Oscar González, director general de la comisión Mexicana de ayuda a refugiados, en el debate de XXXV periodo de sesiones de Comité Ejecutivo del Alto Comisionado de Naciones Unidas para Refugiados. Washington, D. C. Embassy of Mexico, October 1984.

Nicaragua

Decreto 52 de 21-8-1979: The Basic Law.

Decreto 867: Ley de nacionalidad de 19-11-1981: Nationality Law.

Decreto 1031 de 4-5-1982: Immigration Law.

600 NIC of 28-12-1982: Draft Regulations on the Nicaraguan National Office for Refugees.

Reglamento de 6-4-1984 de la ley creadora de la oficina nacional para refugiados: Law creating the National Office for Refugees.

Panama

Decree 100 of 6 July 1981: Creadora de la comisión para el tratamiento del problema de los refugiados.

Venezuela

Ley de inmigración y colonización de 1918: Immigration and Colonization Law.

Ley de extranjeros y su reglamento, Caracas, from editorial La Torre, 29 June 1942.

United States

U.S. Congress. House Refugee and Humanitarian Problems in Chile: Subcommittee to Investigate Problems Connected with Refugees and Escapees. 93rd cong., 1st sess., 28 September 1973.

-----. House Foreign Affairs Committee. Human Rights in Chile. 93rd cong., 2nd sess., December 1973-June 1974.

-----. Senate Committee on the Judiciary. World Refugee Crisis: The International Community's Response. Washington, D. C.: Congressional Research Service, 1979.

U. S. General Accounting Office. Central American Refugees: Regional Conditions and Prospects and Potential Impact on the United States (GAO/NSIAD-84-106) Washington, D. C.: Government Printing Office, 1984.

INTERNATIONAL ORGANIZATION DOCUMENTS

League of Nations

Council of the League. Report to the 5th Assembly of the League Work of the Council (A.8 1924), 10 June 1924.

Intergovernmental Advisory Commission for Refugees. Resolution Submitted by the Committee of Experts to the Intergovernmental Advisory Commission for Refugees (Legal [V] 1-8 C.266-M136 1933), 18 May 1933.

-----. Report of the Intergovernmental Advisory Commission for Refugees on the Work of its 5th Session (C.266-M136 1933), 18 May 1933.

ILO. Minutes of the 36th session of the Governing Body of the International Labor Organization, May-June 1927.

Nansen International Office. Report to the Governing Body (A.24 1932), 16 August 1932.

-----. Report to the Governing Body (A.23-1936), 3 September 1936.

-----. Managing and Finance Committees: 20th Joint Session (J.C. 214-1936), 1 July 1936.

-----. Managing and Finance Committees: 22nd Joint Session (J.C. 223-1936), 1 July 1936.

-----. International Assistance to Refugees (A.73-1936), n.d.

Office of the High Commissioner. 4th Meeting of the Governing Body of the High Commission for Refugees Coming from Germany, London, 1935.

-----. Refugees Coming from Germany: Report to the 17th Session by the High Commissioner Neill Malcolm (A.19-1936), 1 September 1936.

Organization of American States

Constitution of the United States of Brazil (1967, as amended 1969) Law and Treaty Series no. 36, Washington, D.C., 1971.

Constitution of the Republic of Nicaragua (1974) Law and Treaty Series no. 36, Washington, D.C., 1976.

Constitution of the Republic of Panama (1972) Law and Treaty Series no. 36, Washington, D.C., 1974.

Convention on Territorial Asylum (ser. A/10 Sep. F) Law and Treaty Series no. 19, Washington, D.C., 1954.

Convencion Interamericana sobre extradicion (ser. A/36) Law and Treaty Series no. 60, Washington, D.C., 1981.

Council of the OAS. Decisions Taken at the Meetings (ser. G.III vol. 10), 1957.

-----. Decisions Taken at the Meetings (ser. G.III vol. 11), 1958.

-----. Decisions Taken at the Meetings (ser. G.III vol. 12), 1959.

-----. Decisions Taken at the Meetings (ser. G.III vol. 13), 1960.

-----. Decisions Taken at the Meetings (ser. G.III vol. 14), 1961.

-----. Decisions Taken at the Meetings (ser. G.III vol. 15), 1962.

-----. Decisions Taken at the Meetings (ser. G.III vol. 16), 1963.

-----. Decisions Taken at the Meetings (ser. G.III vol. 17), 1964.

-----. Decisions Taken at the Meetings (ser. G.III vol. 18), 1965.

-----. Decisions Taken at the Meetings (ser. G.III vol. 19), 1966.

-----. Decisions Taken at the Meetings (ser. G.III vol. 20), 1967.

-----. Decisions Taken at the Meetings (ser. G.III vol. 21), 1968.

-----. Decisions Taken at the Meetings (ser. G.III vol. 22), 1969.

-----. Decisions Taken at the Meetings (ser. G.III vol. 23), 1970.

Human Rights: The Inter-American System. Part 2. Legislative History of the American Convention. Washington, D. C.: OAS, 1970.

Inter-American Commission on Human Rights Report on the Work Accomplished during Its 4th Session (ser. L/V/II.4 doc. 34), April 1962.

-----. Report on the Work Accomplished during Its 7th Session (ser. L/V/II.8 doc. 35), October 1963.

-----. Report on the Work Accomplished during Its 8th Session (ser. L/V/II.9 doc. 24), April 1964.

-----. Report on the Work Accomplished during Its 9th Session, (ser. L/V/II.10 doc. 21), October 1964.

-----. Report on the Work Accomplished during Its 10th Session (ser. L/V/II.11 doc. 19), March 1965.

-----. Report on the Work Accomplished during Its 12th Session (ser. L/V/II.13 doc. 26), October 1965.

-----. Report on the Work Accomplished during Its 13th Session (ser. L/V/II.14 doc. 35), April 1966.

-----. Report on the Work Accomplished during Its 16th Session (ser. L/V/II.17 doc. 24), April 1967.

-----. Report on the Work Accomplished during Its 17th Session (ser. L/V/II.18 doc. 25), April 1968.

-----. Report on the Work Accomplished during Its 23rd Session (ser. L/V/II.23 doc. 27), April 1970. 6 -----. Report on the Work Accomplished during Its 31st Session (ser. L/V/II.31 doc. 54 rev. 1), October 1973.

-----. Report on the Work Accomplished during Its 32nd Session (ser. L/V/II.32 doc. 31 rev. 1), April 1974.

-----. Report of the Work Accomplished during Its 33rd Session (ser. L/V/II.33 doc. 15 rev. 1), July-August 1974.

-----. Third Report on the Situation of Human Rights in Chile (ser. L/V/II.40 doc. 10), February 1977.

-----. Informe sobre la situacion de los derechos humanos en Paraguay (ser. L/V/II.43 doc. 13 corr. 1), 31 January 1978.

-----. Annual Report of the Inter-American Commission on Human Rights 1977 (ser. L/V/II.43 doc. 21), March 1978.

-----. Report on the Situation of Human Rights in El Salvador (ser. L/V/II.46 doc. 23 rev. 1), November 1978.

-----. Annual Report of the Inter-American Commission on Human Rights 1978-1979 (ser. L/V/II.47 doc. 13 rev. 1), June 1979.

-----. Report on the Situation of Human Rights in the Republic of Argentina (ser. L/V/II.49 doc. 19 corr. 1), June 1980.

-----. Annual Report of the Inter-American Commission on Human Rights 1979-1980 (ser. L/V/II.50 doc. 13 rev. 1), October 1980.

-----. Report on the Situation of Human Rights in the Republic of Bolivia (ser. L/V/II.53 doc. 6), 13 October 1981.

-----. Report on the Situation of Human Rights in the Republic of Guatemala (ser. L/V/II.53 doc. 21 rev. 2), October 1981.

-----. Annual Report of the Inter-American Commission on Human Rights 1981-1982 (ser. L/V/II.57 doc. 6 rev. 10), 20 September 1982.

-----. Inter-American Commission on Human Rights: Ten Years of Activities, 1971-1981, Washington, D.C., 1982.

-----. Annual Report of the Inter-American Commission on Human Rights 1982-1983 (ser. L/V/II.61 doc. 22 rev. 1), 27 September 1983.

-----. Annual Report of the Inter-American Commission on Human Rights 1983-1984 (ser. P/ AG doc.1778/84), 5 October 1984.

-----. Annual Report of the Inter-American Commission on Human Rights 1984-1985 (ser. L/V/II.66 doc. 10 rev. 1), October 1985.

-----. Annual Report of the Inter-American Commission on Human Rights 1985-1986 (ser. L/V/II.68 doc. 8 rev. 1), 26 September 1986.

-----. Annual Report of the Inter-American Commission on Human Rights 1986-1987 (ser. L/V/II.71 doc. 9 rev. 1), 22 September 1987.

-----. Report on the Situation of Human Rights in Paraguay (ser. L/V/II.71 doc. 19 rev. 1), 28 September 1987.

Inter-American Court of Human Rights. Annual Report of the Inter-American Court of Human Rights to the General Assembly 1980 (ser. L/V/III.3 doc. 13 corr. 1), October 1980.

-----. Advisory Opinion: The Effect of Reservations on the Entry into Force of the American Convention on Human Rights (ser. B no. 1 advisory opinion OC-2/82), 24 September 1982.

-----. Advisory Opinion: Other Treaties Subject to the Advisory Jurisdiction of the Court (ser. B no. 1 advisory opinion OC-1/82). 24 September 1982.

-----. Annual Report of the Inter-American Court of Human Rights, 1984 (ser. L/V/III.10 doc. 13), 15 August 1984.

Inter-American Juridical Committee. Extraordinary Meeting of the Inter-American Juridical Committee (ser. I/VI.2 CIJ-85). April 1966.

Inter-American Treaties and Conventions on Asylum and Extradition (ser. XII-Series no. 34), Washington, D.C.. 1967.

Inter-American Yearbook on Human Rights 1960-1967. Washington, D.C: OAS, 1968.

International Council of Jurists, Third Meeting of the International Council of Jurists (ser. I/VI.2 CIJ-24), Mexico City, 17 January 1956.

-----. Final Act of the Fourth Meeting (ser. I/VI.2 CIJ-43). Santiago de Chile, 1959.

-----. Subsecretariat for Legal Affairs. A Study Comparing United Nations International Instruments and Inter-American Instruments on Asylum. Refugees and Displaced Persons (SER/ser.D/5.2), 20 September 1984.

Pan-American Union

Pan-American Union. The Codification of International Law and the Americas. Law and Treaty Series no. 20, Washington, D.C.: PAU, 1939.

-----. Constitution of Argentina (1853 as amended 1860, 1866, 1898 and 1957). Law and Treaty Series no. 36, Washington, D.C.: PAU, 1968.

-----. Constitution of the Unites States of Brazil (1946--as amended 1956). Law and Treaty Series no. 36, Washington, D.C.: PAU, 1958.

-----. Constitution of the Republic of Costa Rica, 1949. Law and Treaty Series no. 35, Washington, D.C.: PAU, 1951.

-----. Constitution of Ecuador, 1967. Law and Treaty Series no. 36, Washington, D.C.: PAU, 1968.

-----. Constitution of the Republic of El Salvador, 1950. Law and Treaty Series no. 36, Washington, D.C.: PAU, 1953.

-----. Constitution of the Republic of Honduras, 1965. Law and Treaty Series no. 36, Washington, D.C.: PAU, 1966.

-----. Constitution of the Republic of Nicaragua, 1950. Law and Treaty Series no. 36, Washington, D.C.: PAU, 1954.

-----. Constitution of the Republic of Uruguay, 1967. Law and Treaty Series no. 36, Washington, D.C.: PAU, 1969.

-----. Constitution of the Republic of Venezuela, 1953. Law and Treaty Series no. 36, Washington, D.C.: PAU, 1954.

-----. Constitution of the Republic of Venezuela, 1961. Law and Treaty Series no. 36, Washington, D.C.: PAU, 1968.

-----. Diario de la sexta conferencia internacional americana, no. 10, Havana, 25 January 1928. República de Cuba: Havana, 1928.

-----. Documentos oficiales de la VII conferencia internacional americana (C.2 no. 4), Washington, D.C., 1933.

-----. Documents for the Use of Delegates to the Seventh International Conference of American States. Washington, D.C., 1933.

-----. Human Rights in the American States. Washington, D.C.: PAU, 1960.

-----. International Commission of Jurists. Sessions Held in Rio de Janiero, Brazil, 1927. Washington, D.C., 1928.

-----. Septima conferienca internacional americana: Acta final. Montevideo, 1933.

-----. Sixth International Conference of American States: Final Act. Havana, 1928.

-----. Tenth Inter-American Conference: Final Act. Washington, D.C.: PAU, 1954.

-----. Treaties and Conventions Signed at the Seventh International Conference of American States. Law and Treaty Series no. 37, Washington, D.C.: PAU, 1952.

United Nations

Economic and Social Council, Commission on Human Rights, 33rd sess., Report on the Ad Hoc Working Group Established under Resolution 8 (XXXI) of the Commission on Human Rights to Inquire into the Present Situation of Human Rights in Chile (E/CN.4/1221), 10 February 1977.

-----. 35th sess., Report of the Ad Hoc Working Group Established Under Resolution 8 (XXXI) of the Commission on Human Rights to Inquire into the Present Situation of Human Rights in Chile (E/CN.4/1310), 2 January 1979.

-----. 36th sess., Report Prepared by the Special Rapporteur on the Situation of Human Rights in Chile, Pursuant to Commission on Human Rights Resolution 11 (XXXV) (E/CN.4/1313), 29 January 1980.

-----. 37th sess., Report on the Situation of Human Rights in Bolivia (E/CN.4/1500), 31 December 1981.

-----. 37th sess., Study on Human Rights and Massive
Exoduses (E/CN.4/1503), 31 December 1981.

-----. 37th sess., Report on the Situation of Human Rights in
Bolivia (E/CN.4/1500/add. 1), 22 February 1982.

-----. 40th sess., Report on the Situation of Human Rights in
Guatemala (E/CN.4/1985/19), 8 February 1985.

-----. 40th sess., Women's International Democratic Foundation
(E/CN.4/1985/NGO/11), 8 February 1985.

General Assembly, 7th sess., Report of the Economic and
Social Council (A/2172), 1952.

-----. 7th sess., Report of the United Nations High
Commissioner for Refugees (A/2126), 1952.

-----. 8th sess., Report of the United Nations High
Commissioner for Refugees (A/2394), 1953.

-----. 9th sess., Report of the United Nations High
Commissioner for Refugees (A/2648/add. 1/add. 2), 1954.

-----. 10th sess., Report of the Economic and Social Council
(A/2943), 1955.

-----. 10th sess., Report of the United Nations High
Commissioner for Refugees (A/2902/add. 1), 1955.

-----. 11th sess., Report of the United Nations High
Commissioner for Refugees (A/3123/rev. 1), 1956.

-----. 11th sess., Addenda to the Report of the United Nations
High Commissioner for Refugees (A/3123/rev. 1/add. 1/add.
2), 1957.

-----. 12th sess., Report of the United Nations High
Commissioner for Refugees (A/3585/rev. 1), 1957.

-----. 13th sess., Report of the United Nations High
Commissioner for Refugees (A/3828/rev. 1), 1958.

-----. 14th sess., Report of the Economic and Social Council
(A/4143), 1959.

-----. 14th sess., Report of the United Nations High
Commissioner for Refugees (A/4104/rev. 1), 1959.

-----. 15th sess., Report of the Economic and Social Council (A/4415), 1960.

-----. 16th sess., Report of the United Nations High Commissioner for Refugees (A/4771/rev. 1), 1961.

-----. 17th sess., Report of the United Nations High Commissioner for Refugees (A/5211/rev. 1), 1962.

-----. 19th sess., Report of the United Nations High Commissioner for Refugees (A/5811/rev. 1), 1964.

-----. 20th sess.. Report of the United Nations High Commissioner for Refugees (A/6011/rev. 1), 1965.

-----. 24th sess.. Report of the United Nations High Commissioner for Refugees (A/7612), 1969.

-----. 25th sess., Report of the United Nations High Commissioner for Refugees (A/8012), 1970.

-----. 26th sess., Report of the United Nations High Commissioner for Refugees (A/8412), 1971.

-----. 27th sess., Report of the United Nations High Commissioner for Refugees (A/8712), 1972.

-----. 28th sess., Report of the United Nations High Commissioner for Refugees (A/9012), 1973.

-----. 29th sess., Report of the United Nations High Commissioner for Refugees (A/9612), 1974.

-----. 30th sess., Report of the United Nations High Commissioner for Refugees (A/10012), 1975.

-----. 31st sess., Report of the United Nations High Commissioner for Refugees (A/31/12), 1976.

-----. 32nd sess., Report of the United Nations High Commissioner for Refugees (A/32/12), 1977.

-----. 33rd sess., Report of the United Nations High Commissioner for Refugees (A/33/12), 1978.

-----. 34th sess.. Report of the United Nations High Commissioner for Refugees (A/34/12), 1979.

-----. 34th sess., Protection of Human Rights in Chile (A/34/583), 21 November 1979.

-----. 35th sess., Report of the United Nations High Commissioner for Refugees (A/35/12), 1980.

-----. 36th sess., Report of the United Nations High Commissioner for Refugees (A/36/12), 1981.

-----. 37th sess., Report of the United Nations High Commissioner for Refugees (A/37/12), 1982.

-----. 38th sess., Report of the United Nations High Commissioner for Refugees (A/38/12), 1983.

International Labor Organization, Migraciones laborales e integración del refugiado en Bolivia (RLA/83/VAROV), Buenos Aires, May 1984.

-----. Migraciones laborales e integración del refugiado en República Dominica (RLA/83/VAROV), Buenos Aires, July 1984.

-----. Migraciones laborales e integración del refugiado en Honduras (RLA/83/VAROV), Buenos Aires, July 1982.

-----. Migraciones laborales e integración del refugiado en Nicaragua (RLA/83/VAROV), Buenos Aires, May 1984.

-----. Venezuela: Informe de avance sobre migraciones internacionales y empleo (RLA/83/VAROV), Buenos Aires, 1984.

International Refugee Organization, General Committee. Report on the Policy of the IRO regarding Repatriation and Resettlement (IRO/GC/4), 13 September 1948.

-----. General Committee. Report of the Director-General on the Activities of the Organization since 1 July 1948. Information Bulletin 60 (IRO/GC/60), 22 March 1949.

-----. General Committee. Report of the Director-General to the General Committee of the IRO (1948-1949), Information Bulletin 100 (IRO/GC/100), March 1950.

-----. General Committee. Semi-Annual Report 1 July 1951 to 31 December 1951 (IRO/GC/256), January 1952.

-----. General Committee. Summary Record of the Second Meeting (IRO/GC/SR 2), 13 October 1948.

-----. General Committee. Summary Record of the Third Meeting (IRO/GC/SR 3), 12 November 1948.

-----. General Committee. Summary Record of the Twenty-fifth Meeting (IRO/GC/SR 25), 21 April 1949.

-----. General Committee. Summary Record of the Forty-first Meeting (IRO/GC/SR 41), 4 July 1949.

-----. General Committee. Summary Record of the Fifty-eighth Meeting (IRO/GC/SR 58), 22 October 1949.

-----. Information Bulletin 7 (IRO/PI/IB/7), 15 December 1948.

-----. Information Bulletin 9 (IRO/PI/IB/9), 1 February 1949.

-----. Information Bulletin 11 (IRO/PI/IB/11), 1 March 1949.

-----. Information Bulletin 15 (IRO/PI/IB/15), 30 April 1949.

-----. Information Bulletin 16 (IRO/PI/IB/16), 15 May 1949.

-----. Information Bulletin 18 (IRO/PI/IB/18), 15 June 1949.

-----. Information Bulletin 19 (IRO/PI/IB/19), 1 July 1949.

-----. Information Bulletin 20 (IRO/PI/IB/20), 15 July 1949.

-----. Information Bulletin 21 (IRO/PI/IB/21), 1 August 1949.

-----. Preparatory Committee Information Bulletin 1 (PC/PI/IB/1), 8 September 1947.

-----. Preparatory Committee Information Bulletin 9 (PC/PI/IB/9), 9 October 1947.

-----. Preparatory Committee Information Bulletin 12 (PC/PI/IB/12), 15 November 1947.

-----. Preparatory Committee Information Bulletin 13 (PC/PI/IB/13), 24 November 1947.

-----. Preparatory Committee Information Bulletin 16 (PC/PI/IB/16), 24 January 1948.

-----. Preparatory Committee Information Bulletin 22 (PC/PI/IB/22), 26 May 1948.

-----. Preparatory Committee Information Bulletin 23 (PC/PI/IB/23), 12 July 1948.

-----. Preparatory Committee Information Bulletin 24 (PC/PI/IB/24), 27 August 1948.

United Nations High Commissioner for Refugees. Press release (Ref/258), 22 November 1955.

-----. 4th sess., Executive Committee. Summary Record of the 10th Meeting (A/AC.96/SR 10), 15 June 1959.

-----. 6th sess., Executive Committee. Summary Record of the 36th Meeting (A/AC.96/SR 36), 8 February 1961.

-----. 7th sess., Executive Committee. Summary Record of the 58th Meeting (A/AC.96/SR 58), 15 May 1962.

-----. 8th sess., Executive Committee. Summary Records of the 64th-68th Meetings (A/AC.96/SR 64-68), 6 March 1963.

-----. 15th sess., Report on the Constitution of the Republic of Argentina. Buenos Aires, 13 May 1964.

-----. 15th sess., Executive Committee. Summary Record of the 133rd Meeting (A/AC.96/SR 133), 17 May 1966.

-----. 15th sess., Executive Committee. Summary Record of the 135th Meeting (A/AC.96/SR 135), 18 May 1966.

-----. 15th sess., Executive Committee. Summary Record of the 140th Meeting (A/AC.96/SR 140), 24 May 1966.

-----. 17th sess., Executive Committee. List of Representatives and Observers (A/AC.96/371), 9 June 1967.

-----. 17th sess., Executive Committee. Summary Record of the 163rd Meeting (A/AC.96/SR 163), 29 May 1967.

-----. 18th sess., Executive Committee. Summary Record of the 175th Meeting (A/AC.96/SR 175), 7 November 1967.

-----. 19th sess., Executive Committee. Summary Records of the 179th Meeting (A/AC.96/SR 179), 22 October 1968.

-----. 19th sess., Executive Committee. List of Representatives and Observers (A/AC.96/404), 21 November 1968.

-----. 20th sess., Executive Committee. Summary Record of the 198th Meeting (A/AC.96/SR 198), 24 October 1969.

-----. 20th sess., Executive Committee. List of Representatives and Observers (A/AC.96/425), 5 November 1969.

-----. 21st sess., Executive Committee. List of Representatives and Observers (A/AC.96/445), 16 October 1970.

-----. 23rd sess., Executive Committee. List of Representatives and Observers (A/AC.96/481), 9 November 1972.

-----. Press release (Ref/1154), 17 October 1973.

-----. 24th sess., Report on the 24th Session of the Executive Committee of the High Commissioner's Programme (A/AC.96/497), 18 October 1973.

-----. Press release (Ref/1157), 26 October 1973.

-----. 24th sess., Executive Committee. Summary Records of the 239th-249th Meetings (A/AC.96/SR 239-249), 14 December 1973.

-----. 24th sess., Executive Committee. List of Representatives and Observers (A/AC.96/501/rev.1), 20 February 1974.

-----. 25th sess., Report on the 25th Session of the Executive Committee of the High Commissioner's Programme (A/AC.96/511), 31 October 1974.

-----. 25th sess.. Executive Committee. List of Representatives and Observers (A/AC.96/512), 6 November 1974.

-----. 26th sess.. Executive Committee. Summary Record of the 267th Meeting (A/AC.96/SR 267), 9 October 1975.

-----. 26th sess.. Executive Committee. List of Representatives and Observers (A/AC.96/522/corr. 1), 29 December 1975.

-----. 26th sess.. Report on UNHCR Assistance Activities in 1975-1976 (A/AC.96/526), 16 August 1976.

-----. 27th sess., Executive Committee. List of Representatives and Observers (A/AC.96/533), 22 October 1976.

-----. 28th sess., Executive Committee. Summary Record of the 289th Meeting (A/AC.96/SR 289), 7 October 1977.

-----. 28th sess., Executive Committee. List of Representatives and Observers (A/AC.96/548), 27 October 1977.

-----. 28th sess., Report on Meeting of the Sub-Committee of the Whole on International Protection Held Monday 30 October 1977 (EC/SCP/6), 7 November 1977.

-----. Press release (Ref/1319), 5 December 1977.

-----. Press release (Ref/1354), 25 September 1978.

-----. 29th sess., Executive Committee. Summary Record of the 295th Meeting (A/AC.96/SR 295), 10 October 1978.

-----. 29th sess.. Executive Committee. Summary Record of the 302nd Meeting (A/AC.96/SR 302), 13 October 1978.

-----. Press release (Ref/1354), 25 September 1978.

-----. Press release (Ref/1371), 6 November 1978.

-----. Report on the Regional Seminar on Protection of Refugees in Latin America, Mexico City 20-24 August 1979, Geneva: UNHCR, 1979.

-----. 30th sess., Note on Voluntary Repatriation (EC/SCP/13), 27 August 1979.

-----. 30th sess., Report of the 30th Session of the Executive Committee of the High Commissioner's Programme (A/AC.96/572), 19 October 1979.

-----. 30th sess.. Report on UNHCR Assistance Activities for 1979-1980 (A/AC.96/577), 14 August 1980.

-----. 31st sess., Sub-Committee on International Protection. Summary Record of the 46th Meeting (A/SCP/35/SR 46), 1 December 1980.

-----. Press release (Ref/863 NY), 12 May 1981.

-----. 31st sess.. Report on the Meeting of the Expert Group on Temporary Refuge in Situations of Large-Scale Influx (EC/SCP/10/add. 1), 17 July 1981.

-----. 31st sess., Note on Procedures for the Determination of Refugee Status under International Instruments (A/AC.96/INF 152/rev.3), 4 September 1981.

-----. 31st sess., Executive Committee. Summary Record of the 334th Meeting (A/AC.96/SR 334), 15 October 1981.

-----. 31st sess., Note on Procedures for the Determination of Refugee Status under International Instruments (A/AC.96/INF 152/rev.5), 30 October 1981.

-----. 32nd sess., Follow-up on Earlier Conclusions of the Sub-Committee: The Determination of Refugee Status (EC/SCP/22/rev.1), 3 September 1982.

-----. 32nd sess., Note on Internatuonal Protection of Refugees in Armed Conflict Situations (EC/SCP/25), 4 October 1982.

-----. 32nd sess., Executive Committee. Summary Record of the 347th Meeting (A/AC.96/SR 347), 14 October 1982.

-----. 32nd sess., Executive Committee. Summary Record of the 350th Meeting (A/AC.96/SR 350), 15 October 1982.

-----. 33rd sess., Report by Ambassador Felix Schnyder (EC/SCP/26), 15 March 1983.

-----. 33rd sess., Report on UNHCR Assistance Activities for 1982-1983 (A/AC.96/620), 1 August 1983.

-----. Fact Sheet no. 12, January 1985.

-----. 35th sess., Report on UNHCR Assistance Activities for 1984-1985 (A/AC.96/657), 5 August 1985.

-----. 38th sess., Note on Procedures for the Determination of Refugee Status Under International Instruments (A/AC.96/INF.152/rev. 7), 24 July 1987.

NONGOVERNMENTAL ORGANIZATIONS

Americas Watch. Honduras: On the Brink. Washington, D.C.: Americas Watch, February 1984.

Amnesty International. Chile: Un informe de Amnestia Internacional. London: AI, 1974.

-----. Report of an Amnesty International Mission to Argentina 6-15 November 1976. Middlesex, UK: AI, 1977.

-----. "Mexico: Treatment of Refugees and Camp Workers Questioned." Amnesty Action, October 1984, p. 5.

International Commission of Jurists. An Application in Latin America of International Declarations and Conventions Relating to Asylum. Geneva: ICJ, 1975.

-----. Human Rights in Nicaragua Yesterday and Today. Geneva: ICJ, 1980.

------. "The Inter-American Commission on Human Rights." Review of the International Commission of Jurists, no. 16 (June 1976): 23-24.

-----. "Uruguay Encouraging Return to Democracy." The Review of the International Commission of Jurists, no. 34 (June 1985): 20, 23, 27.

Intergovernmental Committee for European Migration. Reunion especial sobre el problema de los refugiados: Acta resumida de la Primera Sesion. Geneva, November 1958.

International Committee of the Red Cross. Red Cross Action in Aid of Refugees (ICRC/LCRS/CD/8/1), Geneva, August 1983.

World Peace Through Law Center. Towards the Second Quarter Century of Refugee Law. Washington, D.C.: WPTLC, 1976.

MAGAZINES

"The Geography of Refuge." Refugees, no. 2 (February 1982): 5, 7.

"Emergency in Southern Mexico." Refugees, no. 15 (March 1983): 1-2.

"Situation Improves in Honduran Refugee Camps." Refugees, no. 16 (April 1983): 4, 12.

"Dispersal and Self-Sufficiency." Refugees, no. 17 (May 1983): 1, 8.

"Agricultural Cooperatives." Refugees, no. 17 (May 1983): 6.

"Haitians in the Dominican Republic." Refugees, no. 21 (September 1983): 1, 5.

"News in Brief." Refugees, no. 2 (February 1984): 7.

"Health Services Adjust to Miskito Dispersal." Refugees, no. 2 (February 1984): 20.

"Guatemalan Refugee Rights Guaranteed." Refugees, no. 3 (March 1984): 37.

"Interview: Dante Caputo, Minister of Foreign Affairs." Refugees, no. 4 (April 1984): 43.

"Killing Time Which Kills Us." Refugees, no. 6 (June 1984): 10.

"News in Brief." Refugees, no. 7 (July 1984): 7.

"Priority to Rural Integration." Refugees, no. 9 (September 1984): 18-19.

"News in Brief." Refugees, no. 10 (October 1984): 7.

"News In Brief." Refugees, no. 11 (November 1984): 7.

"Exiles Welcome Home--A One-Way Ticket from Geneva to Montevideo." Refugees, no. 19 (July 1985): 31-33.

"Influx of Refugees from Nicaragua to Costa Rica." Refugees, no. 20 (August 1985): 20-22.

"News in Brief." Refugees, no. 22 (October 1985): 7.

"Current Problems in International Protection." Refugees, no. 22 (October 1985): 5.

"Armed Attacks on Refugee Camps: No International Consensus." Refugees, no. 24 (December 1985): 5.

"News in Brief." Refugees, no. 24 (December 1985): 7.

"Guatemalans Tame the Land." Refugees, no. 24 (December 1985): 15-16.

"UNHCR's Executive Committee-the 36th Session." Refugees, no. 24 (December 1985): 17-30.

"Returnees and Refugees in Argentina and Uruguay." Refugees, no. 25 (January 1986): 19-28.

"Homecoming in Uruguay." Refugees, no. 25 (January 1986): 28-29.

"Trouble in Limon." Refugees, no. 26 (February 1986): 17-18.

"OAS. General Assembly: An Inter-American Initiative on Refugees." Refugees, no. 27 (March 1986): 5.

"Guatemalans in Quintana Roo." Refugees, no. 27 (March 1986): 17-18.

"Refugees in Central America: What Lies Ahead?" Refugees, no. 31 (July 1986): 7.

"Dossier: Central American Refugees." Refugees, no. 31 (July 1986): 19-30.

"Limon: Under New Management." Refugees, no. 32 (August 1986): 8.

"Interview: Ghassan Arnaout." Refugees, no. 34 (October 1986): 16-17.

"Guatemalan Refugees in Chiapas." Refugees, no. 34 (October 1986): 20.

"The Relocation Experience: Refuges in Campeche and Quintana Roo." Refugees, no. 34 (October 1986): 27-29.

"Salvadorans in Mexico." Refugees, no. 34 (October 1986): 30-31.

"Interview: Jorge Carillo Olea." Refugees, no. 34 (October 1986): 31.

"The Humanitarian Need Must Be Addressed Before All Others." Refugees, no. 35 (November 1986): 5.

"News in Brief." Refugees, no. 35 (November 1986): 7.

"Dossier: The 37th Session of the EXCOM." Refugees, no. 35 (November 1986): 17-31.

"Dossier: Refugees, A 1986 Overview." Refugees, no. 36 (December 1986): 21-22.

"Refugee Rights Human Rights." Refugees, no. 38 (February 1987): 5.

"Haiti: Hope, Return, Disillusion." Refugees, no. 39 (March 1987): 15-29.

"Playa Blanca: A New Settlement for Nicaraguan Refugees." Refugees, no. 40 (April 1987): 16-17.

"News in Brief." Refugees, no. 41 (May 1987): 7.

"Liberalization: A New Era." Refugees, no. 41 (May 1987): 33-34.

"Protection: Twenty Years After the Protocol." Refugees, no. 46 (October 1987): 17-34.

"Asylum and Protection in Latin America: the Cartagena Declaration." Refugees, no. 47 (October 1987): 32-33.

"Agreement on Military Attacks." Refugees, no. 47 (November 1987): 13.

"Large-Scale Return to El Salvador Unprecidented Operation." Refugees, no. 47 (November 1987): 14.

"Growing Concerns." Refugees, no. 47 (November 1987): 15-16.

"Guatemalan Refugees Arrested by the Honduran Army." Refugees Magazine, no. 4 (August 1983): 20.

"40.000 Refugees in Mexico." US-Mexico Report 5, no. 12 (December 1986): 9.

"Central Americans in Mexico." US-Mexico Report 6, no. 6 (June 1987): 20.

NEWSPAPERS

"Pinochet's Long-Term Prospects in Question." Christian
Science Monitor, 18 March 1986, pp. 11, 18.

"Returning Chilean Exiles Find It Tough to Readjust."
Christian Science Monitor, 17 April 1986, p. 15.

"Honduras Disarms Contra Forces." The Guardian (London),
16 May 1985.

"Nicaragua Steps Up Raids on Rebels on Honduran Border,
US Aides Say." International Herald Tribune, 20 May
1985.

"Honduras Puts Controls on Nicaraguan Rebels." International
Herald Tribune, 21 May 1985.

"Rumors, Conflicts Complicate Mexico's Relocation of
Refugees." Washington Post, 15 July 1984.

Index

ABOUT THE AUTHOR

KEITH YUNDT is a graduate of Pennsylvania State University and received his M.A. and Ph.D. at Kent State University, Kent. Ohio. He has been a visiting lecturer at Kent State Univeresity and New Mexico State University, Las Cruces. Currently he is a lecturer in international relations at Southwest Texas State University, San Marcos, Texas.